T0355994

"Munther Isaac is a profound prophetic voice that comes along once in a generation. While there may not be universal agreement with his conclusions, Isaac offers—as a Christian pastor and leader from the Holy Land—a critical and invaluable perspective that demands attention and must not be ignored. The global Christian community must heed the cries of their brothers and sisters in Christ from Palestine, cries that are poignantly voiced in *Christ in the Rubble*. The very witness of the gospel is at stake."

—**Mae Elise Cannon**, executive director of
Churches for Middle East Peace

"I shall never forget a Palestinian pastor saying to me, some years back, when he was painfully lamenting the fact that the plight of the Palestinians was virtually ignored by his fellow Christians in the West, 'A baby in its crib is ignored unless it cries out. Perhaps we Palestinians have not known how to cry out.' Palestinian Lutheran pastor Munther Isaac knows how to cry out. *Christ in the Rubble* is an extraordinarily eloquent cry of lament over the suffering of the Palestinians, today and over the past seventy-six years. May this powerful cry from the crib at last awaken Western Christians to understanding, empathy, and action!"

—**Nicholas Wolterstorff**, Yale University

"Writing while a genocide against Palestinians in Gaza is being live streamed, Munther Isaac calls on the world to be ethically consistent. One cannot care for the lives and safety of some and disregard the lives and safety of others. Speaking from his perspective as a Christian Palestinian leader, Isaac demystifies apocalyptic, messianic, and vengeful Christian and Jewish forms of Zionism, all of which have translated into violations of Palestinian humanity manifested in the escalation of the ongoing Nakba into a genocidal assault. *Christ in the Rubble* is a must read for anyone outraged by Palestinian suffering and by the ways that selective appeals to biblical references have authorized the displacement, destruction, and denial of Palestinian materialities, histories, and futures."

—**Atalia Omer**, University of Notre Dame

"Regarding conflict in the Middle East, it goes without saying that global outsiders tend to oversimplify what they believe to be solutions. What aren't always as obvious are the ways we become entwined in structures that reinforce chaos and bloodshed. Munther Isaac lives, prays, weeps, and works for peace in Gaza. His pastoral heart, scholarly acuity, and prophetic passion are not only eye-opening, but inspiring—inviting us to walk a tangible path towards interreligious solidarity and informed action."

—**John A. Nunes**, California Lutheran University

"Munther Isaac has written a heartbreaking indictment of world leaders, religious leaders, and humanity for failing the Palestinian people. With striking moral clarity, Isaac delivers an impassioned argument for the defense of Palestinian life and freedom, one that speaks deeply to universal religious and human values. *Christ in the Rubble* is an SOS and a call to action, especially for church leaders and Christians around the world, whose institutions and religious extremists have used their immense power to support the West's evangelical project in the State of Israel at an unforgivable cost to Palestinians, Jewish people, and all of humanity."

—**Lily Greenberg Call**, former Biden administration political appointee

"Incisive. Penetrating. Convicting. Munther Isaac is here the chronicler of Israel's astonishing history that few in the church have heard. But he has also become a prophetic voice showing the disturbing violence employed by Israel from its inception. Isaac's voice brings us the necessary courage we need for our time."

—**Gary M. Burge**, Wheaton College

"Munther Isaac has become one of the most prominent Christian leaders in the world today. His message 'Christ in the Rubble' has become an anthem for freedom, as he reminds us all that God is under the rubble in Gaza, near to all who suffer from violence and occupation. This is one of the most important books of our generation."

—**Shane Claiborne**, author, activist, and
cofounder of Red Letter Christians

"*Christ in the Rubble* is, in many ways, disturbing, startling, and uncomfortable. Most of all, it is truthful. It is prophetic. I truly believe that the church will look back on our current historical moment and will ask in bewilderment: *What were we thinking? Where was the church? Why were they silent?* Or even worse: *Why were they complicit?* If you want a life-changing wake-up call, you must read *Christ in the Rubble*. It is, quite simply, the most important book of our generation."

—**Preston Sprinkle**, *New York Times* bestselling author and
host of the *Theology in the Raw* podcast

Christ in the Rubble

Faith, the Bible, and the Genocide in Gaza

Munther Isaac

WILLIAM B. EERDMANS PUBLISHING COMPANY
GRAND RAPIDS, MICHIGAN

Wm. B. Eerdmans Publishing Co.
2006 44th Street SE, Grand Rapids, MI 49508
www.eerdmans.com

31 30 29 28 27 26 25   1 2 3 4 5 6 7

ISBN 978-0-8028-8554-8

Library of Congress Cataloging-in-Publication Data

A catalog record for this book is available from the Library
of Congress.

For the children of Gaza

"If you are neutral in situations of injustice, you have chosen the side of the oppressor. If an elephant has its foot on the tail of a mouse and you say that you are neutral, the mouse will not appreciate your neutrality."

—*Desmond Tutu*

"Christianity stands or falls by its revolutionary protest against violence, arbitrariness and pride of power, and by its apologia for the weak. I feel that Christianity is doing too little in making these points rather than doing too much. Christianity has adjusted itself much too easily to the worship of power. It should give much more offense, more shock to the world, than it is doing. Christianity should take a much more definite stand for the weak than for the potential moral right of the strong."

—*Dietrich Bonhoeffer*

"In the end, we will remember not the words of our enemies, but the silence of our friends."

— *Martin Luther King Jr.*

Contents

Foreword

M unther Isaac is Palestinian and Christian. Simply placing those two words together announces something that much of the Christian world is failing to hear at this urgent moment—a call to discipleship. That urgent moment has been with those who are Palestinian ever since the British Empire extended its living space into the land, homes, and lives of those who inhabit what was designated through colonial logic as the "Middle East." Urgency always marks the call to discipleship as we who call ourselves Christian seek to discern how the Spirit is moving, drawing us into the desire of Jesus to be present, seen in and seen by suffering flesh. "Suffering" is a massive word. It is a desert that extends in every direction—vast, inhospitable, and ever widening. Everyone who steps on its rugged terrain is at great risk of getting lost, especially lost in the suffering they witness. We require a map and a guide through the desert of suffering. The way of Jesus is a map through suffering. This map turns us toward places and people that must be seen and understood in the concrete reality of their suffering. The map is always bound to the living guide, this same Jesus, who by the Spirit draws us ever closer to those whose broken bodies and tormented minds must become our constant concern. We are alive to God in the desert of suffering— listening, learning, yielding, responding, and pressing toward the end of oppression and suffering.

Munther Isaac knows what we should all know: the wider Christian world has too often failed to be alive to God and see Palestinian suffering on the map and has failed to walk alongside our Palestinian Christian kin as they traverse this impossible terrain. That long history of failure shines very bright in the flashing bombs and daylight devastation of Gaza. We can identify two fundamental sources for that epic failure. The first source is the couplet of Jewish-Christian Zionism, which founds a theologically totalizing vision of land and people woven through a relentless commitment to territoriality and nationalism as sacred realities. The second source is a racial vision of peoplehood woven through distorted Jewish and Christian practices of reading holy texts, interpreting history, and establishing vision for habitations. Together these sources have led to the fetishization of Jewish people and the erasure of Palestinians. We must hold these two effects together, because they constitute the kind of theological blindness and deafness that is noted in Isaiah and quoted in the Gospels by Jesus:

They have shut their eyes, so that they might not look with their eyes, and hear with their ears, and understand with their hearts and turn—and I would heal them. (Matt. 13:15b)

How we arrived at the condition of seeing but not seeing, of hearing but not hearing, and of thwarting the healing work of God goes back to several beginnings. There is the supersessionist beginning that positioned Jewish people as objects of scorn and hatred, and then as objects of evangelism, and then as signs for discerning the actions of God in history, and culminating in positioning them as good-luck charms for the well-being of every nation that "blesses Israel." There is also the colonialist beginning of empire building and world making that enabled the occupation of Palestine, turned Palestinians and Bedouins into aliens and hostile forces in their own land and home, and began the long-continuing violence of the Nakba. There is the nationalist beginning that forced upon the world the idea that no people exist unless they exist as a nation-state, and every nation-state must defend itself by trafficking in weapons and violence. There are the racial beginnings that embedded the logic of whiteness that binds together segregation, security, and population control into practices of policing that are nothing less than genocidal military operations. There are the geographic beginnings that continue to reformat the land and landscape of Israel-Palestine, turning it into a biblical Disneyland that resembles a European countryside. All these beginnings are woven together into a cord that has bound too many Christians into an inexcusable apathy and inaction in relation to Palestinian suffering.

Christian apathy and inaction are, however, not the central problem for Palestinians, especially Palestinian Christians, but the active, even enthusiastic, articulations of a theology that supports the military and colonial operations of the nation-state of Israel aimed at Palestinians. Make no mistake—this is a theological cord that ties all these beginnings together. Munther Isaac in this book cuts the cord. With a first-person account that is also a theological account that is also a historical account, Munther brings a sharp knife to this fight. It is a fight not against flesh and blood but against principalities that are working very hard to keep the cord in place. Munther cuts, aiming not to draw blood but to free Christians from captivity. It is a captivity he and so many of our Palestinian kin have seen firsthand.

Imagine living as a Christian in Israel-Palestine and every day you know that there is a military force that sees you as a criminal and an enemy combatant, even if you are still in your mother's arms. Imagine growing up and having every aspect of your life shaped by oppression and occupation, and yet learning the arts of survival and thriving amid hostilities as thick as constant smoke. Imagine being a Christian and having a constant stream of Christians from other parts of the world showing up and telling you to "behave, because this land was promised by God to God's chosen people, Israel." Imagine watching your homes, your gardens, and your farms taken by a government that needs little justification for the taking and leaves you no way to challenge that theft. Now imagine you pray, worship, and love the God of Israel and you seek as best you can to walk in the way of the Jewish Jesus and live out the command to love your enemies. This is thick Christianity, serious faith that is at risk every day.

For a couple of years now, I and a few other African American Christian scholars have been meeting regularly on Zoom with a few Palestinian Christian scholars including Munther Isaac. The similarities, as is well known, between black diaspora life and Palestinian life are uncanny, and the African diaspora wager of being Christian is also marked by similar precarity. The deepest question that always flowed between us as we met together is, Why are we yet Christian? We together feel the weight of trying to articulate to our co-suffering comrades why following a Jewish Jesus makes any sense. Together we feel the weight of that cord, all of us cutting it as fast as we can only to see it reweave itself. We keep cutting, but why? We have not come up with a definitive answer. The only thing that might be said at this point is that we are inside someone else's cutting. We feel the hand of a God made flesh who has taken hold of that cord and says to us, "Right here, cut, keep cutting." We discern a presence with us, holding us, sustaining us. We sense the Spirit of God cutting.

I have a dear friend who, when the conversation turns to Palestinian suffering, will always say the same thing: "The situation in the Middle East is complicated." This is no doubt true, but what in life is not complicated? Complication is not the enemy of clarity and certainly not a barrier to seeking justice. That seeking requires of us today the unraveling of thought and practices formed from these beginnings, tracing out each one and then thinking and acting against each of them. This is work that Christians and their theologians and their Bible scholars and their pastors and social-media pundits have not begun to do with the seriousness that it requires. This is why we must be thankful for Munther Isaac and what he offers us in this book. He will not release Christians to a piety that excuses violence; a theology that baptizes territory, nation, state, property, and military actions as ordained by God; and a faith that believes that God uses peoples like chess pieces on a board and sanctifies homicide or genocide as holy collateral damage for God's glory. This is the time for bold intervention—like Jesus rubbing spit and dirt together and placing it on a person's eyes so they might see again. We must remember, however, that a question, implicitly or explicitly, always marks such an intervention, and it is the same question that Munther is asking with this book: do you want to see?

Willie James Jennings
Hamden, Connecticut

Introduction

W hy would a pastor write a book exposing the horrific realities of Gaza? Is it the role of the church to speak publicly—even urgently and insistently—about politics and warfare? And how did a Palestinian pastor find himself engaged in such a task?

I am not a politician. I am a theologian by training and a pastor to multiple churches, and, for me, speaking about Gaza is primarily a pastoral mandate. I have always taken my calling as a pastor to mean, among other things, speaking on my people's behalf, both giving voice to them and supporting them in their challenges and suffering. Families in my congregation, like all Palestinians, are victims of colonialism, occupation, and apartheid. Palestinian Christians, like all Palestinians, have been displaced and dehumanized for over seventy-six years. Their property and their lands have been confiscated, and they have been denied the right to return. They are imprisoned and harassed at checkpoints. Their families are displaced and separated. I have no choice but to address these realities from a standpoint of faith. In Palestine, addressing the political challenges we face daily is a pastoral call.

Today in Gaza, Christians, like all other Gazans, are victims of a vindictive war. And the church in Palestine has been hard-pressed to respond pastorally to such a horrifying reality. Though occupied in a distinctly different way than the West Bank, Gaza is a part of Palestine and its people are our people. Many Palestinians living in the West Bank have friends and family in Gaza. This is why I, a pastor in Bethlehem, only forty-five miles from Gaza, am committed to advocating for Gaza. Over the last year, I lobbied persistently for a cease-fire in Gaza, using my pulpit and platform as a pastor to elevate the voices of Palestinians. I traveled the world, meeting policy makers and church leaders in efforts to call for a cease-fire. I have spoken on hundreds of webinars and podcasts, and I have addressed small and large crowds in person. I have been on the major news channels, both progressive and conservative. And I have done so from a distinctly Christian position. Many in the West were shocked to discover that Palestinian Christians exist, and were further surprised to hear one advocate on behalf of all Palestinians.

Some say Christians should avoid politics. This is a naive instruction anywhere, and in Palestine it is impossible. Worse, it reflects a shallow spirituality. The church must speak on issues of injustice, taking a stand against it, if we believe that Christ's call to love and care for one another applies to all spheres of life. In order to do this, the church must address corrupt politicians and rulers, demanding in the name of God that they rule with justice and equality. The Bible says,

> Learn to do good;
> seek justice,
> rescue the oppressed,
> defend the orphan,
> plead for the widow. (Isa. 1:17)[1]

When the church chooses silence in the face of political injustice, it agrees with injustice. Silence in the face of political oppression is profane, nullifying our belief in the God of justice and compassion. Silence suggests that we condone evil and that God does not care

---

1. Unless otherwise indicated, biblical quotations in this book are from the New Revised Standard Version.

about injustice and bloodshed. How can we be silent as a war of genocide unfolds live on air? This is what we are seeing in Gaza today. Through their silence, entire communities are saying much—to those committing the genocide, to the victims themselves, and about the nature of God. They are condoning the bloodshed. This book is, among other things, my cry against the silence of many in response to this war, for silence is complicity.

There is another important reason why I as a pastor, as a theologian, and indeed as a Christian must address what is happening in Palestine and Gaza. A distinctly shameful feature of the tragedy in Palestine compels me to speak out in anger and rage: it is being justified in the name of God and the Bible. When injustice is defended in the name of the Bible and theology, we must declare: "Not in our name!" and "Not in the name of God!" When Christians promote the idea of a racist, tribal God and argue that this is the God of the Bible revealed in Jesus Christ, we must denounce this claim as antithetical to the teachings of Christianity. When Christian leaders openly call for a genocide—we must, in anger, call them out and call them to repent.

Palestinian and Christian

This book about the war in Gaza is my cry as Palestinian pastor about the pain and suffering of my people. I have written from an unapologetically Palestinian and Christian perspective, highlighting the Palestinian story as we have lived it. It aims to give voice to the people of Palestine and Gaza while their voices are being silenced, distorted, and even demonized by many, including Western Christian leaders.

Positioning myself as a Palestinian Christian is not an admission of bias. Rather, I position myself both as an insider and a person of faith. I am not addressing the issues that shape this catastrophe in Gaza from a distance. I am Palestinian, and Palestine is the only home I have. For hundreds of years, my family has lived in the fields known as the Shepherds' Field, the place believed to be the site where the shepherds heard the ancient hymn

"Glory to God in the highest heaven,
and on earth peace among those whom he favors!"

(Luke 2:14)

Speaking and writing about the reality in Palestine is putting words to my daily experience and life journey, and that of my family and friends.

Further, I am a pastor, theologian, and Bible scholar. The Bible is my strong foundation. My faith and my lived reality are built upon it. I build upon it throughout this book as I wrestle with questions about pain, death, and hope. I build upon it as I seek to articulate hope amid despair and darkness.

This book challenges dominant Western Christian theologies and perspectives about Israel, the land, and the Palestinian people. It presents alternative historical and theological perspectives to counter dominant narratives about Palestine and Gaza. My alternative perspectives will unsettle many readers. A genocide has taken place. An uncomfortable conversation is required.

In this book, I use terms like "genocide," "ethnic cleansing," and "apartheid." I do so not to be provocative but because these words accurately name the reality. When it comes to the present war on Gaza, I lean on the witness of many experts who have classified it as a war of genocide. The following chapters will make all this clear.

Further, I write this book from a clear recognition that what we have in Palestine is not a "conflict," as if two equal (or close to equal) entities were warring. Rather, our context is that of seventy-six years of systematic oppression and domination, of occupiers over the occupied. Honest assessment of the recent history of Palestine exposes the reality that the State of Israel is a case of settler colonialism. The vocabulary that best fits the reality includes words like "oppression," "domination," "erasure," and "apartheid."

Finally, I must reiterate that this book is written from a Christian perspective, out of devotion to the ethics of Jesus, which entails devotion to love, justice, and equality. My Christian faith requires unwavering commitment to nonviolence, peace, and reconciliation rooted in truth and justice. Further, being a peacemaker unavoidably entails willingness to sacrifice, take sides, and speak truth to power.

4

Christ in the Rubble

"If Christ were to be born today, he would be born under the rubble in Gaza." I spoke these words during one of the most brutal periods of this war, during Christmas of 2023. The phrase "Christ in the rubble" refers to the manger scene that we created in the Evangelical Lutheran Christmas Church in Bethlehem; a photo of the scene captured global attention and gave me, as the pastor of that church, a platform to address the world. It is also the title of the sermon I gave on December 23, in which I called out the silence of the world in response to genocide in Gaza. The sermon was heard by tens of millions of listeners around the world and contributed to the creation of a global Christian movement for a cease-fire in Gaza. "Christ in the Rubble" is also a prophetic protest of a world in which genocide is permissible. As a faith leader, I believe it is my calling to speak out about the pain and cries of my people. Palestinians have been marginalized, dehumanized, and demonized to the extent that the killing of more than sixteen thousand Palestinian children is seen as a normal outcome of just another war. In response, I insisted that we must see Jesus's image in every child pulled from under the rubble.

This Book

This book is about faith, the Bible, and the genocide in Gaza. It is a combination of historical, political, theological, and pastoral perspectives on the war on Gaza—as seen from the distinct viewpoint of a Palestinian pastor. The first three chapters introduce the broad historical and political context. Chapter 1 tells the horrifying stories of the October 7 attacks and the genocidal response to those attacks. It highlights the magnitude of the tragedy and the pain and trauma suffered by its Israeli victims. I then delve into the genocide that unfolded thereafter, and explain why I, like many others, have named what happened in Gaza in the last year a genocide. In chapters 2 and 3, I argue that context matters and explain in detail that this war did not begin on October 7. I walk through both the wider context of the seventy-six years since the creation of the State of Israel and the more immediate context of the siege on Gaza for the last sixteen years before October 7. These chapters explain the Nakba—the ethnic cleansing of Palestine beginning in 1948—and argue for the importance of understanding Israel as a settler-colonial entity and an apartheid regime. I also explain the blockade against Gaza as the necessary context for any accurate understanding of current events. Chapter 4 argues that three factors enabled this genocide—and Western support for it: coloniality (political, economic, and control of narrative), racism, and theology (primarily Christian Zionism). Chapter 5 looks in detail at several responses from influential pastors, Christian politicians, theologians, church leaders, and denominations regarding the unfolding genocide. These responses varied from calling for peace to justifying the violence to turning a blind eye to the atrocities. Some called for peace with no force or tangible plan. Chapter 6 highlights the utterances of Palestinian Christians, including my own, especially the "Christ in the Rubble" manger and the sermons I gave during Christmas and Lent, which called out the silence of the Western church. I, then, in chapter 7, share about my pastoral work during the genocide, explaining the theology behind "Christ in the Rubble" and offering my understanding of the meaning of the cross as God's solidarity with humanity in its pain. Finally, chapter 8 builds on the words from my sermon that were quoted in the International Court of Justice and calls the church to action. This chapter features the solidarity responses that emerged from around the world and shows how a new community was created of those who advocated from different faith traditions for an end to the war.

A Book I Wish I Had Never Had to Write

Pastoring in the midst of war is challenging, and writing a book in such times felt, at many points, like an impossible task. Emotionally, spiritually, and psychologically, it has been a very difficult year. The book was written in the midst of watching and reading daily reports of the war, while living in fear that the war could extend to the West Bank, where I live. In fact, as I finished the manuscript of this book, the war had already extended to Lebanon, killing thousands, while the seeds of genocide and ethnic cleansing are planted in the West Bank. I cannot also deny that there was always an element of risk in my activism; speaking out against Israel does come at a cost. My family and friends fear that I will be arrested and continue to plead with me to calm things down. And traveling in the midst of war is always filled with challenges and difficulties. Advocating while the war is still taking place is a mentally taxing task. Once when I was taking the pulpit to speak on Gaza, I received breaking news on my phone that more than a hundred people had just been killed in an attack on a mosque in Gaza. As much as I wanted to take a break that night, feeling helpless, I had to continue and to keep pleading and praying.

The pain, frustration, anger, powerlessness, and fear in my community have been overwhelming. The book was written in tears and anger. I cannot put into words how I felt as I watched with the world the images from the attack on the Al-Ahli hospital ten days into the war that left hundreds killed and injured. The images were brutal and traumatizing. Bodies, body parts, and blood all over the outside courtyard of the hospital. It was a massacre of innocent civilians who took refuge in the fields and courtyards of the hospital. When this particular attack happened, the churches in my hometown of Beit Sahour decided to ring the bells of our churches as a sign of mourning and anger. Our church has one of those old bells that you ring manually. It was very late in the night, and I did not want to wake up our gatekeeper, so I headed to the church myself and released my anger and anguish by pulling the rope to ring the bell as hard as I could for over fifteen minutes. I was traumatized. I was in tears. I was angry at God.

In fact, writing the book is, in itself, an act of protest—not only against those who enabled this war actively or through their silence, but also against the God of justice and mercy, for justice and mercy were sorely lacking in Gaza in the last year. The book is partially about my personal journey of protest, anger, and faith. I must admit, this was an unexpected journey, in that I never planned to be a public figure in this war. Since the creation of the "Christ in the Rubble" manger, it felt like I was put on trial, not knowing where I would be taken next. It truly felt as if someone was controlling this trial and taking me to unexpected and unplanned places.

Through this journey, I discovered the deep thirst for the Divine among the peoples of the world, from many diverse backgrounds. The crisis of this war evoked many spiritual and existential questions. During the war, I spoke not just about the war and the Palestinian perspective, but about faith and God amid suffering. Many resonated with my portrayal of a God who suffers with humanity in its brokenness and pain as much as they did with my political perspective on Palestine. People were moved by my efforts to humanize the children of Gaza. This points to a deep spiritual void within human beings and the need for faith leaders to speak into this void by amplifying the comforting voice of God. When I go through the thousands of comments on my interviews, sermons, and talks, I realize how much this voice is needed, and how much it is missing from our world. The comments also opened my eyes to common perceptions of religious leaders as divisive, narrow-minded figures who create conflicts rather than solve them. The positions of many faith leaders during this war exemplified this failing.

We live in a world full of suffering and human-created tragedies. Palestine is one place in this world, and the suffering of Palestinians is not above other sufferings. We should be aware of and speak out against the violence suffered by those in Sudan, Ukraine, Yemen, and other places of war and suffering. As I was finishing this book, the war against Gaza had already spread into Lebanon, and Israeli strikes had killed and displaced thousands in a mere few days. All lives are precious. We must not accept a world in which wars, mass killings, and displacements are normal. And we should not be comfortable when Christians not only accept war but promote it.

This book is a call to lament—for a genocide has taken place for all the world to see. It has unfolded before the silence of many who turned a blind eye to it—and those funding and empowering it. This book exposes and refutes the misuse and abuse of biblical texts in service of any form of violence. It is an indictment of Western Christian traditions and theologies of supremacy. It is also, therefore, a call to repentance.

It is also about faith, hope, and the presence of God in the midst of suffering. It presents a daring proposition: the concept of a suffering God who is found under the rubble in Gaza, and who allies in solidarity with those who suffer from the brutality of war, colonialism, racism, and colonial theologies. It is about resilience and defiance.

In reflecting on his priestly training in South Africa in the 1960s, Archbishop Desmond Tutu recalls learning that "engaged spirituality" was "central to an authentic Christian existence." This spirituality, while rooted primarily in contemplative Christian practice, manifests itself in sociopolitical engagement and activism in service of the most disenfranchised communities. How desperately this engaged spirituality is needed in our world today! Where profit for the privileged is protected at the expense of the minoritized, and the myth of safety generates overpolicing and militarization, we must advocate on behalf of the most vulnerable.

And so we must tear down the walls that insulate Western communities of faith from the reality of the genocidal war that has been raging in Gaza for over a year. We must insist that our brothers and sisters in Christ face the harsh realities of the world, and their own role in enabling them. In so doing, we aim to liberate not only ourselves but them as well. Like Tutu, I believe this liberatory work is at the core of the Christian faith. Not just faith leaders but everyday Christians must be attuned to the cry of the poor, the hungry, and the massacred because our faith has been built upon such a call.

1

A Genocide in Gaza

"Come take me. Will you come and take me? I'm so scared, please come!"

These were the last words heard from six-year-old Hind Rajab in Gaza. She was trapped in a car with five of her relatives, all of them dead. Israeli shelling had forced them to flee their homes. Due to poor weather, the mother had made the difficult decision to send her daughter in the vehicle along with her aunt, uncle, and three cousins while the rest of the family fled on foot. But the Israeli military ambushed the car, and Hind was the only survivor. She managed to call an emergency line in Gaza and pleaded for more than three hours on the phone for help.

"The tank is next to me. It's moving."

"I'm scared of the dark, come get me."

Twelve days later, Hind was found dead in the car with her relatives. A few meters away were the remains of another vehicle—completely burned, its engine spilling onto the ground. It was the ambulance of the Red Crescent, sent to rescue Hind. Tragically, the two crew members—Yusuf al-Zeino and Ahmed al-Madhoun—were killed when the ambulance was hit by Israeli forces. Yusuf and Ahmed sacrificed their lives trying to rescue Hind.[1]

1. Lucy Williamson, "Hind Rajab, 6, Found Dead in Gaza Days After

11

Hind's story is one of many such stories. For the last year, Palestinians—and people around the world—have seen a genocide unfold before our eyes. This was not a genocide in which the horrors were discovered after the fact. No one can claim to be shocked. No one can claim not to have known—even if the full extent of this genocide is still to be determined, since thousands are still believed to be under the rubble, and since many stories remain to be told, and many investigations to be carried out. Yet, what we have witnessed is horrifying enough. The stories and images from Gaza were horror stories and images.

Over and over we have witnessed children and entire families pulled from under the rubble. We have agonized over images of first responders searching the rubble, hoping to find any sign of life, and we have cried in pain with parents calling out the names of their missing children, hoping to find them alive. We have stood in grief before images of numerous bodies wrapped in white plastic bags, awaiting an undignified burial in a field near a hospital or school. We have been traumatized by gruesome images of collected body parts, or bodies of children without legs or even heads, and by the footage of living people being burned to death. We have been broken by images of starved children, who looked like walking skeletons, and angered by the images of children in incubators, at risk of dying if the fuel powering the generators ran out. We have been outraged by the images of abandoned babies found decomposed in an evacuated hospital. We have seen packed hospitals, with wounded people lying on the ground without the basic elements of medical care. We have seen too many pools of blood on hospital floors. We have heard too many stories of surgery without anesthesia, of children undergoing amputations without anesthesia. We have seen children separated from their parents in a shelling, calling out their parents' names in hospitals, hoping to find them alive. We have learned a new acronym

Phone Calls for Help," *BBC News*, February 10, 2024, https://tinyurl.com/ye3jrur8; Meg Kelly et al., "Palestinian Paramedics Said Israel Gave Them Safe Passage to Save a 6-Year-Old Girl in Gaza. They Were All Killed," *Washington Post*, April 16, 2024, https://tinyurl.com/yeyrumk6.

that is unique to Gaza: WCNSF—wounded child, no surviving family. There are thousands of WCNSFs.[2]

We have been shattered by recurring images of hundreds upon hundreds of families leaving their homes and neighborhoods on foot, moving from one so-called designated safe area to another, which brought memories and nightmares of the 1948 Nakba. We wept with the elderly man who, when he was being interviewed, cried because they keep telling him to move from place to place and he is exhausted from walking long distances carrying his remaining possessions.

We have been troubled by the images of thousands of refugees in tents. We have grieved when we have seen them running in desperation from bombing, or toward the rare sight of a food truck. We have shouted in anger at the images of children being forced to beg in streets for food, or sell drinks in exchange for bread. Gazans have been killed in this war by bombs, missiles, tank shells, and bullets. Some have been killed by roofs collapsing because of bombs. Some have been burned alive. Some have been killed through starvation. Some have been killed by heat when forced to walk from place to place on foot. Some have been killed through deprivation of medicines. Some have been killed through the destruction of hospitals. Some have been killed when air-dropped food packages have landed on them. Some have been killed through being left bleeding for hours because no one could help them without being shot at. Some have been killed through torture in Israeli prisons and detention centers. And we have seen or heard it all. For a full year we have pleaded: enough!

Thousands upon thousands have been severely wounded, and thousands have lost body parts; they are forced to live the rest of their lives handicapped, knowing that the entire health sector has collapsed in Gaza.

Thousands have been arrested, detained without trial or charges, tortured, and in some cases even raped.[3]

2. Dalia Haidar, "'Wounded Child, No Surviving Family': The Pain of Gaza's Orphans," *BBC News*, December 4, 2023, https://tinyurl.com/3xhzr9f6.
3. Jonah Valdez, "Video of Sexual Abuse at Israeli Prison Is Just Latest

Far too many children have been killed in this war. I think, for example, of Mohamed Abu Al-Qumsan, a Palestinian displaced from northern Gaza to a so-called safe zone in Deir al-Balah. Mohamed and his wife Jumana were blessed with newborn twins. They were four days old. Mohamed went to obtain birth certificates for his twins. When he returned, he discovered that an Israeli airstrike had killed his wife and the twins.

The images of Mohamed holding the birth certificates of his two children are heart wrenching. Their names were Aser and Aysel. They joined nearly seventeen thousand children killed in this war. This includes more than two thousand infants. Nameless. Faceless. Numbers. I wish I could say their names. They are not nameless to God: "For the kingdom of heaven belongs to such as these."

The numbers alone tell of the horror Gaza witnessed in one year following October 7, 2023. By October 6, 2024, almost 42,000 people, including nearly 17,000 children, had been killed in Gaza, with close to 100,000 people injured. In addition, more than 10,000 were missing.[4] More than 900 families were wiped out, erased from the Palestinian civil registry.[5]

The devastation across Gaza is total. According to the latest data from the United Nations Office for the Coordination of Humanitarian Affairs, the World Health Organization, and the Palestinian government, as of October 6, 2024, Israeli attacks have damaged or destroyed more than half of Gaza's homes, 80 percent of commercial facilities, 87 percent of school buildings, 68 percent of road networks,

Evidence Sde Teiman Is a Torture Site," *Intercept*, August 9, 2024, https://tinyurl.com/4nrs8vjw.

4. Data according to "Occupied Palestinian Territory," United Nations Office for the Coordination of Humanitarian Affairs, accessed November 19, 2024, https://tinyurl.com/y6hde9aa; "Israel-Gaza War in Maps and Charts: Live Tracker," *Al Jazeera*, accessed November 19, 2024, https://tinyurl.com/5fjeyrk5. The main source for these numbers is the Palestinian Ministry of Health in Gaza.

5. Mohammed Hussein, Mohammed Haddad, and Konstantinos Antonopoulos, "Know Their Names. Palestinian Families Killed in Israeli Attacks on Gaza," *Al Jazeera*, October 8, 2024, https://tinyurl.com/y6zz9eps.

and 68 percent of cropland; and when it comes to health-care facilities, only seventeen of thirty-six hospitals are *partially* functional.[6] Nearly the entire population of Gaza—1.9 million people—has been displaced, many of them multiple times, with no safe place to go.[7]

The numbers are horrifying, yet, as Joyce Msuya, the acting undersecretary-general and emergency relief coordinator in the United Nations, said: "No statistics or words can fully convey the extent of the physical, mental, and societal devastation that has taken place." It has indeed been, as many have described it, hell on earth.

Throughout, Israel and its allies have continued to insist that this was a limited war, aimed at the Palestinian militant group Hamas. It was a war of self-defense, in response to the attacks of October 7. We should not bypass October 7, and I will talk about what happened on that day next, and its impact. I will also consider the question: Can we truly consider the war on Gaza as a response to October 7?

A Massacre on October 7

October 7 is a day that no Israeli or Palestinian can ever forget. Everyone remembers where they were when they first heard the news, and how they felt. It was a Saturday morning. On that day, I was leading the daily morning prayer for the students in the Lutheran school in Beit Sahour, as I do every day. My phone was beeping like crazy with breaking news. A teacher at the school kept showing me headlines and videos of Hamas militants who broke the siege and were already in the streets of Israeli towns and kibbutzim outside of Gaza, shooting whatever they encountered. It was hard to finish the prayer with such distraction. We were shocked. We could not believe that anyone, let alone a large number of militants, could infiltrate the fence around Gaza, given the heavy Israeli security. Somehow I managed to finish the prayer and dismiss the students to their classes, only to

6. "Israel-Gaza War in Maps and Charts."

7. "One Year of Unimaginable Suffering Since the 7 October Attack," United Nations Office for the Coordination of Humanitarian Affairs, October 7, 2024, https://tinyurl.com/292s9dws.

be distracted by the sound of Israeli alarm sirens from Jerusalem, which is only a few miles away from the Bethlehem area, indicating that Hamas missiles were heading toward Jerusalem. We then heard a big explosion from a missile that hit near Jerusalem—and naturally, we were terrified. We realized immediately that this was war. This was different from previous times. My first priority was to secure the children of our school. In Palestinian schools, we have no shelters. Keeping hundreds of children in one place was a risk we were not willing to take. We immediately activated an emergency plan, evacuating the school and making sure that all 450 students got safely home. Amid this panic, I forgot to check on my own kids, who attend a different school. They were both home by then, and the youngest was beginning to panic, having heard that war was about to break out. I headed home immediately and comforted him. After that, like all Palestinians and Israelis, I was glued to my TV and my mobile phone, looking for any update, trying to figure out what on earth was happening in and around Gaza.

News and videos kept streaming in on social media. The videos were shocking. As Palestinians, we were under the impression that the siege on Gaza was unbreakable. We were amazed that anyone could break out—and in such numbers! Images of destroyed Israeli tanks and empty military bases were even more shocking. We thought the Israeli army was invincible.

The photographs were also disturbing. Unfiltered social media images showed dead Israelis stripped and dragged through the streets of Gaza, and hostages treated inhumanely. It was hard to watch, and a clear indication of the ugliness and messiness of what was unfolding that day. Although we did not quickly grasp the full extent of the massacre that took place on that day, clearly this was a major attack. It took days and weeks to learn the full extent of the massacre. More than 1,100 Israelis, and some foreign nationals, were killed on that day.[8] Around 240 were taken hostage inside the Gaza Strip by Hamas. A year after the abduction, Israel says 97 hostages remain in captivity, including the bodies of at least 34. The rest either were released in the

8. "Israel-Gaza War in Maps and Charts."

exchange deal in November 2023 or have been killed during the war.[9] Hamas committed war crimes on that day.[10] We witnessed some of them in videos that circulated on social media.

The attacks were planned for months. Shockingly, Israeli intelligence was notified about these plans but never took them seriously. According to the *New York Times* and major Israeli news outlets, Israeli officials obtained Hamas's battle plan for the October 7 attack more than a year before it happened, but the Israeli military and intelligence officials dismissed the plan as aspirational, considering it too difficult for Hamas to carry out.[11] Even on the day of the attack, there were notifications on the movement of the militants, but there was no adequate response.[12] October 7 is considered a major Israeli intelligence failure.[13] The fact that hundreds of militants were able to approach the fence in different locations at exactly the same time without setting off a big alarm for the Israelis could be an even bigger failure.

The attacks began at 6:30 a.m. An estimated 1,200 Hamas militants attacked the fence from ten locations. At the same time, Hamas fired thousands of rockets toward Israel, creating a distraction. Militants also used boats to attack by sea, and, by air, paragliders flew across the fence. Simple drones bombed surveillance points and radars atop watchtowers. Military bases were ambushed, and Israeli soldiers were caught by surprise. Many were killed on their beds, and others taken hostage. After taking control of the military bases,

9. Peter Saidel, Summer Said, and Anat Peled, "Hamas Took More Than 200 Hostages from Israel. Here's What We Know," *Wall Street Journal*, October 7, 2024, https://tinyurl.com/yk4p8wuw.

10. "October 7 Crimes Against Humanity, War Crimes by Hamas-Led Groups," Human Rights Watch, July 17, 2024, https://tinyurl.com/bdeftdys.

11. Ronen Bergman and Adam Goldman, "Israel Knew Hamas's Attack Plan More Than a Year Ago," *New York Times*, updated December 2, 2023, https://tinyurl.com/3ctntsyh.

12. "More Details Unveiled of IDF Intel on Oct. 7 Plans, Consults Hours Before Hamas Attack," *Times of Israel*, December 5, 2023, https://tinyurl.com/9ctam4mu.

13. Oren Liebermann and Tamar Michaelis, "Calls for Accountability Grow over October 7 Failures, but Israel's Leadership Is Unlikely to Act," *CNN*, June 20, 2024, https://tinyurl.com/3eefnfx9.

Hamas militants went outside the strip, and the towns and kibbut-zim were at their mercy. But no mercy was shown, as evident by the massacre from the Supernova music festival.

The festival was an overnight event in an open area approxi-mately five kilometers outside of Gaza. More than four thousand Israeli and international young men and women were partying all night in the open space. It is hard to know whether the militants were aware of the festival, but official Israeli reports concluded that the attack on the music festival was not planned.[14] Once the militants arrived at the location of the festival, chaos ensued. What happened in the festival was horrifying and evil. Hamas militants mercilessly shot hundreds dead—executed them, murdered them—and took many others hostage. The images of dead bodies scattered across the area were brutal and traumatizing; so were those of the panicking participants fleeing for their lives or being taken hostage.[15]

Similar things happened in the towns, villages, and kibbutzim around the Gaza Strip. Militants and gun-wielding civilians from Gaza entered these communities, shooting at cars, homes, and anything else in their way. They entered homes, shot at people, and took many hostages, including children and elderly people. It was a horror movie, except it was real, and it was recorded by the militants' own head cameras. Even Thai workers who were in these areas for labor were not spared; the militants killed many and took others hostage.

It took hours before the Israeli army and police responded. As word spread in the Gaza Strip that the fence was compromised, hun-dreds if not thousands of Gazans headed toward the openings in the fence and toward the Israeli communities, looting homes and steal-

14. "Hamas Had Not Planned to Attack Music Festival, Israeli Report Says," *Al Jazeera*, November 18, 2023, https://tinyurl.com/3e5ay9zv.

15. For more on the festival slaughter, see Roger Cohen, "Slaughter at a Festival of Peace and Love Leaves Israel Transformed," *New York Times*, updated December 27, 2023, https://tinyurl.com/yc8pwnen; David Browne, Nancy Dillon, and Kory Grow, "They Wanted to Dance in Peace. And They Got Slaughtered," *Rolling Stone*, October 15, 2023, https://tinyurl.com/mjmw2wvv.

ing cars, farm machinery, and even horses, all while filming themselves wandering in these communities and, in some instances, abducting hostages or helping in the transportation of the hostages.

About three hours into the attack, Israeli military helicopters appeared. By then, much damage was already done. Israeli pilots launched several air strikes against those heading back toward the Gaza Strip. In the chaos, Israeli pilots may have killed Israeli hostages along with Hamas militants.[16] Israeli tanks arrived at the kibbutzim where Hamas militants were present, in some instances holding hostages in their homes. Clashes erupted, and many were killed. The Israeli newspaper *Haaretz* published a lengthy investigative report that claimed that the Israeli military ordered the use of what is known as the Hannibal Directive on October 7, to prevent Hamas from taking soldiers captive.[17] The Hannibal Directive is an unwritten code that allows the Israeli military to use any force necessary to prevent Israeli soldiers from being captured and taken into enemy territory, even if it leads to those captives' deaths.[18] *Haaretz* reported not knowing "whether or how many civilians and soldiers were hit due to these procedures, but the cumulative data indicates that many of the kidnapped people were at risk, exposed to Israeli gunfire, even if they were not the target."[19] Israel's initial report of the number killed was 1,400. This number was later reduced to less than 1,200, as it was revealed that many of the incinerated bodies found in the houses and kibbutzim attacked by the Israeli military were militants. Israelis and Palestinians may have died together in the Israeli counterattacks.

16. Eric Tlozek, Orly Halpern, and Allyson Horn, "Israeli Forces Accused of Killing Their Own Citizens Under the 'Hannibal Directive' During October 7 Chaos," *ABC News Australia*, September 6, 2024, https://tinyurl.com/yckyx4eh.

17. Yaniv Kubovich, "IDF Ordered Hannibal Directive on October 7 to Prevent Hamas Taking Soldiers Captive," *Haaretz*, July 7, 2024, https://tinyurl.com/mpryfyjh.

18. "Why Did Israel Deploy Hannibal Directive, Allowing Killing of Own Citizens?" *Al Jazeera*, July 9, 2024, https://tinyurl.com/4rtpbtu7.

19. Kubovich, "IDF Ordered Hannibal Directive on October 7 to Prevent Hamas Taking Soldiers Captive."

When the dust settled, the shocking extent of the carnage was revealed. According to a report by the Independent International Commission of Inquiry on the Occupied Palestinian Territory (including East Jerusalem, and Israel), which is part of the Office of the High Commissioner for Human Rights (OHCHR), the leading UN entity on human rights:

> According to Israeli sources, more than 1,200 persons were killed directly by members of the various Palestinian armed groups and others and by rockets and mortars launched from the Gaza Strip. Of these, at least 809 were civilians, including at least 280 women, 68 were foreign nationals and 314 were Israeli military personnel. Among those killed were 40 children (including at least 23 boys and 15 girls confirmed by the Commission) and 25 persons aged 80 and over. In addition, 14,970 people were injured and transferred to hospitals for treatment. At least 252 people were abducted to Gaza as hostages, including 90 women, 36 children, older people and members of Israeli Security Forces. About 20 of these abductees were members of Israeli Security Forces, many of whom have since been killed in captivity.[20]

Human Rights Watch published a detailed investigative report about October 7. The report concluded that "Hamas-led armed groups committed numerous war crimes and crimes against humanity against civilians during the October 7 assault on southern Israel. Palestinian fighters committed summary killings, hostage-taking and other war crimes, and the crimes against humanity of murder and wrongful imprisonment."[21]

October 7 was the deadliest day for the Jews since the Holocaust,

20. "Detailed Findings on Attacks Carried Out on and After 7 October 2023 in Israel. Independent International Commission of Inquiry on the Occupied Palestinian Territory, including East Jerusalem, and Israel," Office of the United Nations High Commissioner for Human Rights, June 10, 2024, https://tinyurl.com/utdktvr3, p. 6.

21. "October 7 Crimes Against Humanity, War Crimes by Hamas-Led Groups."

and has been described as the worst atrocity against Jews since the Holocaust.[22] Many have described it as Israel's 9/11.[23] One could argue that just as September 11 altered the United States, so has October 7 altered Israel. It terrorized the Israeli people and deepened their national trauma and anxiety, especially in the context of rising antisemitism across the globe. And for a nation of Holocaust survivors, it understandably evoked existential questions.

It also evoked a brutal, genocidal response. "We will take mighty vengeance for this black day," declared Israeli prime minister Benjamin Netanyahu.[24] The events of October 7 prompted several world leaders to announce their intention to visit Israel, including US president Joe Biden, French president Emmanuel Macron, German chancellor Olaf Scholz, and British prime minister Rishi Sunak. The intention was to show support, sympathy, and solidarity with Israel. I wonder if they realized that they were also giving the green light to a genocide? That they were signing off to a vengeance campaign? A retribution not of the scale of an "eye for an eye" but forty eyes for an eye, and much more?

Numerous factors—the pain and horror of that day; the desire of a militant government to avenge the killing of Israelis; the mind-set that insists that those who dare to attack Israel will be met with overwhelming destructive force; the backing, support, and cover of the world's superpowers, especially the United States; and the immunity Israel has enjoyed over the years from the international community—led to a genocidal response by Israel to October 7.

A Genocidal Response

"Genocide" is not a term to be used lightly. And it is not just conjecture. The term was created after the Holocaust and subsequently

22. Marcia Bronstein, "October 7 and the Legacy of Tisha B'Av," American Jewish Committee, August 12, 2024, https://tinyurl.com/4p9bwe8u.

23. Jon Schwarz, "Yes, This Is Israel's 9/11," *Intercept*, October 9, 2023, https://tinyurl.com/4uu4rhtj.

24. "Fears of a Ground Invasion of Gaza Grow as Israel Vows 'Mighty Vengeance,'" *Al Jazeera*, October 7, 2023, https://tinyurl.com/y2vz4m4m.

adopted within the Genocide Convention.[25] Article II of this document gives a clear definition of genocide:

> Genocide means any of the following acts committed with intent to destroy, in whole or in part, a national, ethnical, racial or religious group, as such:
> (a) Killing members of the group;
> (b) Causing serious bodily or mental harm to members of the group;
> (c) Deliberately inflicting on the group conditions of life calculated to bring about its physical destruction in whole or in part;
> (d) Imposing measures intended to prevent births within the group;
> (e) Forcibly transferring children of the group to another group.

This definition serves as a framework for our discussion and definition of a genocide, and it was the basis for South Africa's case against Israel in the International Court of Justice (ICJ), "Application of the Convention on the Prevention and Punishment of the Crime of Genocide in the Gaza Strip (South Africa v. Israel)."[26] The question that must be addressed is simple: Do the actions of Israel since October 7 fit the definition of the Genocide Convention?

I first publicly called the assault on Gaza a genocide on October 28, 2023.[27] We had heard that Christians besieged in the two churches were baptizing their infants during the bombardment, bracing for the worst. At that point, it was already clear. The signs of genocidal intent were unmistakable to those paying attention. The definition of genocide states that for a war to be a war of genocide,

---

25. "Convention on the Prevention and Punishment of the Crime of Genocide. 75th Anniversary," United Nations, December 2023, https://tinyurl.com/28c6h49t.

26. To read the full document, visit https://tinyurl.com/mc7w8hxp.

27. @MuntherIsaac, X, October 28, 2023, https://tinyurl.com/4ymmuw4x.

there must an *intent to destroy* the victim group *in whole or in part*. The intentions of Israel were clear from the beginning. Israeli prime minister Netanyahu set the tone on day one:

> We will take mighty vengeance for this black day. . . . We will take revenge for all the young people who lost their lives. We will target all of Hamas's positions. We will turn Gaza into a deserted island. To the citizens of Gaza, I say: You must leave now. We will target each and every corner of the strip.[28]

Netanyahu's words are very clear. This is not a war of "self-defense," as the West repeated over and over. This is clearly a vengeance campaign that aimed at turning Gaza into a "deserted island." Five days after October 7, Israeli president Isaac Herzog continued the pattern, declaring the entire "Palestinian nation" culpable for the actions of a few, thereby dismissing the distinction between armed fighters and innocent civilians.[29] Ariel Kallner, a member of the Israeli parliament, vocally advocated for a repeat of the mass expulsion witnessed in 1948, calling for another Nakba that would overshadow the original.[30] Yoav Gallant, Israel's defense minister, ordered a complete siege of the Gaza Strip, explicitly referring to everyone as "human animals"—including more than one million children:

> I have ordered a complete siege on the Gaza Strip. There will be no electricity, no food, no fuel, everything is closed. . . . We are fighting human animals and we are acting accordingly.[31]

28. "Fears of a Ground Invasion of Gaza Grow as Israel Vows 'Mighty Vengeance.'"

29. Chris McGreal, "The Language Being Used to Describe Palestinians Is Genocidal," *Guardian*, October 16, 2023, https://tinyurl.com/55cz46ak.

30. Joseph Krauss, "Israel's Recent Call for Mass Evacuation Echoes Catastrophic 1948 Palestinian Exodus," *PBS News*, October 13, 2023, https://tinyurl.com/29n4sbyf.

31. Emanuel Fabian, "Defense Minister Announces 'Complete Siege' of Gaza: No Power, Food or Fuel," *Times of Israel*, October 9, 2023, https://tinyurl.com/4utv9fy5.

Tembeka Ngcukaitobi, one of the lawyers who represented South Africa in its case against Israel in the ICJ, stated: "The evidence of genocidal intent is not only chilling, it is also overwhelming and incontrovertible." Further, this intent "to destroy Gaza has been nurtured at the highest level of state."[32]

Now let us consider the actions that constitute genocide as listed above. Proving that Israel did all these things is not difficult. In the ICJ, South African lawyers presented their claims that Israel's actions are part of a broader strategy that aligns with the definition of genocide. The lawyers listed several Israeli actions against Palestinians in Gaza that it asserted are genocidal in nature: killing Palestinians, including children, in large numbers; causing serious bodily and mental harm to Palestinians, including children, and inflicting on them conditions of life intended to bring about their destruction as a group; causing mass displacement and expulsion of Palestinians from their homes, alongside the large-scale destruction of homes and residential areas; depriving Palestinians of access to adequate food and water; depriving Palestinians of access to adequate medical care; depriving Palestinians of access to adequate shelter, clothes, hygiene, and sanitation; causing destruction of life for the Palestinian people; and imposing measures intended to prevent Palestinian births.[33] Again, proving all of this is not difficult, given the mounting evidence. It is important to note that South Africa presented its case in December 2023. As I write this, it has been ten months since then, and there is much more evidence.

In its court case, South Africa illustrated how Israel systematically killed a large number of Palestinians, including children. This is seen as a direct act of genocide because it targets a significant part of the Palestinian population in Gaza. If fifty thousand isn't mass killing—what is?

That Israel's actions are causing severe physical and mental harm to Palestinians is undeniable. This includes putting them in living

32. Stephanie van den Berg, Anthony Deutsch, and Toby Sterling, "At ICJ, South Africa Accuses Israel of Genocide in Gaza," Reuters, January 11, 2024, https://tinyurl.com/msvk7kc8.

33. Alexandra Sharp, "South Africa Presents Genocide Case Against Israel in Court," *Foreign Policy*, January 11, 2024, https://tinyurl.com/ufavs799.

conditions that are likely to destroy them as a group. Large-scale forced removals of Palestinians from their homes and the widespread destruction of residential areas are also genocidal acts. At the time of the trial, half of the buildings in Gaza had already been destroyed. At the time of writing, it's more than 60 percent. Israel has taken over more than 30 percent of all areas of Gaza by systematically demolishing neighborhoods. This is genocide.

The denial of essential resources like food and water occurred almost immediately. In fact, the Israeli leaders told us they were doing it. I have already quoted the words of Minister of Defense Gallant. Further, on October 9, 2023, in a video statement addressed to Hamas and Gaza residents, the Israeli army's Coordinator of Government Activities in the Territories, Major General Ghassan Alian, warned:

> Hamas became ISIS and the citizens of Gaza are celebrating instead of being horrified. Human animals are dealt with accordingly. Israel has imposed a total blockade on Gaza, no electricity, no water, just damage. You wanted hell, you will get hell.[34]

Since October 7, Palestinians in Gaza have been systematically deprived of essential resources. A report by the United Nations OHCHR stated that thirty-four Palestinians have died from malnutrition since October 7, the majority being children.[35] The report cites a chilling testimony by a group of experts in which they unequivocally state:

> We declare that Israel's intentional and targeted starvation campaign against the Palestinian people is a form of genocidal violence and has resulted in famine across all of Gaza.[36]

34. Video address by Ghassan Alian, October 10, 2023, https://tinyurl.com/395spv2k.

35. "UN Experts Declare Famine Has Spread Throughout Gaza Strip," Office of the United Nations High Commissioner for Human Rights, July 9, 2024, https://tinyurl.com/bdjabe66.

36. "UN Experts Declare Famine Has Spread Throughout Gaza Strip." The experts who said this are Michael Fakhri, special rapporteur on the right to food; Balakrishnan Rajagopal, special rapporteur on the right to adequate

Human Rights Watch, in a detailed report, determined that starvation is being used as a weapon of war.[37] Moreover, Israel has blocked access to necessary medical care for Palestinians in Gaza, worsening their living conditions and survival chances. I know people who died in Gaza for lack of medicine and medical care. People with chronic diseases were particularly vulnerable, especially those needing permanent medicine and hospital care, such as kidney dialysis patients and children in incubators.

In this war, the world has witnessed bombing of hospitals, targeting of medics, and abduction and murder of Palestinian doctors, to the extent that Gaza's health infrastructure has been systematically destroyed. In the beginning of April 2024, the World Health Organization warned that the "systematic dismantling of healthcare" in Gaza must end.[38] In the same month, Médecins Sans Frontières, also known as Doctors Without Borders, published a detailed report under the title "Gaza's Silent Killings: The Destruction of the Healthcare System in Rafah." The report concluded: "Gaza's entire healthcare system has been decimated and people are under siege. Without access to medical care, thousands more lives will be lost, beyond those killed in the Israeli bombardments seen in the news—these are Gaza's 'silent killings.'"[39]

---

housing; Tlaleng Mofokeng, special rapporteur on the right of everyone to the enjoyment of the highest attainable standard of physical and mental health; Francesca Albanese, special rapporteur on the situation of human rights in the Palestinian Territory occupied since 1967; Pedro Arrojo-Agudo, special rapporteur on the human rights to safe drinking water and sanitation; Paula Gaviria Betancur, special rapporteur on the human rights of internally displaced persons; George Katrougalos, independent expert on the promotion of a democratic and equitable international order; and Barbara G. Reynolds (chair), Bina D'Costa, Dominique Day, and Catherine Namakula, working group of experts on people of African descent.

37. "Israel: Starvation Used as Weapon of War in Gaza," Human Rights Watch, December 18, 2023, https://tinyurl.com/2s48jckw.

38. "Gaza: 'Systematic Dismantling of Healthcare Must End' Says WHO," United Nations, April 6, 2024, https://tinyurl.com/469kv4f8.

39. "Gaza's Silent Killings: The Destruction of the Healthcare System in Rafah," Médecins Sans Frontières, April 29, 2024, https://tinyurl.com/nkpbek28.

If this is not a genocide, what is? It must be stated that although the United States repeatedly denied that Israel was blocking aid to Gaza, the US Agency for International Development and the State Department's Bureau of Population, Refugees, and Migration both stated later in internal documents that Israel had deliberately blocked deliveries of food and medicine into Gaza.[40] According to ProPublica, US secretary of state Antony Blinken, who told Congress, "We do not currently assess that the Israeli government is prohibiting or otherwise restricting aid," had been informed of these conclusions before he made this declaration. This is complicity.

Going back to the case of genocide, we can also reference the denial of access to adequate shelter, clothing, and sanitation that further marginalizes Palestinians and exposes them to harsh living conditions. Israel has bombed and bulldozed cultural and heritage sites, including a newly built cultural center that belonged to the Orthodox Church in Gaza. In the first 100 days of this war, *all twelve universities* in Gaza were bombed and wholly or partly destroyed.[41] Schools have been blown up, and scholars and scientists were killed,[42] in what has been called "educide"[43] and "scholasticide." UN experts stated in April of 2024:

> With more than 80% of schools in Gaza damaged or destroyed, it may be reasonable to ask if there is an intentional effort to comprehensively destroy the Palestinian education system, an action known as "scholasticide."[44]

40. Bret Murphy, "Israel Deliberately Blocked Humanitarian Aid to Gaza, Two Government Bodies Concluded. Antony Blinken Rejected Them," *ProPublica*, September 24, 2024, https://tinyurl.com/etvvn3ua.

41. Chandi Desai, "Israel Has Destroyed or Damaged 80% of Schools in Gaza. This Is Scholasticide," *Guardian*, June 8, 2024, https://tinyurl.com/39d6hm58.

42. "How Israel Has Destroyed Gaza's Schools and Universities," *Al Jazeera*, January 24, 2024, https://tinyurl.com/yjnnrcfd.

43. Patrick Jack, "Academia in Gaza 'Has Been Destroyed' by Israeli 'Educide,'" *Times Higher Education*, January 29, 2024, https://tinyurl.com/4jdft7ja.

44. "UN Experts Deeply Concerned over 'Scholasticide' in Gaza," Office

And according to the head of the Euro-Mediterranean Human Rights Monitor based in Geneva, the targeting of educational institutions by the Israeli army is systematic and deliberate.[45]

The South African case was concise, comprehensive, and compelling. So was the initial finding of the court in January:

> In the Court's view, the facts and circumstances mentioned above are sufficient to conclude that at least some of the rights claimed by South Africa and for which it is seeking protection are plausible. This is the case with respect to the right of the Palestinians in Gaza to be protected from acts of genocide and related prohibited acts.[46]

The court also said that Israel must ensure "with immediate effect" that its forces not commit any of the acts prohibited by the convention. Palestinian human rights organizations welcomed the ruling and argued that it is "a de facto ceasefire," hoping that it would bring an end to the war. The organizations added: "Through this ruling, the Court conveys a clear message: no State is above the law or immune from legal scrutiny."[47]

Sadly, they were wrong, not in their assessment, but in their assumptions that the world would hold Israel accountable or that at least the ruling would lead to a cease-fire. Months passed, and this genocidal war continued. Later in the war, eleven countries joined South Africa in its ongoing case against Israel: Nicaragua, Belgium, Colombia, Turkey, Libya, Egypt, Maldives, Mexico, Ireland, Chile, and Spain.

---

of the United Nations High Commissioner for Human Rights, April 18, 2024, https://tinyurl.com/yc4uxsza.

45. Sally Ibrahim, "Here Are All the Universities That Israel Has Destroyed in Gaza," *New Arab*, September 20, 2024, https://tinyurl.com/3vrwv5ff.

46. To read the full document, "Application of the Convention on the Prevention and Punishment of the Crime of Genocide in the Gaza Strip (South Africa *v.* Israel)," see https://tinyurl.com/37mu6wc5.

47. "Palestinian Organizations Welcome Landmark ICJ Provisional Measures Order Finding That Israel's Actions in Gaza Are Plausibly Genocidal," Al Haq, January 26, 2024, https://tinyurl.com/2s98fzj8.

In addition, many leading genocide and Holocaust scholars, including Israelis and Jews, concluded that what Israel has done since October 7 amounts to genocide. Raz Segal, associate professor of Holocaust and genocide studies at Stockton University, wrote in a piece for *Jewish Currents*, a progressive Jewish magazine, published on October 13, 2023, that the assault on Gaza is "a textbook case of genocide unfolding in front of our eyes." He concluded:

> Indeed, Israel's genocidal assault on Gaza is quite explicit, open, and unashamed. Perpetrators of genocide usually do not express their intentions so clearly, though there are exceptions. . . . Gallant's orders on October 9th were no less explicit. Israel's goal is to destroy the Palestinians of Gaza. And those of us watching around the world are derelict in our responsibility to prevent them from doing so.[48]

Omer Bartov, professor of Holocaust and genocide studies at Brown University, published an op-ed in the *New York Times* on November 10, 2023:

> As a historian of genocide, I believe that there is no proof that genocide is currently taking place in Gaza, although it is very likely that war crimes, and even crimes against humanity, are happening. . . . There is still time to stop Israel from letting its actions become a genocide. We cannot wait a moment longer.[49]

Nine months later, Bartov, who is a former Israeli soldier, wrote a lengthy piece in the *Guardian*, in which he talked about a contentious visit he made to Israel in June. He now stated that Israel's actions were genocidal:

48. Raz Segal, "A Textbook Case of Genocide," *Jewish Currents*, October 13, 2023, https://tinyurl.com/32pum2n5.

49. Omer Bartov, "What I Believe as a Historian of Genocide," *New York Times*, November 10, 2023, https://tinyurl.com/5jn6rpsj.

By the time I traveled to Israel, I had become convinced that at least since the attack by the IDF [Israel Defense Forces] on Rafah on May 6, 2024, it was no longer possible to deny that Israel was engaged in systematic war crimes, crimes against humanity and genocidal actions.[50]

Amos Goldberg, a Holocaust and genocide researcher at the Hebrew University, also concluded in April:

Yes, it is genocide. It is so difficult and painful to admit it, but despite all that, and despite all our efforts to think otherwise, after six months of brutal war we can no longer avoid this conclusion.[51]

Goldberg lists several scholars who also concluded that it is a genocide, including Jeffrey Sachs, a professor of economics at Columbia University, and "a Jew with a warm attitude toward traditional Zionism, with whom heads of state all over the world regularly consult on international issues,"[52] who speaks of the Israeli genocide as something "taken for granted."[53]

In March 2023 Francesca Albanese, United Nations Special Rapporteur on the Occupied Palestinian Territories, submitted a report on the human-rights situation in the Palestinian territories occupied since 1967, in which she concluded:

By analysing the patterns of violence and Israel's policies in its onslaught on Gaza, this report concludes that there are reasonable

50. Omer Bartov, "As a Former IDF Soldier and Historian of Genocide, I Was Deeply Disturbed by My Recent Visit to Israel," *Guardian*, August 13, 2024, https://tinyurl.com/5n84jcr3.

51. Amos Goldberg (translated by Sol Salbe), "Yes, It Is Genocide," The Palestine Project, April 18, 2024, https://tinyurl.com/43vuddw3. The original article in Hebrew: https://tinyurl.com/3u9hj5jh.

52. Goldberg, "Yes, It Is Genocide."

53. See, for example, Jeffrey Sachs, "US Is Complicit in Israeli Genocide," YouTube, March 17, 2024, https://tinyurl.com/8fb46t77.

grounds to believe that the threshold indicating Israel's commission of genocide is met.[54]

In December 2023, over fifty-five scholars of the Holocaust, genocide, and mass violence warned of "the danger of genocide" in Israel's attack on Gaza.[55] And in May 2024, a joint report by the University Network for Human Rights, International Human Rights Clinic, Boston University School of Law, International Human Rights Clinic, Cornell Law School, Centre for Human Rights, University of Pretoria, and the Lowenstein Human Rights Project at Yale Law School concluded:

> After reviewing the facts established by independent human rights monitors, journalists, and United Nations agencies, we conclude that Israel's actions in and regarding Gaza since October 7, 2023, violate the Genocide Convention. Specifically, Israel has committed genocidal acts of killing, causing serious harm to, and inflicting conditions of life calculated to bring about the physical destruction of Palestinians in Gaza, a protected group that forms a substantial part of the Palestinian people.[56]

The above-mentioned views are only samples; there is much more. Genocide is not a matter of opinion. My *opinion* should not count. I am not an expert. However, given all the facts, studies, and expert testimony, we can say that the burden of the proof now lies with those

54. Francesca Albanese, "Anatomy of a Genocide: Report of the Special Rapporteur on the Situation of Human Rights in the Palestinian Territories Occupied Since 1967," Office of the United Nations High Commissioner for Human Rights, March 25, 2024, https://tinyurl.com/mrxempuk. The final version was posted in July 2024: https://tinyurl.com/2srw8drm.

55. Raz Segal, "Statement of Scholars in Holocaust and Genocide Studies on Mass Violence in Israel and Palestine Since 7 October," Contending Modernities, December 9, 2023, https://tinyurl.com/yhy9sv73.

56. "Genocide in Gaza: Analysis of International Law and Its Application to Israel's Military Actions Since October 7, 2023," University Network for Human Rights, May 15, 2024, https://tinyurl.com/mrxyz7fk.

who deny that it is a genocide. For those who object to the use of this term, I must question not only their analysis but also their motives. And given that this war has been taking place for more than a year, and that with every passing day more people are brutally killed, the failure to acknowledge reality and call things by name only enables the aggressors and gives a green light for Israel to continue its crimes.

As Christians, we must take these reports seriously. We must respect the rule of law in accordance with Romans 13. What message are we sending to the world by choosing to ignore these reports? Or by undermining international law and universal conventions? The fact that many Christian leaders and churches still did not use the word "genocide" to describe the actions of Israel has to do mainly with theologies that they have adopted over the years. These theologies have led them not only to support Israel blindly and unconditionally, but also to ignore clear and obvious war crimes, something that I will unpack more in detail later in this book. Denying that what happened in Gaza is a genocide affects the credibility of our Christian witness.

But What About October 7?

What about October 7? This is a question I am almost always asked when I speak about Gaza. This question implies that what Israeli forces have done in Gaza since October 7 is an appropriate response to what Palestinian militants did on October 7 and therefore cannot be a genocide.

How do we in today's polarizing and toxic environment, where it seems we cannot have any sensible conversation, explain that Palestinians can speak of numerous similar "supernova experiences" before and after October 7 without undermining the terror and trauma of what happened at that festival? When will the world pay attention to *our* suffering and pain? To our Nakba? Since October 7, forty-two thousand Palestinians have been killed, and we are still asking that question.

It is really hard to talk about October 7 as a Palestinian, because anything we say toward explaining the context of it or the Palestinian trauma that led to the day is interpreted as a justification of what was done that day. Palestinians are expected to begin every conversation by condemning October 7, while the other side and their supporters are never asked about the seventy-six years that led to that horrifying day. The trauma and horrifying nature of that day have foreclosed the possibility of any sensible conversation about Palestine and the Palestinians, or even about October 7. While I have always been against all forms of violence, it is important to address October 7 in the context of the dynamic of occupied versus occupier. Many Palestinians would emphasize that occupied people have the right for even *armed* resistance, as clearly stated in the UN resolution titled "Right of Peoples to Self-Determination/Struggle by All Available Means"[57] (something I personally do not endorse). But it is really important to distinguish between attacking military bases and targeting civilians. October 7 was both, and more civilians were killed than army personnel. This must be acknowledged.

Further, Palestinians tried to emphasize that pressure leads to unwanted results. Gazans were in what can be described as a pressure cooker. Sadly, and tragically, we saw this coming, and in 2020 I wrote:

> Things are beyond urgent. The current status quo in the land is not sustainable. My fear, and I hope that I am wrong, is that we are on the verge of a tragic collapse. To simply assume that life under occupation will become the norm is delusional. No people group will accept living under such conditions.[58]

I am not in the business of predictive prophecy. I wrote these words because I live under the dehumanizing apartheid of military occupation—and my life in the West Bank is a walk in the park in comparison to how things were in Gaza for sixteen years *before* October 7. Sadly,

---

57. "Right of Peoples to Self-Determination/Struggle by All Available Means—GA Resolution," United Nations, accessed October 9, 2024, https://tinyurl.com/4sh9vyma.

58. Munther Isaac, *The Other Side of the Wall* (InterVarsity, 2020), 220.

we saw this coming. We warned against it.[59] And on October 7, our fears became a reality.

So, what about October 7? First, let me state the obvious. Like most Palestinian Christian clergy and theologians, I have always opposed all forms of violence, even in the face of oppression.[60] In fact, it feels awkward and even insulting when Palestinian Christians are asked such a question, given our long-standing stances, and our commitment to the ethics of Jesus—especially when the people asking the question are Western Christians who do not share our commitment to the nonviolent ethics of Jesus. I cannot but condemn the killing of innocent people, especially families and children in their homes. Even if one maintains that Palestinians have the right to defend themselves and resist their occupiers and besiegers, killing festival participants or kidnapping children cannot be described as acts of resistance. We cannot and must not deny that horrible and evil crimes took place on October 7.

Second, and having stated the obvious, I must ask in return whether those asking this question have condemned the seventy-six years of Israeli oppression against Palestinians. I would even argue that those who have not condemned all that Israel has been doing toward the Palestinians and Gazans, in particular leading to October 7, are morally unqualified to address what happened on October 7. Throughout this war, I called out the hypocrisy of the Western world for its blatant and racist double standards. They cry "foul" using the strongest terms of condemnation when Israelis are killed and kidnapped, yet remain silent when it is Palestinians who are killed, kidnapped, tortured, and abused.

Third, for those obsessed with asking "but what about October 7?" let me say this: If you believe that what Israel has committed since October 7 can be explained as an appropriate response to what

59. "Open Letter from the National Coalition of Christian Organizations in Palestine," World Council of Churches, June 21, 2017, https://tinyurl.com/bdf7tetw.

60. See, for example, sections 4.2 and 4.3 of the Kairos Document: "A Moment of Truth: A Word of Faith, Hope and Love from the Heart of Palestinian Suffering" [2009], Kairos Palestine, accessed November 20, 2024, https://tinyurl.com/2f87b2n6.

happened that day, then you lack any sense of fairness and moral responsibility. I know this might sound harsh, but I truly believe that it is reprehensible to argue that the brutality of the killing and destruction, the high number of civilians and especially children killed, the utter destruction of the infrastructure, and the forced starvation are an appropriate response to October 7. It is an expression of vile racism to argue that the brutal killing of 42,000 Palestinians is a response to the killing of 1,200 Israelis. I say this not to devalue the lives of Israelis lost but to emphasize that all lives are equally precious. Moreover, I will continue to challenge the evil mind-set that would justify massacring hundreds of Palestinians with one push of a button by arguing that it was done to kill "one Hamas terrorist," as has often been argued throughout this war.

Continuing to cite October 7 as a justification is in fact a defense and an endorsement of a vindictive genocidal war. There is no other way to describe it.

I Am Sorry, My God

Nakba is the Arabic word Palestinians use to describe the mass displacement and dispossession that took place in 1948. The word means catastrophe. The displacement and dispossession of Palestinians are not past tense. This has been a continuous process. This is why we speak about the Nakba in the present tense. The Nakba continues. The war against Gaza is one more very intense episode of this process of the erasure of Palestinians, their displacement and dispossession.

Earlier in this war a Palestinian friend sent me a poem by Palestinian Druze poet Samih al-Qasim. It captures powerfully how we feel today. Al-Qasim wrote these words about Gaza in 2009, yet they seem to describe the Palestinian experience throughout the last seventy-six years, and these words are so relevant today, maybe even in a stronger way. This poem helped me put words to how I and millions of Palestinians felt as we watched this genocide unfold. It is really a psalm of lament. The poem is called "I Am Sorry."[61] Here are my translations

61. Samih al-Qasim, *Ana Muta'sif: Sarbiya* (Dar Al-Shorouq, 2009), 140–42.

of some excerpts from this poem. Naturally, the English translation does not fully capture the emotions of the original.

> I am deeply distressed / The soldiers are driving me away from the door of my house / And I hope for my life through my death. . . .
> My father's homeland has become a graveyard / The homes of those who believe are desolate / The orchards of those who believe are deserted / Their schools are forsaken. . . .My God, my God, is there any forgiveness? Is there no forgiveness? No forgiveness? My God, my torment is long, cruel, and unfortunate / You are forgiving, merciful, and just / My God, my God, I am sorry / I am sorry, God. God, I am sorry / I am sorry / I am sorry.

It is hard to read or listen to this poem without shedding tears for Palestine and Palestinians. The Palestinian experience is an intense, ongoing tragedy. Poetry reaches the depth of our souls and brings deep emotions. This poem describes vividly the experience of being a Palestinian over the last seventy-six years. It expresses emotionally the experience of abandonment by God and the world. But it also expresses faith—for why else would the poet keep praying, even complaining to God, and begging for forgiveness? The poet seems to imply that somehow his sins and those of his people are responsible for this tragedy. This is *not* a doctrinal statement, and it is worth mentioning that the poet was a member of the Communist Party. Yet I feel that in this poem he embodies a profound theological perspective stemming from the deep pit of darkness. This is how Palestinians throughout this war have felt—abandoned in the deep pit of darkness, awaiting our fate, with only our faith to hold firm to. Yet somehow, from deep down the pit of darkness, Palestinians feel closeness to God—calling out the divine, pleading for mercy and forgiveness.

2

This War Did Not Start on October 7

Evangelical leader Anne Graham Lotz, daughter of the late evangelist Billy Graham, was asked to help "the average American understand the conflict in Israel." Her answer:

> The conflict in Israel goes back millennia. . . .
>
> God promised Israel—Jacob and his sons—the land, and He also gave land to the descendants of Ishmael, which is a lot of what we see in the Arab world. They've got a lot of oil under their land. He blessed them, but the covenant nation belongs to Israel. God is the one who ordained that. . . .
>
> Yet there's a wicked agenda, the leadership of Hamas and Hezbollah and in the Gaza strip and Iran and Syria. They don't want to live with Israel. They want to destroy her. They want to push her into the sea. I think it goes back to an anti-Semitic core and that fight that began when Isaac was born with his older brother Ishmael. . . .
>
> Bottom line, God gave the land to Israel and her neighbors are not accepting.[1]

1. Tiffany Jothen, "Anne Graham Lotz Q&A on the Crisis in Israel," Billy Graham Evangelistic Association, June 11, 2021, https://tinyurl.com/2s48xd9j.

This is how many American Christians understand the reality in Palestine. They believe that Arabs and Jews are fighting because Arabs resent Jews and want to destroy them. As someone who lives in Palestine, I am outraged by this misrepresentation, which completely misses the point and engages in a mythical discourse that is detached from reality and historical events. As a Christian scholar and pastor, I am appalled by how it misinterprets and abuses the Bible. I am also angered by the mischaracterization and demonization of my people as hateful and violent.

Lotz believes that Arabs are destined by God to hate Jews. According to her, Palestinians hate Jews and desire their destruction because Palestinians are antisemitic by design. She traces this hatred back to biblical times, suggesting all of this is the fault of Palestinians—that since the time of Ishmael, they have not accepted that God gave the land to the Jewish people. The basis of this fault is simple: Palestinians are not the descendants of Isaac, with whom God made an everlasting covenant, but of Ishmael. And the descendants of Ishmael, Lotz argues, received *other* lands in the region. Theirs are marked by an abundance of oil.

Before we even consider the accuracy of Lotz's claims, let us stop and imagine how this God would sit with Palestinians. Are they expected to accept this theology at face value, this claim that God destined them for displacement rather than promise? This outrageous and hateful rhetoric that Lotz employs is factually and theologically unsound on multiple levels. I refuse to accept that Jews and Arabs are destined to hate one another because the Bible decreed this thousands of years ago. Our destiny here in this land should not depend on our DNA. In addition, can we equate the Jews of today with Abraham, and the Arabs and Palestinians of today with Ishmael? Is this, really, how we should try to comprehend one of the most tragic and complex realities in our world today—by imposing a certain biblical fatalism?

The argument that the conflict underlying the current reality in Palestine and the war on Gaza is millennia old is factually wrong. The current enmity between Palestinians and Israelis does indeed have roots, but they are modern, stemming from the events leading to the creation of the State of Israel in 1948. Palestinian Arabs and Jews did not fight for thousands of years prior to this. Albert Einstein, the famous Jewish scientist, said in 1939, during the Palestinian revolt against Zionism:

> There could be no greater calamity than a permanent discord between us and the Arab people. . . . We must strive for a just and lasting compromise with the Arab people. . . . Let us recall that in former times no people lived in greater friendship with us than the ancestors of these same Arabs.[2]

In fact, an honest assessment of Jewish history shows that Jews suffered most at the hands of Christians, especially in the West, not Arabs or Muslims. A Jewish scholar who participated with me in an interfaith forum once said that if there is such a thing as a "Judeo-Christian" tradition, it consists of Christians persecuting Jews. We can talk about the inquisitions and forced conversions. We can talk about years of theological antisemitism, which produced hateful attitudes toward Jews, which in turn culminated in the evil of the Holocaust, in which six million Jews were killed in the most brutal ways imaginable. European Christians, not Arab Muslims, committed these evils.

When it comes to the war on Gaza, it is crucial to understand that this war did not start on October 7, 2023. Palestinians have repeatedly tried to communicate this reality to Westerners. This war has a context. It did not ignite in a vacuum. It is completely deceptive to portray October 7 as an isolated incident. Saying this is by no means an attempt to defend or justify the actions of Hamas on that day. I do not deny or justify the horrible evils that some Hamas militants and civilians inflicted on innocent Israeli children and civilians on that day, such as killing families in their homes and kidnapping innocent civilians and children. Nor do I legitimize the abuse of corpses and the sexual violence that took place on that day. Such actions cannot be justified as acts of self-defense or resistance. Having said that,

---

2. "Einstein Counsels 'Reason' on Palestine, Urges Arab-Jewish Amity," *Jewish Telegraphic Agency*, May 29, 1939, https://tinyurl.com/2fcpacww, pp. 4–5.

I feel it is important to mention that mischaracterizations of that day gave many the impression that only civilians in their homes were killed on October 7. This is not true or accurate. Hundreds of Israeli soldiers were also killed that day, and the number of children killed was thirty-six. This is horrific and tragic. As a man of faith and follower of Jesus, I lament even the killing of the Israeli soldiers. Every life is precious, and those soldiers were victims of the brutal reality of war.

But October 7 has a context. For Palestinians, October 7 was a response to decades of oppression and suffering. If we are to move forward, we must explain the root causes of the Palestinian tragedy. Ignoring the context, purposefully or not, will lead to disingenuous characterizations of Palestinians as hateful and seeking to eliminate Israeli Jews. It should not come as a surprise that Palestinians are angered when people refer to October 7 as an attack motivated by hatred toward Jews for simply being Jewish. *Palestinians have a problem with Zionism and the State of Israel, not Jews and Judaism.* This chapter seeks to highlight this crucial distinction. What follows is an invitation to try to understand our lived reality for the last seventy-six years. This is not simply a detached overview of historical events, nor is it a political analysis. This is the lived experience of millions of Palestinians, including my family and my community, and certainly that of Gazans.

As you begin to understand the context of the past seventy-six years through our eyes and experience, you will understand the reason behind our frustration and anger. You will understand why I, as a Palestinian pastor, argue that if you were outraged and horrified by the violence of October 7 yet are completely silent and ambivalent over decades of systematic violence against the Palestinians, then you have no moral credibility to engage in this discussion. The systematic violence that I am referring to came to us in the form of *settler colonialism, ethnic cleansing, apartheid,* and *siege*. These terms might come across as exaggerations that aim to cast Israel in a negative light. But these terms have clear definitions, and I only use them because their occurrences have been clearly documented and continue in Palestine today.

Settler Colonialism Explained

One of the biggest misconceptions about the situation in Palestine is that it is a "conflict." The phrase "Palestinian-Israeli conflict" is used often, and it gives the impression that we are talking about two roughly equal entities fighting over ideological, religious, political, or territorial differences. Even the description of the situation as merely an occupation is inaccurate.[3] A careful and honest reading of the past and the present will clearly show that what we are dealing with is settler colonialism. This statement should not be controversial; the identification of Israel as a settler-colonial state is well established among contemporary historians and scholars.[4]

Settler colonialism is a form of colonialism in which the existing inhabitants of a territory are displaced by settlers who take land by force and establish a permanent society where their privileged status is enshrined in law.[5] Palestinian theologian and historian Mitri Raheb explains that "settler colonialism describes contexts where colonization constitutes an ongoing reality rather than a singular event in the past."[6] Leading scholar of settler colonialism Patrick Wolfe explains, "Settler colonialism destroys to replace."[7] Israel's actions in historic Palestine over the last century accurately fit these

3. Mitri Raheb, *Decolonizing Palestine: The Land, the People, the Bible* (Orbis Books, 2023), 19.

4. According to Raheb (*Decolonizing Palestine*, 21): "While settler colonialism theory was first used for contexts like Australia, New Zealand, and North America, several major writers have published works recently applying settler colonialism to the State of Israel, among them Lorenzo Veracini, Magid Shihadeh, Steven Salaita, Shira Robinson, Elia Zureik, Nadim Rouhana, Areej Sabbagh-Khoury, Nahla Abdo, and, most recently, Rashid Khalidi in his comprehensive work, *The Hundred Years' War on Palestine: A History of Settler Colonialism and Resistance, 1917-2017*."

5. Jennifer Schuessler, "What Is 'Settler Colonialism'?" *New York Times*, January 22, 2024, https://tinyurl.com/4u8hx8au.

6. Raheb, *Decolonizing Palestine*, 20.

7. Quoted in J. Kēhaulani Kauanui, "'A Structure, Not an Event': Settler Colonialism and Enduring Indigeneity," *Lateral* 5, no. 1 (Spring 2016): 2, https://doi.org/10.25158/L5.1.7.

definitions. From its inception, the Zionist movement was a colonial movement. Palestinian scholar at the Hebrew University Areej Sabbagh-Khoury argues that the Zionist movement "used the terminology of colonization," and that "permanent settlement was a core goal of the movement's founders." She quotes Theodore Herzl, the father of political Zionism, who in 1902 pleaded with Cecil Rhodes, the empire builder of British South Africa, to support Zionist settlement in Palestine "because it is something colonial."[8] Renowned Palestinian American historian Rashid Khalidi clearly demonstrates the colonial nature of Zionism in his landmark book *The Hundred Years' War on Palestine: A History of Settler Colonialism and Resistance, 1917-2017*. He writes:

> Significantly, many early apostles of Zionism had been proud to embrace the colonial nature of their project. The eminent Revisionist Zionist leader Ze'ev Jabotinsky . . . wrote in 1923: "Every native population in the world resists colonists as long as it has the slightest hope of being able to rid itself of the danger of being colonised. That is what the Arabs in Palestine are doing, and what they will persist in doing as long as there remains a solitary spark of hope that they will be able to prevent the transformation of 'Palestine' into the 'Land of Israel.'" Such honesty was rare among other leading Zionists, who like Herzl protested the innocent purity of their aims and deceived their Western listeners, and perhaps themselves, with fairy tales about their benign intentions toward the Arab inhabitants of Palestine. Jabotinsky and his followers were among the few who were frank enough to admit publicly and bluntly the harsh realities inevitably attendant on the implantation of a colonial settler society within an existing population. . . .
>
> The social and economic institutions founded by the early Zionists, which were central to the success of the Zionist project,

8. Areej Sabbagh-Khoury, "Tracing Settler Colonialism: A Genealogy of a Paradigm in the Sociology of Knowledge Production in Israel," *Politics & Society* 50, no. 1 (2022): 47, https://doi.org/10.1177/0032329221999906.

were also unquestioningly understood by all and described as co-lonial. The most important of these institutions was the Jewish Colonization Association (in 1924 renamed the Palestine Jewish Colonization Association). . . . The JCA provided the massive fi-nancial support that made possible extensive land purchases and the subsidies that enabled most of the early Zionist colonies in Palestine to survive and thrive before and during the Mandate period. . . .

Many cannot accept the contradiction inherent in the idea that although Zionism undoubtedly succeeded in creating a thriving national entity in Israel, its roots are as a colonial set-tler project (as are those of other modern countries: the United States, Canada, Australia, and New Zealand). Nor can they accept that it would not have succeeded but for the support of the great imperial powers, Britain and later the United States. Zionism, therefore, could be and was both a national and a colonial settler movement at one and the same time.[9]

Khalidi further says:

The modern history of Palestine can best be understood in these terms: as a colonial war waged against the indigenous population, by a variety of parties, to force them to relinquish their homeland to another people against their will.[10]

Further, Khalidi contends that the religious dimension of the Zionist movement, and the fact that it dressed itself in biblical attire, is what led to a prevailing blindness to the colonial nature of Zionism and to the characterization of the resulting situation as a "conflict":

Given this blindness [to the reality of colonialism], the conflict is portrayed as, at best, a straightforward, if tragic, national clash

9. Rashid Khalidi, *The Hundred Years' War on Palestine: A History of Settler Colonialism and Resistance, 1917–2017* (Picador, 2017), 12–14.
10. Khalidi, *Hundred Years' War*, 9.

between two peoples with rights in the same land. At worst, it is described as the result of the fanatical, inveterate hatred of Arabs and Muslims for the Jewish people as they assert their inalienable right to their eternal, God-given homeland.[11]

To point out the settler-colonial nature of the State of Israel is not to negate the historical Jewish connectedness to the land, nor to deny that Jews lived in Palestine throughout history. Jews were part and parcel of the rich and diverse history of Palestine. Palestine in history was "a multiethnic, multicultural, and multireligious region that was able to include diverse identities and peoples within its boundaries."[12] However, the spiritual, religious, and historical connection Jews have with the land of Palestine does not translate into political entitlement and does not give European Jews the right to colonize Palestine by force, ethnically cleanse the indigenous Palestinians, and declare Palestine as a national homeland for the Jewish people worldwide.

Furthermore, we cannot ignore the reality that the founding figures of Zionism and those who colonized Palestine were heirs to many years of rejection and persecution in Europe. Zionism emerged at the end of the nineteenth century while oppression and racist violence toward European Jews were on the rise. The Zionist movement gained traction later and took a different shape in the horrors of the Holocaust. We cannot deny that many of the colonizers were traumatized refugees looking for safety and dignity. Yet in their search for refuge, they committed crimes against others. Zionists envisioned that their redemption would be found in aligning with the empires of the day, namely, Great Britain and later the United States. Palestinians continue to wonder why it was they who paid the price of redemption for the Holocaust, and why it was they who were offered at the altar of Western repentance as an atonement for the sin of antisemitism.

11. Khalidi, *Hundred Years' War*, 9.
12. Raheb, *Decolonizing Palestine*, 121.

44

The Nakba as Ethnic Cleansing Explained

Settler colonialism by definition includes the expulsion or displacement of an indigenous population from their land. This is what the Nakba is. *Nakba*—Arabic for "catastrophe"—is what Palestinians call what took place in 1948 with the establishment of the State of Israel, and specifically the mass displacement and dispossession of Palestinians during the 1948 war.[13] Israel was not established on an "empty land," as Zionists often referred to it.

The Institute for Middle Eastern Understanding (IMEU), among many other institutions and scholars, has spent years investigating and documenting the Nakba. The IMEU's "Nakba by the Numbers" project highlights the magnitude of the scale of the disaster that fell upon the Palestinians:[14]

Between 750,000 and 1 million: The number of Palestinians expelled from their homeland and made refugees by Zionist militias and the new Israeli army during Israel's establishment (1947–1949), amounting to approximately 75 percent of all Palestinians.

Several dozen: The number of massacres of Palestinians carried out by Zionist militias and the Israeli army, which played a critical role in prompting the flight of many Palestinians from their homes.

More than four hundred: The number of Palestinian cities and towns systematically destroyed by Zionist militias and the new Israeli army or repopulated with Jews between 1948 and 1950. Most Palestinian communities, including homes, businesses, houses of worship, and vibrant urban centers, were destroyed to prevent the return of their Palestinian owners, now refugees outside of Israel's borders or internally displaced inside of them.

13. "The Question of Palestine," United Nations, accessed November 20, 2024, https://tinyurl.com/2p63nu99.
14. "Quick Facts: The Palestinian Nakba ('Catastrophe')," Institute for Middle East Understanding, April 5, 2023, https://tinyurl.com/ycxbf7hf.

Approximately 8.36 million: The number of Palestinian refugees (as of 2021), including Nakba survivors and their descendants. They're located mostly in the occupied West Bank, East Jerusalem, and Gaza, and neighboring Arab countries such as Lebanon, Jordan, and Syria, and are denied their internationally recognized legal right to return to their homeland.

Approximately 4,244,776: The number of acres of Palestinian land stolen by Israel during and immediately after the establishment of the state in 1948.

This was a catastrophe of biblical proportions. Israel was established on 78 percent of British mandate Palestine. And here is the most important element to keep in mind: This was all done *by design!* This was no unfortunate consequence of a war. According to the IMEU:

> The Nakba was a deliberate and systematic act intended to establish a Jewish majority state in Palestine. Amongst themselves, Zionist leaders used the euphemism "transfer" when discussing plans for what today would be called ethnic cleansing.[15]

The term "ethnic cleansing" is commonly used to describe the events of 1948. Ethnic cleansing is defined by international law as "purposeful policy designed by one ethnic or religious group to remove by violent and terror-inspiring means the civilian population of another ethnic or religious group from certain geographic areas."[16] It is a violation of international law and is designated as a crime against humanity in international treaties, such as that which created the International Criminal Court.[17]

15. "Quick Facts."
16. "International Law: Understanding Justice in Times of War," United Nations Regional Information Centre for Western Europe, March 27, 2024, https://tinyurl.com/327233kv.
17. "Q&A: War Crimes, Crimes Against Humanity, Ethnic Cleansing in West Darfur," Human Rights Watch, May 9, 2024, https://tinyurl.com/ydrew66y.

In his seminal work *The Ethnic Cleansing of Palestine*, Israeli historian Ilan Pappe reviews previously classified documents from early Zionist leaders about the Nakba and events leading to it. In his analysis, Pappe concludes: "The general definition of what ethnic cleansing consists of applies almost verbatim to the case of Palestine."[18]

Another Israeli historian, Benny Morris, attempted to put a spin on things—not by denying that ethnic cleansing took place but by justifying it as inevitable and necessary for the success of the Zionist endeavors. In an interview, he acknowledged that what happened was indeed ethnic cleansing, while claiming that it was necessary to avoid a genocide against the Jews in Palestine. He said:

> A Jewish state would not have come into being without the uprooting of 700,000 Palestinians. Therefore, it was necessary to uproot them. There was no choice but to expel that population. It was necessary to cleanse the hinterland and cleanse the border areas and cleanse the main roads. It was necessary to cleanse the villages from which our convoys and our settlements were fired on.[19]

This is a startling admission from a Zionist scholar. And it is truly inexplicable for a historian of his credentials to claim that ethnic cleansing was a measure of protection for the colonizers against the colonized. Colonizers do not defend themselves. They attack. Those committing ethnic cleansing in 1948 were the invaders, while the indigenous people were "cleansed." The victims are blamed for defending their towns and villages, protecting their families, and resenting the colonization of their land.

Moreover, such "necessary" acts included massacres such as the ones in Deir Yassin and Tantura—massacres that Zionists long denied and concealed. It is estimated that in the Deir Yassin massacre of 1948 more than one hundred Palestinians were brutally killed,

---

18. Ilan Pappe, *The Ethnic Cleansing of Palestine* (OneWorld, 2006), 7.

19. Ari Shavit, "Q&A with Benny Morris," *Jewish Journal*, January 29, 2004, https://tinyurl.com/rmn5mh4r.

including dozens of children, women, and elderly people. The Zionist militias that carried out the massacres were led by future Israeli prime ministers Menachem Begin and Yitzhak Shamir. The massacre at Deir Yassin was one of the worst atrocities committed during the Nakba, and it triggered the flight of Palestinians from their homes in and around Jerusalem and beyond.[20] Previously censored documents contain vivid and shocking descriptions of this massacre *by those who committed it*. These firsthand descriptions included:

> "In the village I killed an armed Arab man and two Arab girls of 16 or 17 who were helping the Arab who was shooting. I stood them against a wall and blasted them with two rounds from the Tommy gun."

> "We confiscated a lot of money and silver and gold jewelry fell into our hands. . . . This was a really tremendous operation."

> "I won't tell you that we were there with kid gloves on. House after house . . . we're putting in explosives and they are running away. An explosion and move on, an explosion and move on and within a few hours, half the village isn't there any more."

> "Our guys made a number of mistakes there that made me angry. Why did they do that? . . . They took dead people, piled them up and burned them. There began to be a stink. This is not so simple."

> "To me it looked a bit like a pogrom. . . . If you're occupying an army position—it's not a pogrom, even if a hundred people are killed. But if you are coming into a civilian locale and dead people are scattered around in it—then it looks like a pogrom."

> "There was a feeling of considerable slaughter and it was hard for me to explain it to myself as having been done in self-defense.

20. "Quick Facts."

My impression was more of a massacre than anything else. If it is a matter of killing innocent civilians, then it can be called a massacre."[21]

This is truly terrorism.

It is important to remember that more than 80 percent of Gaza's population are refugees, most of them descendants of those displaced in 1948.[22] This crucial detail is almost entirely neglected in Western media coverage of the war on Gaza and in the vast majority of church statements on the war. Beyond ignorance, it is baffling that many still argue that Jews are entitled to the land because their ancestors lived here *thousands of years ago*, while denying the right of Palestinians to return to their villages and rebuild them *just seventy-six years later*. Palestinians are told to "move on" despite a clear and direct UN resolution that calls for the right of return for the Palestinians expelled from their towns and villages in 1948.[23] Over the years, Israel did its best to hide the events of the Nakba, even going so far as to plant forests on the remains of the towns and villages destroyed during the Nakba. But the state of Israel cannot undo its history, and it certainly cannot remove the memory of Palestinians. Tragically, Israel has repeated history in Gaza in 2023–2024 by creating a new refugee crisis, driving close to two million Palestinians out of their homes, and destroying virtually all of Gaza's infrastructure.

21. Ofer Aderet, "Testimonies from the Censored Deir Yassin Massacre: 'They Piled Bodies and Burned Them,'" *Haaretz*, July 16, 2017, https://tinyurl.com/d8xd7nzs.

22. Bill Frelick, "No Exit in Gaza," Human Rights Watch, April 1, 2024, https://tinyurl.com/4uhn9nxd.

23. The United Nations General Assembly resolution 194 (III) instructs that "refugees wishing to return to their homes and live at peace with their neighbours should be permitted to do so at the earliest practicable date, and that compensation should be paid for the property of those choosing not to return and for loss of or damage to property which, under principles of international law or in equity, should be made good by the Governments or authorities responsible." United Nations Security Council, accessed September 8, 2024, https://tinyurl.com/meac29wy, p. 5.

Zionism, from the outset, sought to establish a homeland for the Jewish people in Palestine, which was already an inhabited land. As such, Zionism by definition necessitates ethnic cleansing. The first prime minister of Israel, David Ben-Gurion, told the Jewish Agency in June 1938: "I am for compulsory transfer; I do not see anything immoral in it."[24] The same sentiment is echoed today by the Zionists in the Israeli government and by many American politicians, who openly call for emptying Gaza and forcing Palestinians out of it. Ethnic cleansing is still taking place in Palestine today. The Nakba continues. This is the context in which October 7 and the subsequent war campaign must be situated.

The Occupation Explained

In 1948, Israel was established on 78 percent of British mandate Palestine. Since 1948, the Zionist nation-state has continued to expand and hold a strong grip on the land and people of Palestine. In 1967, Israel took the West Bank (including East Jerusalem) and the Gaza Strip (the remaining 22 percent) by force. The reality of military occupation is what I grew up in and what continues to define Palestinian life today. The Israeli military controls the ground, air, and sea, governing virtually every aspect of Palestinians' lives in the occupied territories. They control the water, electricity, and airwaves. They control the entrances and exits of our towns and all movement within the Palestinian territories. They control the exports and imports. They control the family registration system, regulating whom we can marry and where we can live. They control where we can build. And the Israeli military imposes all of the above by force. They can arrest and imprison Palestinians, including children, without trial. Israeli forces can kill Palestinians in their homes and impose sieges on refugee camps without accountability. Israel exercises the right to label any person a terrorist, with no obligation of explanation or proof, and kill that person. Decades of Israel's rampant violations of international law and human rights are well documented,

24. Pappe, *Ethnic Cleansing*, 1.

yet their actions are accepted with impunity by the majority of the international community.

Following the Oslo Accords in 1993, parts of the West Bank were handed over to the Palestinians for self-rule and administration, with the understanding that this was a temporary phase that would lead to a Palestinian State within five years. The West Bank was fragmented and classified into areas A, B, and C. Israel has maintained its grip over the vast majority of the West Bank (Area C), and while Palestinians need a permit from the Israeli military to build anything in this area, even to dig for water, the State of Israel has been engaging in aggressive settlement-building activities in this very same area at an accelerated rate since the Oslo Accords. While Israeli settlements built in Gaza in 1993 were later emptied and dismantled, the most intensive settler activity is taking place in the West Bank. From 2012 to 2022, the population of Israeli settlers in the occupied West Bank, including East Jerusalem, grew from 520,000 to over 700,000. These settlers live illegally in 279 Israeli settlements across the occupied West Bank, including 14 settlements in occupied East Jerusalem, with a total population of more than 229,000 people.[25]

These Israeli settlements, built on land confiscated from Palestinian families, are illegal according to international law.[26] According to an Amnesty International report on Israeli settlements published in 2019, "Israel's policy of settling its civilians in occupied Palestinian territory and displacing the local population contravenes fundamental rules of international humanitarian law."[27] Further, the report details how Israel's settlement policy is one of the main driving forces behind the mass human rights violations resulting from the occupation.[28] The settlements typify the harsh realities of the military occu-

25. "Human Rights Council Hears That 700,000 Israeli Settlers Are Living Illegally in the Occupied West Bank—Meeting Summary (Excerpts)," United Nations, accessed November 20, 2024, https://tinyurl.com/3hw7n7pv.

26. "Israeli Settlements and International Law," Amnesty International, January 30, 2019, https://tinyurl.com/mv2x8x8h.

27. "Israeli Settlements and International Law."

28. These include violations of the rights to life, liberty, security of the

pation of the West Bank. Their existence is not only the main barrier to establishing a Palestinian state on the 1967 borders but also clear proof that Israel was never serious about the two-state solution. The settlements have killed any possibility of a two-state solution.

Everyone was rightly outraged by the kidnapping of Israelis, including children, on October 7. In one of the many webinars I did during the war, a nun asked me, in tears and anger, about the kidnapped Israeli children, and offered to give herself as a ransom to free one of them. I answered by affirming that kidnapping children is evil, saying that I hope we can all agree on this. But then I asked: "What about the Palestinian children kidnapped?" Did you know that for years Israel has been kidnapping Palestinians in the West Bank and East Jerusalem on a much larger scale? According to Amnesty International:

> Every year, 500–700 Palestinian children from the occupied West Bank are prosecuted in Israeli juvenile military courts under Israeli military orders. They are often arrested in night raids and systematically ill-treated. Some of these children serve their sentences within Israel, in violation of the Fourth Geneva Convention. The UN has also documented that many children have been killed or injured in settler attacks.[29]

Palestinian children are the only children in the world who face prosecution in military courts under "administrative detention," a policy allowing incarceration without charge or trial based on so-called secret evidence that is not disclosed to detainees or their lawyers. Often abducted in the middle of the night in violent raids, then blindfolded, Palestinian children are transferred to adult facilities within Israel where

---

person, equal treatment before the law, effective remedy for acts violating fundamental rights; freedom of expression and peaceful assembly, equality and nondiscrimination; right to adequate housing; freedom of movement; enjoyment of the highest attainable standard of physical and mental health; right to water and education; the rights of the child; and the right to earn a decent living through work. "Israeli Settlements and International Law."

29. "Israeli Settlements and International Law."

access for families and even lawyers is not permitted. These abductions disrupt children's education and familial bonds, and often leave them in need of psychosocial support and rehabilitation from unimaginable trauma.[30] Is this not kidnapping? This systematic practice violates international law and perpetuates abuse and torture against Palestinian children, who are unjustly considered adults at age sixteen—a distinction not applied to Israeli children. This is another piece of the context in Palestine that foregrounds the ongoing war on Gaza.

Our question as Palestinians is this: Where is the world's outrage? No one called for besieging and bombing Israel in response to the kidnapping of Palestinians. No Palestinian flags are shown on the Berlin Wall in support.[31] No nun or religious figure has offered to give himself or herself as ransom to free the Palestinian children.[32]

Palestinians continue to ask if we are less worthy than other nationalities—those who are never named as terrorists, no matter how grotesque their campaigns of violence might be. While Israel conveniently labels children as terrorists and claims to arrest and kidnap children as self-defense, the world nods in approval and moves on. With between five hundred and seven hundred children abducted every year, the psychological effect of this systematic violence on Palestinian children is insurmountable—a reality that is hardly considered by Westerners. Again, Palestinians are at an impasse for how to respond to the crushing weight of occupation. How should we respond to years of land confiscation? How should we respond to the blatant discrimination in water allocation whereby Israelis, including those living in settlements, use at least three times the quantity per capita used by Palestinians in the West Bank?[33] How should we

---

30. "Physical Abuse, Infectious Disease Spreading as Conditions for Palestinian Children in Israeli Military Detention Deteriorate," Save the Children, July 22, 2024, https://tinyurl.com/23emaks4.

31. Cf. "Brandenburg Gate in Berlin Lights Up with Israeli Flag in Solidarity," *Times of Israel*, October 7, 2023, https://tinyurl.com/pyhjjj2c.

32. Cf. Philip Pullella, "Jerusalem Catholic Patriarch Offers to Be Exchanged for Gaza Hostages," Reuters, October 16, 2023, https://tinyurl.com/mryebfj7.

33. "Parched: Israel's Policy of Water Deprivation in the West Bank," B'Tselem, May 2023, https://tinyurl.com/2rucjuut.

respond to the orderly degradation and theft of our youth, and with them, our hope in the next generation?

The final crucial technology of the occupation that must be addressed is the separation wall. The separation barrier, which Israel began constructing in 2002, stands as a stark symbol of contention, control, and decades-long defiance of international law. The wall dissects Palestinian territory, splintering it into *territories*. It runs a total length of approximately 700 kilometers, which is more than double the length of the internationally recognized border, and 85 percent of the route runs inside the West Bank. This deviation has not only annexed Palestinian land but also significantly impacted the lives and livelihoods of thousands by isolating about 55,000 dunams (nearly 14,000 acres) of vital agricultural land and water resources. Reports from human rights organizations consistently illustrate that the wall's route strategically encircles these essential resources, deliberately crippling Palestinian economic and social development by severing trade routes and restricting movement. Many Palestinian farmers must obtain special permits simply to access their own land. In 2004, the ICJ explicitly declared the barrier illegal where it encroaches upon occupied Palestinian territory beyond the 1967 borders, mandating its dismantlement and the compensation of affected Palestinian communities.[34]

The Israeli rights organization B'Tselem detailed how the route of the separation barrier enabled the expansion of illegal Israeli settlements in the West Bank.[35] The United Nations Office for the Coordination of Humanitarian Affairs (OCHA) has repeatedly documented how this land seizure impacts Palestinians.[36] The intrusive

34. "Legal Consequences of the Construction of a Wall in the Occupied Palestinian Territory," International Court of Justice, 2004, https://tinyurl.com/yc5kwmys.

35. "Under the Guise of Security: Routing the Separation Barrier to Enable the Expansion of Israeli Settlements in the West Bank," B'Tselem, December 2005, https://tinyurl.com/ms462nht.

36. "10 Years Since the International Court of Justice (ICJ) Advisory Opinion," United Nations Office for the Coordination of Humanitarian Affairs, July 9, 2014, https://tinyurl.com/6dpcahtz; "The Humanitarian Impact

route of the barrier leaves Palestinian communities—approximately eleven thousand people—stuck between the barrier and the Green Line, not including those in East Jerusalem. Most residents over sixteen years of age are obliged to apply for permits just to continue to live in their own homes. Can you imagine such physical barriers of control governing your life? Can you imagine a huge wall dividing your town or neighborhood?

Officially portrayed by Israel as a security measure, this barrier includes stretches of fencing and concrete walls up to 8 meters high, dwarfing the infamous Berlin Wall, which stood at just 3.6 meters. The claim that the wall is a necessary security measure does not hold up against the evidence that shows the timing of its construction in 2002 followed a decline of attacks from the Second Intifada.[37] Rather, the barrier serves Israel's broader political objectives, primarily facilitating further annexation and controlling strategic resources and areas.

The wall not only symbolizes a physical division but also imposes profound psychological repercussions, contributing to a sense of isolation and imprisonment among Palestinians. Critics and human rights organizations argue that the security justification is a facade used to mask broader geopolitical aims, systematically undermining the viability of a future Palestinian state and exacerbating conditions akin to severe, open-air imprisonment. The structure's imposing presence illustrates and enacts the asymmetries of power and the ongoing disregard for the basic rights and dignity of the Palestinian people.

Apartheid Explained

The "A-word" is how apartheid is referred to in some ecumenical and diplomatic circles. "Apartheid" has become a dirty word, not because

---

of 20 Years of the Barrier—December 2022," United Nations Office for the Coordination of Humanitarian Affairs, 2022, https://tinyurl.com/yjaxubnj.

37. For the question of security and the separation wall, see Munther Isaac, *The Other Side of the Wall* (InterVarsity Press, 2020), 17–18.

of what it represents, but because it is considered unacceptable to use as a term to define Israel's actions. It has become taboo to even discuss the topic in relation to Israel's actions. It is as if there is an unspoken global agreement that Israel can do no wrong. However, much more lies beneath the surface. Given the history of apartheid in South Africa, it is a grave indictment to accuse any state of apartheid. But apartheid is real—and (under the 1977 Additional Protocol to the Geneva Conventions) it is a war crime. It is abhorrent for foreign nations, and especially the church, to claim to be appalled by the ugliness of apartheid in South Africa while remaining complicit in and silent about apartheid in Palestine.

When people ask me about the A-word, I answer by underscoring the fact that apartheid is not a matter of opinion. It does not matter what I *think* about the term; rather, it must be assessed based on the definition set by the international community. The question of apartheid is answered by first studying and understanding this definition, and then by examining the evidence on the ground and comparing the facts with the definition. This is how we must engage with the A-word unless we are willing to publicly and officially acknowledge that international law does not matter in the context of Palestine. It is quite a simple yet crucial distinction: we either uphold world treaties, international law, and human rights, or we don't. And the consequences of the answer to this question are critical. If Israel is indeed committing the sin of apartheid, then Israel can no longer be treated as a normal state and must be held accountable for its war crimes.

In 2022, I was part of a team that prepared a document called "A Dossier on Israeli Apartheid." The dossier was a collaboration between Kairos Palestine and the Global Kairos for Justice Coalition. In what follows, I will quote it at length in order to fully elucidate the definition of apartheid and its relevance in the context of Palestine.[38]

---

38. This section is from the document "A Dossier on Israeli Apartheid: A Pressing Call to Churches Around the World," by Kairos Palestine and the Global Kairos for Justice Coalition, which I lead. I was one of the writers

Three important documents define the crime of apartheid and describe its features: The Geneva Conventions; The International Convention on the Suppression and Punishment of the Crime of Apartheid; and the Rome Statute of the International Criminal Court.

A careful analysis of the documents reveals three decisive elements necessary to define the crime of apartheid and its paradigms: 1) the implementation of a system of separation or segregation based on race, creed, or ethnicity designed with the intent to maintain domination by one racial group over another is the first element that makes up the crime of apartheid; 2) the use of legislative measures to enforce separation and segregation, essentially legalizing separation from within its own legal system; 3) the commission of inhumane acts, human rights violations, denial of freedoms, and forced ghettoization, i.e., the practices used to impose and enforce separation within its regime.

Between the river and the sea, it is abundantly clear that Israel meets the definition of the crime of apartheid under international law. Both through the laws the state has adopted and its inhumane practices, Israel actively works to promote separation and segregation through a biased legal regime that offers specific rights and privileges to one group at the expense of the other to maintain its domination. For an Israeli Jew, there are no restrictions to movement or limitations to deciding where to live throughout Israel and the West Bank, while Israel limits the choices for Palestinians. Israeli Jews enjoy certain laws, administrative structures and privileges—such as education, social and health benefits. These are not afforded to Palestinians.

For decades, Palestinian civil society organizations have pointed to the harsh realities of Israel's apartheid regime. Over the years, a few internationally recognized leaders have con-

---

and the lead editor of this document. It is used with permission. The entire document can be found at https://tinyurl.com/48py3kz7. The original document directed readers to sources via hyperlinks. I have provided source citations in footnotes.

curred, including U.S. President Jimmy Carter and South African Archbishop Desmond Tutu. But over the past few years a rapidly growing number of globally respected human rights organizations have issued thoroughly researched reports describing Israel's laws, policies and practices as apartheid. It is important to note that, while each of the following documents have been subjected to repeated accusations of "anti-Semitism" and "delegitimization of the State of Israel," there has not been a single response that disputes the charges in these reports.

Reports

Yesh Din: "The Israeli Occupation of the West Bank and the Crime of Apartheid: Legal Opinion"[39]

Yesh Din–Volunteers for Human Rights is an Israeli organization registered as a non-profit in Israel and subject to Israeli law. A team of volunteers serve alongside a professional staff including lawyers and human rights experts. In June 2020, Yesh Din published a legal opinion charging that "the crime against humanity of apartheid is being committed in the West Bank. The perpetrators are Israelis, and the victims are Palestinians." The 58-page report offered this conclusion:

> The crime [of apartheid] is committed because the Israeli occupation is no "ordinary" occupation regime (or a regime of domination and oppression), but one that comes with a gargantuan colonization project that has created a community of citizens of the occupying power in the occupied territory.... The crime of apartheid is being committed in the West Bank because, in this context of a regime of domination and oppression of one national group by another, the Israeli authorities implement policies and practices that constitute inhuman acts as the term is de-

39. "The Israeli Occupation of the West Bank and the Crime of Apartheid: Legal Opinion," Yesh Din, June 2020, https://tinyurl.com/mpmyvte7.

fined in international law: Denial of rights from a national group, denial of resources from one group and their transfer to another, physical and legal separation between the two groups and the institution of a different legal system for each of them.

B'Tselem: "A Regime of Jewish Supremacy from the Jordan River to the Mediterranean Sea: This Is Apartheid"[40]

While Yesh Din's finding of Israeli apartheid was limited to the West Bank, in January 2021 B'Tselem—The Israeli Information Center for Human Rights in the Occupied Territories issued a report, charging that "The essence of the apartheid regime in place between the Jordan River and the Mediterranean Sea is to promote and perpetuate the supremacy of one group over another." B'Tselem (in Hebrew, "in the image") is an independent, non-partisan, globally award-winning Israeli organization. Summarizing the findings in the eight-page report, B'Tselem's executive director wrote, "Israel is not a democracy that has a temporary occupation attached to it: it is one regime between the Jordan River and the Mediterranean Sea, and we must look at the full picture and see it for what it is: apartheid. This sobering look at reality need not lead to despair, but quite the opposite. It is a call for change. After all, people created this regime, and people can change it."

Human Rights Watch: "A Threshold Crossed: Israeli Authorities and the Crimes of Apartheid and Persecution"[41]

Human Rights Watch (HRW) is an international non-governmental organization based in New York City with a staff of around 450 people including lawyers and journalists and over

40. "A Regime of Jewish Supremacy from the Jordan River to the Mediterranean Sea: This Is Apartheid," B'Tselem, January 12, 2021, https://tiny url.com/4msybce7.

41. "A Threshold Crossed: Israeli Authorities and the Crimes of Apartheid and Persecution," Human Rights Watch, 2021, https://tinyurl. com/32awezh5.

70 nationalities described as "country experts." In the summary of its April 2021 213-page report, HRW writes, "Laws, policies, and statements by leading Israeli officials make plain that the objective of maintaining Jewish Israeli control over demographics, political power, and land has long guided government policy. In pursuit of this goal, authorities have dispossessed, confined, forcibly separated, and subjugated Palestinians by virtue of their identity to varying degrees of intensity. In certain areas, as described in this report, these deprivations are so severe that they amount to the crimes against humanity of apartheid and persecution."

Amnesty International: "Israel's Apartheid Against Palestinians: Cruel System of Domination and Crime Against Humanity"[42]

Amnesty International is a non-governmental organization based in the United Kingdom with regional offices in cities around the world. Amnesty describes itself as "a global movement . . . independent of any political ideology, economic interest or religion." In the Executive Summary of its 278-page February 2022 report documenting Israel's apartheid regime, Amnesty writes, "Over decades, Israeli demographic and geopolitical considerations have shaped policies towards Palestinians in each of the different areas of Israel, East Jerusalem, the rest of the West Bank and the Gaza Strip in different ways. . . . Palestinians experience this system in different ways and face differing levels of repression based on their status and the area in which they live." Amnesty "has assessed that almost all of Israel's civilian administration and military authorities, as well as governmental and quasi-governmental institutions, are involved in the enforcement of the system of apartheid against Palestinians."

United Nations: "Report of the Special Rapporteur on the Situation of Human Rights in the Palestinian Territories Occupied Since 1967"[43]

42. "Israel's Apartheid Against Palestinians: Cruel System of Domination and Crime Against Humanity," Amnesty International, 2022, https://tinyurl.com/42bsuxdv.
43. "Report of the Special Rapporteur on the Situation of Human Rights

In an April 2022 report to the United Nations Human Rights Council, Special Rapporteur Michael Lynk applied tests from the Convention Against Apartheid and the Rome Statute to conclude that Israel's "political system of entrenched rule in the occupied Palestinian territory . . . satisfies the prevailing evidentiary standard for the existence of apartheid." In his meticulously footnoted 18-page report, Lynk documents violations of international humanitarian law and international human rights law, including arbitrary detention, ill-treatment and torture, gender-based violence, restrictions of the rights to freedom of movement, expression, association and peaceful assembly, and violations of the rights to life and physical integrity. Lynk insisted that, because of the vast asymmetry of power, an international intervention is indispensable using a rights-based approach.

The dossier is worth reading in full. These reports are a few among many that leave no room for dispute. We either take these investigations seriously, and by implication international law and the rule of law, or we give Israel the green light to do whatever it wants with no accountability. The latter is the current reality that persists. As we wrote in the dossier:

> To call Israel an apartheid regime, is not a political epithet, nor does it require comparisons with South Africa, but an examination of the actual facts on the ground, which fulfills the legal elements established for the crime of Apartheid. These elements are so clearly there, that it is no surprise that Israel is worried about the International Criminal Court, or that it seeks to label as "terrorist organizations" those organizations that are carefully documenting its behavior on the ground, in preparation for the day when the ICC will hear this case.

The question that haunts me is this: Why are churches—let alone the international community—ignoring these reports, while con-

---

in the Palestinian Territories Occupied Since 1967," Human Rights Council, March 21, 2022, https://tinyurl.com/47nfap6t.

tinuing to regard Israel as a typical, democratic nation? Why is someone like Archbishop Tutu celebrated and respected almost unanimously around the world for his activism against apartheid in South Africa, yet his accusations of apartheid committed by Israel are ignored?[44]

In 2022, I was part of a group of Christian activists from Palestine and around the world who attended the general assembly of the World Council of Churches in Germany to press for a resolution from the council linking Israel's actions with apartheid. We were aided by a powerful letter to the council from the Anglican Church in South Africa that prophetically challenged the assembly to adopt a resolution naming Israel as an apartheid state. This letter, along with our activism, created discomfort for many in the council who resented the idea. The German churches in particular were against it.[45] The resolution did not pass, and instead, the assembly asked the member churches to study the reports calling Israel an apartheid state and discern for themselves. Over the years, I and many of my friends held conversations with church leaders about this issue, and even today there is still strong hesitation against it. We are told it is not helpful—a bad strategy that burns bridges and stops dialogue with partners. We are sometimes told that we should leave it to the relevant courts to decide, and that it is not up to the church to do so (which is not what happened in South Africa).

The real question is not whether Israel's actions can be classified as apartheid or not. The alignment of the facts with the definition is indisputable, as numerous human rights organizations have shown. The more pressing question for me is why churches are so slow to respond to these reports, sometimes dismissing or ignoring them altogether. In the dossier, we say:

---

44. Chris McGreal, "When Desmond Tutu Stood Up for the Rights of Palestinians, He Could Not Be Ignored," *Guardian*, December 30, 2021, https://tinyurl.com/mxwj65jj.

45. Jeff Wright, "World Council of Churches General Assembly Puts Israeli Apartheid on the Global Church's Table," *Mondoweiss*, September 10, 2022, https://tinyurl.com/28bxu8dn.

"Words matter." The words the Church uses says a lot about the Church and its response to the issues of the day. We urge our brothers and sisters not to choose words that soften the harshness of the crimes perpetrated upon Palestinians. When the Church refuses to call Israel's laws and actions apartheid, the Church contributes to the continuation of apartheid.

We are troubled when our sisters and brothers are more concerned about their relations with religious dialogue partners than they are concerned about our reality under harsh occupation. We are troubled when our sisters and brothers are more concerned about their image than they are concerned about our suffering. Often, when we speak boldly about our oppression and Israeli apartheid, we are told that our cry is too loud. But when we spoke softly, we were ignored. Too much is at stake—for Palestinians, for the Palestinian church, for the global Church—for us to speak softly and employ euphemisms to describe our suffering.

The church should not wait for the international community to officially describe and condemn Israel's apartheid. No, a prophetic church should shape and lead the international community. A prophetic, faithful church does not watch from the sideline and act when it is safe, when it has nothing to lose. The prophetic church speaks truth to power. When it comes to justice, human dignity and human rights, we join Peter and the apostles who counseled, "We must obey God rather than any human authority (Acts 5:29)."

Zionism Today Explained

Consider for a moment how you would respond to the following statement:

"Arab Muslims have an exclusive and inalienable right over all areas of the Land of Palestine."

If a Palestinian leader made such a statement at a Christian gathering in the United States, with the understanding that what is meant by

"Land of Palestine" is all of mandated Palestine (from the river to the sea), then that person would be immediately rebuked and likely labeled a racist antisemite. Such an exclusionary ideology would be dismissed as radical and inflammatory. This statement, however, is actually an altered quote. The original comes from the Guiding Principles of the *Israeli* Government, elected and sworn in in 2023. The real statement reads as follows:

> "The Jewish people have an exclusive and inalienable right over all areas of the Land of Israel."[46]

Consider your initial reflection on the statement again—do you see it in a different light?

It is important to clarify that those upholding such a statement unquestionably define "all areas of the Land of Israel" far beyond the 1948 borders. They have very little, if any, regard for the Palestinians. The Israeli coalition government that took over early in 2023 is "nationalist, exclusionist, and far, far right" and is considered "the most extreme Israeli government in the nation's history."[47] Much has been written about the radical and hateful ideology of some of the openly racist ministers in this government, especially that of Bezalel Smotrich and Itamar Ben-Gvir. To this government, all the land is the land of Israel, and building settlements within the 1967 borders is a national priority.

This right-wing government represents a natural progression in the accelerating shift from the center, to center-right, to the extreme right in Israeli politics. The leading Palestinian-led human rights organization, Adalah, asserts that this declaration from the new government regarding an "exclusive and inalienable right" is a step further than that of the already controversial Jewish Nation State

46. "Adalah's Analysis of the New Israeli Government's Guiding Principles and Coalition Agreements and Their Implications on Palestinians' Rights," Adalah, January 10, 2023, https://tinyurl.com/4ex9ksra.

47. Jonathan Guyer, "Israel's New Right-Wing Government Is Even More Extreme Than Protests Would Have You Think," *Vox*, January 20, 2023, https://tinyurl.com/yyhckf2c.

Law, which was adopted in 2018 and bears "distinct apartheid characteristics." Article 1 of the law "defines self-determination as unique to the Jewish people within the 'State of Israel,' rather than as an exclusive right to only the Jewish people in all of the areas it considers as the historic 'land of Israel.'"[48] The Nation State Law is racist and discriminatory in its very essence. As mentioned, it states that "the right to exercise national self-determination" in Israel is "unique to the Jewish people." It further establishes Hebrew as Israel's official language and downgrades Arabic—a language widely spoken by Arab Israelis—to a "special status." The law ordains aggressive settlement of the land by asserting "Jewish settlement as a national value" and mandating that the state "will labor to encourage and promote its establishment and development."[49]

This law ensures that the 1.7 million Palestinian citizens of Israel—the native inhabitants who survived the Nakba and managed to remain in their homes when the Zionists established their state in 1948—shall be without sovereignty or agency, forever living at the mercy of Israel.[50] And when it comes to the West Bank, East Jerusalem, and Gaza, there are virtually no acts beyond the law for the Israeli state. The extremist government can establish settlements as they wish, adding to Israel's national value, in their eyes.

Again, can you imagine if Palestinian leaders declared that the right for self-determination is exclusive to Palestinians? The Nation State Law has clear exclusive and racist features that echo Jim Crow segregation and apartheid South Africa. Zionism and apartheid are two sides of the same coin. The Zionism of today is reflected in the exclusivism and supremacy of the Zionism of the Nation State Law and that of the Guiding Principles of the Israeli Government of 2023.

48. "Adalah's Analysis of the New Israeli Government's Guiding Principles and Coalition Agreements and Their Implications on Palestinians' Rights."

49. "Basic Law: Israel—the Nation State of the Jewish People, Unofficial Translation, 25 July 2018," Adalah, July 25, 2018, https://tinyurl.com/mv4ynz7t.

50. Susan Abulhawa, "Israeli 'Nation-State' Law Follows in Footsteps of Jim Crow, Indian Removal Act, and Nuremberg Laws," *Mondoweiss*, July 23, 2018, https://tinyurl.com/2s45u3vb.

Much recent conversation about the radical, violent settlers in the West Bank has included calls to hold them accountable. This logic assumes that the actions of a settler who is not physically violent toward Palestinian farmers are lawful. But the violent settlers are not the only problem. They are the product of more serious problems: the Zionist ideology that renders the land as theirs for settlement and the Israeli government's protection of these settlers. Similarly, there are many reports about the racist, fanatical views of people like Bezalel Smotrich and Itamar Ben-Gvir, who were once considered terrorists by Israel itself and now have become leaders in the government and shapers of its policies.

In one instance in 2023, the US State Department "strongly condemned" the "inflammatory comments" and "all racist rhetoric" by Ben-Gvir.[51] Again, this gives the impression that Smotrich and Ben-Gvir are the exception to the rule. But this could not be further from the truth. The truth is that they represent the fruit of Zionism. Their views are consistent with mainstream Zionism. Benjamin Netanyahu has openly and consistently asserted that there will never be a Palestinian state under his watch. He has never shied away from displaying his racist, discriminatory views.[52] Netanyahu once declared that Israel is "the national state, not of all its citizens, but only of the Jewish people."[53] The Nation State Law became a reality because of Netanyahu. And it was Netanyahu himself, in his thirst for power but also in his deep Zionist convictions, who brought these extreme voices into power. The presence of these figures in positions of power is an existential threat to all. An analysis in the Israeli *+972 Magazine* demonstrates this clearly:

51. Tom Bateman, "US Condemns Israeli Minister Ben Gvir's 'Inflammatory' Palestinian Comments," *BBC News*, August 25, 2023, https://tinyurl.com/mry2z3wh.

52. Jodi Rudoren and Julie Hirschfeld Davis, "Netanyahu Apologizes; White House Is Unmoved," *New York Times*, March 23, 2015, https://tinyurl.com/2u6pxwpv.

53. Bill Chappell and Daniel Estrin, "Netanyahu Says Israel Is 'Nation-State of the Jewish People and Them Alone,'" *NPR*, March 11, 2019, https://tinyurl.com/cxcxcmwj.

That right-wing politicians have long held such violent and discriminatory views, and regularly exploited them rhetorically for political gain, is not news. Now, however, these politicians have full control of the state apparatus, and upon nullifying the judiciary, can ensure that they face no external check on their rightward march. With little internal ideological dissent, the coalition can easily transform their words into reality.[54]

The manifestation of the extreme right in Israeli politics today is consistent with Zionist ideology and the values that Zionism has stood for from the outset. Zionism is Jewish supremacy, and any form of racist supremacy is racism. It is not hateful to say this, and in fact, we must emphatically resist the equation of Zionism with Judaism. This critique of Zionism is not about Judaism as a religion or the Jewish people as a whole. Palestinians are profoundly grateful for the growing number of Jewish people and organizations that are speaking out against Zionism and asserting that anti-Zionist Judaism is not contradictory. One of those organizations is Jewish Voice for Peace (JVP). Regarding Zionism, JVP asserts:

> Jewish Voice for Peace is guided by a vision of justice, equality and freedom for all people. We unequivocally oppose Zionism because *it is counter to those ideals. . . .*
>
> Through study and action, through deep relationship with Palestinians fighting for their own liberation, and through our own understanding of Jewish safety and self-determination, we have come to see that Zionism was a false and failed answer to the desperately real question many of our ancestors faced of how to protect Jewish lives from murderous antisemitism in Europe.
>
> While it had many strains historically, the Zionism that took hold and stands today *is a settler-colonial movement, establishing*

---

54. Nate Orbach, "You've Heard of Bibi and Ben Gvir. Now Meet the Rest of the New Government," *+972 Magazine*, December 29, 2022, https://tinyurl.com/24n3cxsk.

an apartheid state where Jews have more rights than others. Our own history teaches us how dangerous this can be.

Palestinian dispossession and occupation are by design. Zionism has meant profound trauma for generations, systematically separating Palestinians from their homes, land, and each other. Zionism, in practice, has resulted in massacres of Palestinian people, ancient villages and olive groves destroyed, families who live just a mile away from each other separated by checkpoints and walls, and children holding onto the keys of the homes from which their grandparents were forcibly exiled.

Because the founding of the state of Israel was based on the idea of a "land without people," Palestinian existence itself is resistance. We are all the more humbled by the vibrance, resilience, and steadfastness of Palestinian life, culture, and organizing, as it is a deep refusal of a political ideology founded on erasure.[55]

As a Palestinian Christian, indeed as a person of faith and a human being, I say: Amen to this!

Facts Matter

In July 2024, the ICJ, in what was described as a landmark ruling, declared that Israel's occupation of the Gaza Strip and the West Bank, including East Jerusalem, is unlawful, along with the associated settlement regime, annexation, and use of natural resources. The ICJ added that Israel's legislation and action violate the international prohibition on racial segregation and apartheid. It mandated that Israel end its occupation, dismantle its settlements, provide full reparations to Palestinian victims, and facilitate the return of displaced people.[56]

55. "Our Approach to Zionism," Jewish Voice for Peace, accessed November 20, 2024, https://tinyurl.com/44bpzpt5 (emphasis added). I strongly recommend reading the whole declaration, which talks about the danger of Zionism to Judaism and Jews themselves.

56. "Experts Hail ICJ Declaration on Illegality of Israel's Presence in the Occupied Palestinian Territory as 'Historic' for Palestinians and Interna-

The reality in Palestine today is the cumulative outcome of decades of normalizing oppression, military occupation, and continual ethnic cleansing. The West framed this reality as a "conflict," or ignored it, or outright endorsed it. This paved the way for acceptance of the crimes witnessed now in real time in Gaza—crimes still being disregarded by many who claim to champion human rights and many who claim to stand for the gospel of Jesus. The genocide of Gaza exhibits nothing short of profound hypocrisy and moral failure on a global scale.

It is crucial that we understand that the Palestinian situation is not a series of isolated incidents but a systematic, long-term effort aimed at the eradication of Palestinian identity and livelihood. Acts of genocide don't usually happen overnight. Understanding history is key to understanding not just this moment but everything that led up to it. Zionist ideological foundations, which reflect a stark vision of exclusion and erasure, have formed the backbone of the daily discriminatory practices against Palestinians in the land for many years.

The systematic oppression and ethnic cleansing of Palestinians have escalated over decades. Many steps along the way have seemed minor, and every step has been "justified" under the guise of security, nationalism, or retaliation, making the reality less perceptible to the international community. Laws allowing Jewish people anywhere in the world to claim "birthright" have contrasted starkly with the denial of the Palestinian refugees' right of return. This combination has slowly solidified a system under which one group's rights are paramount and another's have been systematically diminished. Military checkpoints, the Gaza blockade, and the regular military incursions in Palestinian communities—each act has escalated the severity of the conditions faced by Palestinians.

These measures cumulatively contribute to conditions that oppress and systematically dismantle the Palestinian community's ability to sustain itself economically, socially, and politically. The passing of the Nation State Law, declaring Israel as the state exclusively for

---

tional Law," press release, Office of the United Nations High Commissioner for Human Rights, July 30, 2024, https://tinyurl.com/3sknmbek.

the Jewish people, was yet another move toward overt codification of racial and national superiority within the legal system of the state.

So, by the time social media began broadcasting undeniable evidence of genocidal acts, the international community had become acclimated to the "both sides" narrative that somehow justified progressive acts of violence as "self-defense." The tragic irony is that, like the metaphorical frog in a pot of boiling water, the gradual nature of these escalations has led to a situation where the boiling point seemed sudden to outside observers but was a long time in the making.

Facts matter. Truth matters. The war on Gaza is a perfect illustration as to how reality can be distorted and altered. One analysis after another, one statement after another—all seemed to ignore, intentionally or not, the context that led to October 7. Gaza has elucidated the power of empire in creating "myths" and introducing them into public discourse as facts. Israeli historian Ilan Pappe has recognized this, as the title of his book *Ten Myths about Israel* suggests. The myths that Pappe dismantles in his book include: Palestine was an empty land, Zionism is Judaism, Zionism is not colonialism, the Palestinians voluntarily left their homeland in 1948, and Israel is the only democracy in the Middle East.[57] Pappe's book shows the power of myths in shaping not only narratives but opinions. If I can add just one myth to Pappe's list, I would add the myth that the conflict is "religious in nature." These myths and others have shaped global perceptions of Palestinians over the years, giving the impression that there is a religious conflict in which Muslims are refusing to accept Israel for ideological and religious reasons, while Israel is constantly engaged in existential wars of self-defense. This is why whenever I speak mainly in Western contexts, I am always asked about radical Islam, and in particular Hamas and Hezbollah. These groups are often the narrow focus of Westerners as if they are *the* problem. To be sure, Islamism or political Islam is a problem in its attempt to mandate Islamic teachings by force, and in its attempt to forcefully bring the "will of God" among people. But we would be completely wrong

57. Ilan Pappe, *Ten Myths about Israel* (Verso, 2017).

to ignore what has been done in the land since 1948 by a violent, Zionist state and focus on Islamic fundamentalism as the problem. In fact, those who do this are themselves part of the problem.

The histories I've unpacked in this chapter must be viewed as the context for the rise of Palestinian Islamic resistance movements such as Hamas. In our attempts to understand any contemporary realities in Gaza, we must be comprehensive in our research, and we must tell the truth, the whole truth. We must engage in critical analysis of history, aiming to move beyond simplistic answers and understand the motives behind actions. We must get to the roots.

Understandings of settler colonialism, ethnic cleansing, and apartheid must shape any honest and faithful discourse about Gaza and Palestine today. In the next chapter, I will deal with yet one more key factor in understanding Gaza, namely, the blockade on Gaza. Since 1948, Israel has been engaged in what Pappe explains as a strategy "of taking as much of Palestine as possible with as few Palestinians in it as possible."[58] It has managed to do so by multiple means, and creating myths and altering history is one of those means. This is why we as Palestinians will continue to insist: "Context matters!"

58. Pappe, *Ten Myths about Israel*, 146.

3

The Relevant Context of Gaza

Sitting in a relaxed atmosphere on the set of the American TV show *The View*, Hillary Clinton unflinchingly responded to a question about a cease-fire in Gaza, saying that "there was a ceasefire on October 6."[1] This was not ignorance. Clinton is an experienced politician who served as the US secretary of state for four years. She knows the truth about the blockade and the many wars waged against Gaza. She is well aware that Gaza is still considered occupied under international law.[2] Clinton understands that even after the disengagement in 2005, Israel has retained "effective military, economic, and administrative control over the Gaza Strip and will therefore continue to occupy the Gaza Strip."[3]

We cannot talk about the war on Gaza, or October 7, without addressing the siege on Gaza that started sixteen years before October

---

1. "Hillary Clinton: 'There Was a Ceasefire on October 6. Hamas Chose to Break It,'" *Times of Israel*, November 9, 2023, https://tinyurl.com/2p8v6srv.

2. Safaa Sadi Jaber and Ilias Bantekas, "The Status of Gaza as Occupied Territory Under International Law," *International & Comparative Law Quarterly* 72, no. 4 (2023): 1069–88, DOI: https://doi.org/10.1017/S0020589323000349.

3. "The Israeli 'Disengagement' Plan: Gaza Still Occupied," United Nations, PLO Negotiations Affairs Department, September 2005, https://tinyurl.com/n338tsmn.

2023 and the multiple wars waged on Gaza during that period. The siege is perhaps the most acute aspect of the context of the war. We must understand the nature of this siege and how it came to be. If the seventy-five years of colonialism and oppression toward Palestinians serve as the wider context for October 7, the siege of Gaza is the immediate context for October 7.

The Recent History of Gaza

The Gaza Strip comprises 360 square kilometers (141 square miles) of land along the Mediterranean Sea, next to Sinai. It is 41 kilometers (25 miles) long and from 6 to 12 kilometers (3.7 to 7.5 miles) wide. Can you imagine how small this territory is? For reference, the entire strip is only two-thirds the size of Manhattan. With a population of 2.1 million, it is one of the most densely populated areas in the world. The strip gets its name from the city of Gaza, which has a long and rich history.

The history of Gaza is rich and ancient. It has witnessed many civilizations and cultures. From a Christian perspective, Gaza is home to one of the oldest Christian communities in the world. The city embraced the Christian faith under the leadership of Bishop Porphyrius (Saint Porphyry of Gaza), who became bishop of Gaza in 395 CE. The church in Gaza was consecrated on April 14, 407, Easter Sunday, and was dedicated to Porphyrius in 442.[4] It is still a functioning church today, and its ancient building sheltered hundreds of Palestinian Christians throughout the war. Tragically, the compound was hit by an Israeli bomb in October 2023, and a building adjacent to the sanctuary collapsed, killing eighteen people.[5]

Gaza was important in the history of Palestinian monasticism, mainly because of the pioneering efforts of Hilarion (ca. 291–371 CE). Hilarion was born in Gaza, and, after being initiated by the anchorite Antony in Alexandria, he founded a monastic community close

---

4. Jean-Pierre Filiu, *Gaza: A History* (Oxford University Press, 2014), 12.

5. Karen Zraick and Ameera Harouda, "Israel Airstrike Hits Greek Orthodox Church Compound in Gaza City," *New York Times*, updated December 21, 2023, https://tinyurl.com/4hy427yc.

to Gaza.[6] When Hilarion died in Cyprus, his remains were brought back to Gaza. Today, his tomb is located at the monastery of Umm al-Amr, a UNESCO World Heritage site that sits on the edge of the Nuseirat refugee camp, south of Gaza City.[7] Today, fewer than one thousand Christians live in Gaza. This number has declined significantly since 2007 as a part of a larger phenomenon I will unpack in the subsequent section.

Throughout its long history, the Gaza Strip has always been considered part of what was commonly known as Palestine. It was controlled by the Ottoman Empire starting in the sixteenth century, and then by the British Mandate from 1923 to 1948. The Gaza Strip survived the Nakba of 1948 and became home to thousands of Palestinian refugees. Before the 2023 war on Gaza, 1.7 million of Gaza's 2.1 million inhabitants were refugees from the Nakba. These refugees and their descendants lived in eight refugee camps: Rafah, Jabalia, Khan Younis, Al-Shati, Nuseirat, Bureij, Maghazi, and Deir al-Balah. These camps were largely in miserable condition before the war and were then completely destroyed as a result of the war. Life in refugee camps, especially in the early years, was full of hardships and marked by psychological trauma. These refugees often lived just a few kilometers away from their homes, to which they desperately wanted to return. They were not permitted to do so.

The strip was under Egyptian administrative control from 1948 to 1967, and during that period Gazans were "stateless"—the territory was not annexed or considered part of Egypt. This short era of Egyptian control was interrupted in 1956–1957 by a four-month Israeli occupation during which many massacres took place, especially in the early weeks. According to French historian Jean-Pierre Filiu:

> There were two massacres of civilians . . . one in the central square of Khan Yunis, with the execution by machine gun of victims lined up along the wall of the old Ottoman caravanserai,

6. Filiu, *Gaza*, 14.

7. "Saint Hilarion Monastery/Tell Umm Amer," UNESCO World Heritage Convention, accessed November 20, 2024, https://tinyurl.com/mrxyjm23.

and the other in the refugee camp, where the victims were also shot. The corpses were left for hours, sometimes overnight, before the families were permitted to recover the bodies. UNRWA [United Nations Relief and Works Agency] later assembled a list it regarded as "credible" of the names of 275 people who were executed on 3 November 1956, including 140 refugees.[8]

Israeli historian Benny Morris also wrote that although Israel's conquest of the strip in 1956 was "anything but peaceful," the following four months were undisturbed by acts of resistance, probably partly because of "the wave of massacres that took place during the first weeks of the occupation."[9] Moreover, Morris contends that the experience of life in the strip's refugee camps, and of the brief Israeli occupation, did produce what he calls "fanatical Israel haters." He names Sheikh Ahmad Yassin, the founder of Hamas, as one of those figures.[10] Filiu also states that Abdulaziz Rantissi, who became the leader of Hamas in 2004, was an eight-year-old child in the refugee camp at Khan Yunis when the massacres took place and has spoken about hundreds killed there "in cold blood."[11] These incidents undoubtedly contributed to the collective intergenerational trauma of Gazans and shaped their attitudes toward Israel and its military.

In 1967, Israel occupied the Gaza Strip in the Six-Day War, as well as the West Bank (including East Jerusalem), Sinai, and the Golan Heights. One of the ten myths Israeli historian Ilan Pappe addresses in his book *Ten Myths about Israel* is that from an Israeli perspective the war of 1967 was a war of no choice.[12] Rather, it was always part of the Zionist plan:

> The takeover of the West Bank and the Gaza Strip represents a completion of the job that began in 1948. Back then, the Zion-

8. Filiu, *Gaza*, 97.

9. Benny Morris, "Israel's Occupation of Gaza in 1956–57," *Quillette*, January 13, 2024, https://tinyurl.com/2s8nuxhv.

10. Morris, "Israel's Occupation of Gaza in 1956–57."

11. Filiu, *Gaza*, 97.

12. Ilan Pappe, *Ten Myths About Israel* (Verso, 2017), 68.

ist movement took over 80 percent of Palestine—in 1967 they completed the takeover. The demographic fear that haunted Ben-Gurion—a greater Israel with no Jewish majority—was cynically resolved by incarcerating the population of the occupied territories in a non-citizenship prison.[13]

Menachem Begin, an observer-participant in these events who became prime minister of Israel in 1977, was very clear about Israel's intentions. In a speech he made on August 8, 1982, at Israel's National Defense College, he called Gaza part of Israel's homeland. The occupation of Gaza in 1967, he asserted, was a correction of Israel's withdrawal from Gaza in 1957:

> After 1957, Israel had to wait 10 full years for its flag to fly again over *that liberated portion of the homeland*. In June 1967, we again had a choice. The Egyptian Army concentrations in the Sinai approaches do not prove that Nasser was really about to attack us. We must be honest with ourselves. *We decided to attack him.*[14]

There are two important admissions in this quote. First, Begin, a leader of the Zionist movement and the founder of Likud—and as such the founder of right-wing politics in Israel—considered Gaza part of Israel's homeland. Second, Israel's decision to wage the 1967 war was a deliberate choice; Israel was not forced into the Six-Day War. And so, following June 1967, the Gaza Strip was under the control of the Israeli military. It was an occupied territory, alongside East Jerusalem and the West Bank. East Jerusalem was illegally annexed, while the West Bank and Gaza remained under Israel's military control despite UN Resolution 242, which called for the "withdrawal of Israel armed forces from territories occupied in the recent conflict." Life under the military occupation left its mark on all Palestinians, myself included. I remember those days too well. We were powerless, yet united. The

13. Pappe, *Ten Myths About Israel*, 81.
14. "Excerpts from Begin Speech at National Defense College," *New York Times*, August 12, 1982, https://tinyurl.com/2v6r3hcw (emphasis added).

Israeli army was the ultimate authority in our towns. Gradually, over twenty years of this intense reality, Palestinians in the West Bank and Gaza began to revolt.

The first Palestinian intifada (uprising) against the Israeli occupation in 1987 actually began in Gaza, when an Israeli army vehicle hit Palestinian cars containing workers, killing four and injuring seven others. The incident led to demonstrations in the Jabalia refugee camp that gradually expanded to the rest of the strip and the West Bank. The resistance of Palestinians during the First Intifada was led by grassroots groups and marked by Palestinians demonstrating in the streets, throwing rocks at soldiers, and marching peacefully, which acts were met by curfews imposed by the Israeli military and violence. Schools and universities played an important role in the grassroots mobilization of the people, and were therefore closed for extended periods. Neighborhoods had coordination committees, and we arranged homeschools when schools were closed by the military. The Israeli military responded to the demonstrations with tear gas, rubber bullets, and live ammunition. Over the course of almost six years (December 1987 to September 1993), the Israeli army killed at least 1,070 Palestinians, including 237 children.[15] Among Israelis, 47 civilians and 43 soldiers were killed during that same period, mainly through stabbing incidents.[16]

The Oslo Accords brought a sense of hope for Palestinians. The basis of the peace talks was the understanding that this process would ultimately lead to a "two-state solution," in which Palestinians would gain independence and sovereignty over the West Bank and Gaza. Not only did this agreement not materialize, but throughout the years following, Israel continued and even intensified the building of settlements inside the West Bank and East Jerusalem. Oslo failed, and this led to the Second Intifada, which was far more violent than the first, and tragically many more were killed. It is estimated that between 2000 and 2007 more than 4,200 Palestinians, 1,000 Israelis,

15. "Fatalities in the First Intifada," B'Tselem, accessed November 21, 2024, https://tinyurl.com/mvnr5vrc.
16. "Fatalities in the First Intifada."

and 63 foreign citizens were killed. In this period, Palestinian militant groups resorted to suicide bombings against Israeli civilians. Also, Israel assassinated many Palestinian politicians and militants through targeted airstrikes and bombs. Most Hamas leaders at the time were assassinated in Gaza, elevating their profiles as folk heroes in the eyes of Gazans and increasing the popularity of Hamas amid the failed peace process and the corruption of the Palestinian Authority at the time.

From August to September of 2005, Israel conducted a unilateral withdrawal of all Israeli security forces and settlements from the Gaza Strip. This is known as Israel's disengagement from Gaza, in which nine thousand Israeli settlers left twenty-one settlements in Gaza, some by force. Israel and its allies continue to present this disengagement as a positive gesture whereby Israel handed over land to the Palestinians, claiming that since 2005 Gaza is no longer occupied. This can be added to the number of myths I have discussed thus far in the book. A legal analysis conducted by the Palestinian Negotiations Affairs Department demonstrates how in this unilateral move "Israel will retain effective military, economic, and administrative control over the Gaza Strip and will therefore continue to occupy the Gaza Strip—even after implementation of its 'Disengagement Plan.' Because Israel will continue to occupy Gaza, it will still be bound by the provisions of 1907's Hague Regulations, the Fourth Geneva Convention and relative international customary law."[17] Israeli legal center Gisha made a similar argument, naming this event the "disengagement illusion," arguing that Israel still controls many aspects of life in Gaza, and consequently the lives of Gaza's residents. It concluded:

> While Israel does face security challenges, it cannot address them by permanently denying the human rights of Gaza's two million residents, who are subject to Israeli control over many aspects of their lives. . . . The reality today is not disengagement—it is remote (but not too remote) control.[18]

17. "The Israeli 'Disengagement' Plan."
18. "The Illusion of Disengagement," Gisha, September 12, 2019, https://tinyurl.com/42bw6ary.

Dov Weisglass, senior advisor to former Israeli prime minister Ariel Sharon, the architect of the disengagement, claimed that

> The significance of the disengagement plan is the freezing of the peace process. . . . Effectively, this whole package called the Palestinian state, with all that it entails, has been removed indefinitely from our agenda . . . all with a presidential blessing and the ratification of both houses of Congress.[19]

This brief history shows that normality in Gaza (like in all Palestine) is a normality of war and tragedies. There are hardly any periods of rest and stability in Gaza's recent history. The only stability is that of being attacked. The intergenerational trauma of this majority-refugee community is heartbreaking. Gazans are born into inescapable situations of military occupation and control, confinement, and violent attacks. Can you imagine this life? Gaza is a continuous tragedy embodied. And the history I've shared to this point all occurred *before* 2007. What is yet to come is far more intense, violent, and catastrophic.

Hamas Comes to Power

Hamas is an Islamic political and militant group that was founded in 1987 by Ahmed Yasin, and his aide Abdul Aziz al-Rantissi, shortly after the start of the first Palestinian intifada. Hamas was viewed as an alternative to the more secular approach of the Palestinian political movement at the time, especially that of the Fatah party. Hamas gets its name from the Arabic acronym for the Islamic Resistance Movement. The ideology behind Hamas comes from the well-known Muslim Brotherhood movement. The founding charter, written in 1988, clearly lays the foundation for a religious (rather than national) movement while trying to maintain an inclusive position: "[Hamas] strives to raise the banner of Allah over every inch of Palestine, for under the wing of Islam followers of all religions can coexist in se-

19. Cited in "The Israeli 'Disengagement' Plan."

79

curity and safety." The charter declares the land of Palestine as an Islamic trust from God, a *waqf*:

> The Islamic Resistance Movement believes that the land of Palestine is an Islamic Waqf consecrated for future Moslem generations until Judgement Day. It, or any part of it, should not be squandered: it, or any part of it, should not be given up. Neither a single Arab country nor all Arab countries, neither any king or president, nor all the kings and presidents, neither any organization nor all of them, be they Palestinian or Arab, possess the right to do that. Palestine is an Islamic Waqf land consecrated for Moslem generations until Judgement Day.[20]

For Hamas, the Palestinian question is a religious matter: "It is necessary to instill in the minds of the Moslem generations that the Palestinian problem is a religious problem."

The charter sees no place for negotiations or for any peaceful talks with Israel: "Initiatives, and so-called peaceful solutions and international conferences, are in contradiction to the principles of the Islamic Resistance Movement." In fact, the introduction of the charter gives a clear indication of the vision of Hamas with regards to Israel. After quoting a qur'anic verse about the polemic relationship between those who embraced Islam and those who did not, the charter quotes Hassan al-Banna, the founder of the Muslim Brotherhood: "Israel will exist and will continue to exist until Islam will obliterate it, just as it obliterated others before it." The charter evokes very polemical and dangerous religious rhetoric: "Our struggle against the Jews is very great and very serious. It needs all sincere efforts. It is a step that inevitably should be followed by other steps . . . until the enemy is vanquished and Allah's victory is realised."

In 2017, Hamas revisited and modified the charter, in what can be described as a pragmatic move.[21] The main principles of the first

20. "Hamas Covenant 1988," Yale Law School, Lillian Goldman Law Library, The Avalon Project, https://tinyurl.com/yff8xpmj.

21. "Hamas in 2017: The Document in Full," *Middle East Eye*, May 2, 2017, https://tinyurl.com/ymxaz3n2.

charter remain the same, yet there are significant revisions, most notably the acceptance of the two-state solution, and a distinction between Zionism and Judaism. With regards to the two-state solution, the new charter says:

> There shall be no recognition of the legitimacy of the Zionist entity. . . . Hamas believes that no part of the land of Palestine shall be compromised or conceded, irrespective of the causes, the circumstances and the pressures and no matter how long the occupation lasts. Hamas rejects any alternative to the full and complete liberation of Palestine, from the river to the sea. However, without compromising its rejection of the Zionist entity and without relinquishing any Palestinian rights, Hamas considers the establishment of a fully sovereign and independent Palestinian state, with Jerusalem as its capital along the lines of the 4th of June 1967, with the return of the refugees and the displaced to their homes from which they were expelled, to be a formula of national consensus.[22]

This is a confusing statement, but it presents a compromise, even if understated, toward accepting the two-state principle. (By comparison, the position of the Palestinian Liberation Organization [PLO] and the Palestinian Authority has acknowledged the existence of Israel within the 1967 borders and looks for peace and coexistence with Israel.) And in a notable shift, the new charter of Hamas states:

> Hamas affirms that its conflict is with the Zionist project not with the Jews because of their religion. Hamas does not wage a struggle against the Jews because they are Jewish but wages a struggle against the Zionists who occupy Palestine. Yet, it is the Zionists who constantly identify Judaism and the Jews with their own colonial project and illegal entity.[23]

The new charter clearly aims at positioning Hamas anew in line with the main Palestinian political discourse represented by the Palestinian

22. "Hamas in 2017," sections 19–20.
23. "Hamas in 2017," section 16.

Authority. But the October 7 attacks ended any possibility toward that end, unless there is a dramatic shift of course. Since its foundation, Hamas has been involved in armed resistance through its military wing, the Izz al-Din al-Qassam Brigades, with the aim of liberating historic Palestine. Hamas looks at it as "Holy Jihad," or a religious duty, given the religious nature of the conflict as they understand it. Hamas rejected the Oslo Accords, yet later agreed to adopt and join the political system established by the Oslo Accords, namely, the Palestinian Authority, during the campaign for the parliamentary elections in 2006. During the Second Intifada, Hamas militants conducted many suicide attacks against Israeli military targets and civilians. Today, the United States and the West in general look at Hamas as a terrorist organization, whereas in Palestine it is mainly viewed as a resistance movement. It is important to note that Hamas drew its popularity from the network of charities, clinics, mosques, and schools that it set up in the West Bank and Gaza. Due to the perceived religious devotion of its leaders, it was at times viewed as the counter to the perceived corruption and ineffectiveness of the elite Palestinian Authority. The fact that Israel has over the years assassinated many Hamas leaders, including its founders, has only served to elevate the movement's popularity among Palestinians. Many view the positions of the Palestinian Authority as weak compromises. By contrast, Hamas dared to stand up against and challenge Israel and the West.

Hamas represents a sector in the Palestinian society. It is distinct in its Islamic and religious ideology. Today, it stands in opposition with the main rival, Fatah, not in its desire to end the occupation but in method: Hamas believes in armed resistance, while the leadership of the PLO has adopted the path of diplomacy, international pressure, and building the institutions of a future Palestinian state. Hamas does not represent all Palestinians, and many religious and secular Muslim leaders openly disagree with Hamas and sometimes criticize its actions. The rivalry between Fatah and Hamas has developed into enmity at times, and the Palestinian Authority in the West Bank is known to make life difficult for Hamas leaders there.

The years in which Hamas was in charge of Gaza have not been convenient for Christians, though Hamas did not target them directly. Palestinian Christians do not support Hamas's religious ideology or its characterization of the Palestinian struggle as a religious one. They also are opposed to Hamas's vision of a religious state. The state, according to the Kairos Palestine document, a widely accepted Palestinian Christian document, must be for all its citizens:

> Trying to make the state a religious state, Jewish or Islamic, suffocates the state, confines it within narrow limits, and transforms it into a state that practices discrimination and exclusion, preferring one citizen over another. We appeal to both religious Jews and Muslims: let the state be a state for all its citizens, with a vision constructed on respect for religion but also equality, justice, liberty and respect for pluralism and not on domination by a religion or a numerical majority.[24]

And Palestinian theologians, unlike Hamas and other Palestinian factions that believe in armed resistance, support creative nonviolence and condemn the killing of civilians.

Hamas must be viewed in the context of the Israeli occupation. Just as the Muslim Brotherhood aimed partially at responding to Western colonialism in the Middle East, Hamas is a response to Israeli colonialism. If people are genuine in their desire to destroy Hamas, I suggest we begin by getting rid of the occupation and apartheid.

In the January 2006 Palestinian elections, the Islamic party Hamas won a majority of legislative seats with 44 percent of the vote. The vote was as much a vote against the ruling secular Fatah party as it was a vote for Hamas and its agenda. Many voted for Hamas because they were frustrated with the failed peace process led by Fatah leaders, which led to more settlements and an intensified occupation. Many votes were also in protest of the corruption of the Palestinian Authority at the time, which had become controlled by a rich elite minority. Widely respected Palestinian independent politician Mustafa Barghouti told CNN that "mostly, they were voting

---

24. Kairos Document 9.3, Kairos Palestine, https://tinyurl.com/u52ddy45.

for opposition and voting against Fatah—against corruption, against nepotism, against the failure of the peace process, and against the lack of leadership."[25]

Throughout the recent war, Gazans have been blamed for electing Hamas to power, as though a majority of the people living in Gaza on October 6, 2006, voted for Hamas. This logic has been used as a justification for the mass killing of civilians, contributing to an image of most, if not all, Gazans as Islamic militant terrorists. This is a gross distortion of the facts. A *Washington Post* article cited Lara Friedman, president of the Foundation for Middle East Peace, who observed that in 2006 Hamas did not win a majority of the votes in even one district in Gaza. The *Washington Post* also reported that in 2023, children made up roughly half of Gaza's population, meaning that only a fraction of the territory's population ever cast a ballot for Hamas.[26]

When Hamas militants took over Gaza by force in 2007, toppling the security forces of the Palestinian Authority, Israel announced a total blockade on Gaza, by ground, air, and sea, beginning in June 2007. This is collective punishment, a tactic prohibited under international law. The blockade has enabled Israel to control all access points and allow only humanitarian supplies into the strip. This policy's stated intent is to "keep Gaza's economy on the brink of collapse" and thus dependent on external actors.[27]

Meanwhile, Hamas ruled Gaza with force, and with limited freedom of expression, especially for opponents. It was authoritarian rule of a distinctly Islamic nature. The early months of the takeover were characterized by chaos and the appearance of many factions that were more extreme than Hamas in their Islamic ideology. The small Christian community of Gaza was the target of attacks by these groups in 2007, and a member of that community was killed. Some

25. Ishaan Tharoor, "The Election That Led to Hamas Taking Over Gaza," *Washington Post*, October 24, 2023, https://tinyurl.com/43mfvzft.

26. Tharoor, "Election."

27. Jeffrey Heller, "Israel Said Would Keep Gaza Near Collapse: WikiLeaks," Reuters, January 5, 2011, https://tinyurl.com/35mx6xrw.

Christians decided to flee Gaza then, and over time many Christians, due to the hardships of the blockade and the nature of Hamas's rule, took advantage of the special permits Israel gave to Christians during holidays to visit Bethlehem and Jerusalem and never returned to Gaza. Others emigrated when it was possible to leave through Egypt, so that by 2023 the number of Christians in Gaza had declined from three thousand to one thousand.

As time passed, Hamas gained full control over the strip, almost without any remaining opposition. The highly religious nature of Hamas's reign and the freedoms Hamas restricted were rightly a matter of concern, not merely for the small Christian community that remained in Gaza but also for many Muslim Gazans. The leadership of Hamas invested much in its military arsenal and its underground tunnels. For years, the tunnels were mainly between Egypt and Gaza and were used to bring in goods, which turned into a profitable business for Hamas. There were other outward indications of corruption as well.[28] One survey showed that Hamas was losing its popularity before October 7: 67 percent of the four hundred Palestinians surveyed in Gaza "had little or no trust in Hamas in that period right before the attacks."[29]

The Blockade Explained

Beginning in June 2007, Israel significantly intensified existing movement restrictions, virtually isolating the Gaza Strip from the rest of the occupied Palestinian territories and the world. This land, sea, and air blockade has significantly exacerbated previous restrictions, limiting the number and specified categories of people and goods allowed in and out through the Israeli-controlled crossings.[30] At the

28. "Gaza: Journalist Facing Prison Term for Exposing Corruption in Hamas-Controlled Ministry," Amnesty International, February 25, 2019, https://tinyurl.com/mree48hh.

29. "Rare Survey Details How Gazans Wary of Hamas Before Israel Attack," *France 24*, November 28, 2023, https://tinyurl.com/26svmep2.

30. "The Gaza Strip: The Humanitarian Impact of 15 Years of Blockade," UNICEF, June 2022, https://tinyurl.com/4pdpxzfy.

same time, the Egyptian authorities have closed the Rafah border crossing with Gaza for extended periods since 2007.

Since the start of the blockade, Israel has subjected Gazans to highly inhumane policies. In addition to years of merciless bombing while the blockade and Israeli control of Gaza remained in place, Israeli authorities mandated that Gazans should receive minimal food, with fewer fruits and vegetables than the average Israeli, just enough to avoid malnutrition. As a result, by 2021, 69 percent of households in Gaza were food insecure and 80 percent of Gazans relied on aid to survive.

The restrictions on Gaza's resources did not stop at food. Throughout the years, the changing list of prohibited items has included building materials such as plaster, tar, wood for construction, cement, and iron. Even fabric and sewing machines for clothing have been barred. Just two decades ago, the targets of these bans—the construction and garment industries—were key sectors of Gaza's economy and its largest employers.

Chicken cages were allowed, but not chickens. What security threat is posed by fishing rods and nets, space heaters, and musical instruments? How might chocolate or children's toys be weaponized against an occupying power with an air force, navy, and army? The restrictions imposed on Gaza since 2007 have clearly aimed to stifle life and livelihood in Gaza by whatever means possible. The West has not only ignored this crucial aspect of Gaza's context but parroted the talking points of those dropping the bombs. This purposefully ignored context is a crucial element of the story. It is a fact. We cannot tell the story of Gaza without these fundamental components of its history and present. Before October 7, a majority of Gaza's children suffered from symptoms of PTSD. Psychologists instead began using the term "complex continuous trauma" to describe the effect the chronic, never-ending warfare had on children, because there is no such thing as *post*traumatic stress for those trapped inside Gaza.[31] They are an imprisoned population of more than two million inno-

---

31. Iman Farajallah, "The Invisible Wounds of Palestinian Children," *Psychiatric Times*, March 28, 2024, https://tinyurl.com/mn6z5z5z.

cent people, half of them children, who have been intentionally kept on the brink of survival for over sixteen years. What type of defense is this? How many of the children in Gaza watched as friends and families were massacred in recent years while the world called their suffering "collateral damage"? How many of them have decided to pick up arms after witnessing constant indiscriminate violence?

Throughout the siege, young people in Gaza have had virtually no employment opportunities. Hopelessness has pervaded Gazan society as the siege has stretched on indefinitely. A study in 2020 estimated that 38 percent of young people in the Gaza Strip have considered suicide at least once. The youth unemployment rate at the time was at 70 percent, with young graduates making up 58 percent of unemployed youth.[32] This is the context that precedes October 7—a context of hopelessness and despair. In 2022, the unemployment rate in Gaza was 45 percent. With 800,000 of Gaza's 1 million children never knowing life without a blockade, youth suicides reached an all-time high, and 80 percent of children had depression.

Israel has granted tens of thousands of work permits to Palestinians from Gaza, mostly for physical-labor jobs in Israel such as construction and agriculture. Many Gazans are reliant on these jobs due to the high unemployment rates resulting from the Israeli-imposed blockade. Thus Israel has effectively been using Gaza as its labor pool. Some observers refer to Gaza no longer as an open-air prison but as a concentration camp.[33] That term is shocking, but as far back as 2004 the director of Israel's National Security Council used it in describing Gaza.[34]

---

32. "On the Brink: Gaza's Youth Are Turning to Suicide amid Growing Desperation," ReliefWeb, November 30, 2020, https://tinyurl.com/7w8nmhkm.

33. See Jeremy Scahill, "Blacklisted Academic Norman Finkelstein on Gaza, 'The World's Largest Concentration Camp,'" *Intercept*, May 20, 2018, https://tinyurl.com/3r9cwmm8; Haidar Eid, "On the Gaza 'Shoah' and the 'Banality of Evil,'" *Al Jazeera*, December 30, 2023, https://tinyurl.com/mry6njtk; Hilal Kaplan, "Gaza as an Extermination Camp," *Daily Sabah*, May 1, 2024, https://tinyurl.com/4u9jxdsd.

34. Giora Eiland's use of this language is reported in a leaked US diplomatic cable. See Jonathan Ofir, "Influential Israeli National Security Leader

For sixteen years before October 7, Gazans lived under an Israeli blockade in one of the most densely populated places on earth. While Israeli kibbutz residents around Gaza have lived prosperously with amenities such as swimming pools and music concerts almost within earshot of Gaza, Gazans have remained trapped in some of the worst living conditions on earth. "If there is a hell on earth, it is the lives of children in Gaza," remarked UN Secretary-General António Guterres in 2021.[35] His words cut to the core of the context of Gaza today.

Four Wars in Fourteen Years

To make an already horrible reality even more atrocious, Gaza endured four wars with Israel from 2008 to 2021. Israel and Hamas blame each other for starting these wars. Israel consistently plays the role of the victim and characterizes each war as a war of self-defense, while Hamas uses the language of liberation and military resistance. What cannot be disputed is the asymmetry of power in these wars and the brutality of the Israeli aggression against Gaza: large and tragic numbers of Palestinian civilians were killed as Israel pounded Gaza with large-tonnage bombs that destroyed buildings and the entire infrastructure. In total, about five thousand Gazans were killed during these wars; most of the dead were civilians, and at least 1,020 were children. The total number of Israelis killed in these wars, including soldiers, did not exceed two hundred.[36] All lives are precious. Yet the asymmetry of power is evident, and the ruthlessness of the Israeli military was on full display, preparing the way for what we have witnessed since October 7.

Makes the Case for Genocide in Gaza," *Mondoweiss*, November 20, 2023, https://tinyurl.com/mr7dz55c.

35. "Gaza Children Living in 'Hell on Earth' Secretary-General Tells General Assembly, as Calls for End to Violence Crescendo, News of Israel-Hamas Ceasefire Breaks," United Nations, May 20, 2021, https://tinyurl.com/mr2vv2rt.

36. "Data on Casualties," OCHA-OPT, accessed November 21, 2024, https://tinyurl.com/yeu7bmuv.

Imagine life under siege and poverty, and then consistent bombing over fourteen years in one of the most densely populated areas in the world. Again, try to imagine the generations of trauma. Can you imagine the anger and despair? We must stop playing the political blame game and instead humanize the experience of Gazans. It was truly hell on earth in Gaza before October 7, and one of the factors that enabled these realities to prevail is the systematic dehumanization of Palestinians and Gazans.

Mowing the Lawn

Since the start of the blockade, inhumane policies have been central to the cruel intent of making life hell on earth for Palestinians in Gaza. The most chilling is the strategy commonly known as "mowing the lawn," whereby the Israeli military intermittently bombs this tiny enclave every few years to wear down and reduce the population.[37]

This metaphor illustrates how Palestinian lives are viewed as disposable and civilians are not distinguished from resistance fighters. All Palestinians are nuisances requiring maintenance rather than individuals with inherent dignity. The mowing metaphor implies that the relentless bombardments and military operations against a majority-refugee population—a population that is half children—are unremarkable, a routine domestic chore. Similarly dehumanizing language appeared, in July 2014 social media posts by Israeli Knesset member Ayelet Shaked. She openly called for genocide, labeling all Palestinians snakes. The following year she was promoted to the cabinet as Israel's minister of justice.[38]

Rather than address this blatantly murderous approach for what it is—grounds for investigation, immediate cease-fire, weapons embar-

---

37. An opinion column advocating this approach: Efraim Inbar and Eitan Shamir, "Mowing the Grass in Gaza," *Jerusalem Post*, July 22, 2014, https://tinyurl.com/2ddkwc7h.

38. Judy Maltz, "What Does Israel's New Justice Minister Really Think About Arabs?" *Haaretz*, May 11, 2015, https://tinyurl.com/2v6jpe6r; "'Mothers of All Palestinians Should Also Be Killed,' Says Israeli Politician," *Daily Sabah*, July 14, 2014, https://tinyurl.com/48p4sepd.

goes, and charges of war crimes—international organizations offered their statements of condemnation and critique while Western governments widely accepted Israel's cover of "self-defense," ignoring the violent racism of this practice.

After thousands upon thousands of innocent children, men, and women were "mowed down" in attacks on Gaza in 2008–2009, 2012, 2014, and 2021, the mainstream media in the United States merely reported the events, and sometimes (rarely) reported on disagreements about the morality or effectiveness of the strategy.[39] But we did not see full, accurate, and persistent portrayal of the horrors, and we did not hear a powerful moral outcry, either in the media or in the churches. Rather, the US government, and seemingly its people, including Christians, have accepted the racism inherent in the "mowing" metaphor. They unquestioningly support continued US funding of weapons to bomb Gaza and "mow the lawn," resulting in a smaller population and infrastructure, as if this strategy somehow protects Israel or promotes stability.

Israel's Role in October 7 Explained

We cannot bypass one important factor that led to the events of October 7, and consequently to the tragedy of Gaza. Any attempt to understand Hamas must consider that Netanyahu himself, backed by the Israeli government, deliberately enabled Hamas to stay in power so as to weaken the Palestinian Authority and maintain division among Palestinians. Yes, you read that correctly: Netanyahu himself supported Hamas. It is now well documented that Netanyahu has adopted a policy of "divide and conquer" to keep Palestinians divided, weaken the Palestinian Authority, and eradicate any possibility of a Palestinian state. Senator Chris Van Hollen confirmed this in an address to Congress:

39. Here is a rare and slight example from 2021: Adam Taylor, "With Strikes Targeting Rockets and Tunnels, the Israeli Tactic of 'Mowing the Grass' Returns to Gaza," *Washington Post*, May 14, 2021, https://tinyurl.com/bdct4n3y.

But what we rarely, if ever, discuss is the inconvenient truth that, until the unexpected horror of the Hamas attack on October 7, Prime Minister Netanyahu himself saw it as in his interest to keep Hamas in control in Gaza.

Don't take my word for it. He told us this back in 2019 at a Likud Party meeting, where he said: "Anyone who wants to prevent the creation of a Palestinian state needs to support strengthening Hamas. This is part of our strategy to divide the Palestinians between those in Gaza and those in Judea and Samaria."[40]

In fact, the Israeli government under Netanyahu channeled upward of hundreds of millions of dollars over the years from Qatar to Hamas in Gaza. Although these actions are well documented in Israeli sources,[41] Israel's support of Hamas does not seem to be a main talking point in most Western coverage of the war. Netanyahu might claim that he allowed this for humanitarian reasons, but as a report in Israeli newspaper *Haaretz* shows:

> Allowing cash transfers, as the Qatari envoy comes and goes to Gaza as he pleases, agreeing to the import of a broad array of goods, construction materials in particular, with the knowledge that much of the material will be designated for terrorism and not for building civilian infrastructure. . . . All these developments created symbiosis between the flowering of fundamentalism and preservation of Netanyahu's rule.

40. *Congressional Record*, Vol. 170, no. 46 (March 14, 2024): S2387–S2394, https://tinyurl.com/2vmztkpe. See also Lahav Harkov, "Netanyahu: Money to Hamas Part of Strategy to Keep Palestinians Divided," *Jerusalem Post*, March 12, 2019, https://tinyurl.com/7d2uv3dv; Tal Schneider, "For Years, Netanyahu Propped Up Hamas. Now It's Blown Up in Our Faces," *Times of Israel*, October 8, 2023, https://tinyurl.com/yk444s64.

41. Jacob Magid, "Documents Show Israel Sought, Valued Qatari Aid for Gaza in Years Leading to Oct. 7," *Times of Israel*, March 22, 2024, https://tinyurl.com/mvptv3v7; Nima Elbagir et al., "Qatar Sent Millions to Gaza for Years—with Israel's Backing. Here's What We Know About the Controversial Deal," *CNN*, December 12, 2023, https://tinyurl.com/22ah3ar6.

Take note: It would be a mistake to assume that Netanyahu thought about the well-being of the poor and oppressed Gazans—who are also victims of Hamas—when allowing the transfer of funds. His goal was to hurt Abbas and prevent division of the Land of Israel into states.[42]

A *New York Times* columnist gives a similar account of this affair, citing previous Israeli Prime Minister Ehud Barak. The columnist states that "Netanyahu's aim, according to Barak and others, was to buttress Hamas so as to weaken the rival Palestinian Authority and undermine any possibility of a two-state solution."[43]

This is the same Netanyahu who was welcomed as a hero in the US Congress over half a year into the war. This kind of policy is not new to Israel, nor indeed to the United States, its biggest supporter. Did not the United States play a role in toppling the Iranian coup in the 1950s, to support its own interests? Did not the United States help the Taliban fight against the Soviet Union? Did not the United States help create ISIS in its attempt to overthrow the Syrian regime? And did not Israel play a role in creating Hamas, so that it could weaken the PLO? Again, all of the above is well documented.[44]

So, again, I ask, how is Netanyahu still regarded as the victim in this context? Or even the hero? Why is this very critical component of the war on Gaza ignored? Why do world leaders and some church leaders continue to deal with Israel and Netanyahu as if none of this happened? This is beyond my comprehension. Perhaps because to admit Netanyahu's role would be to admit America's guilt as well?

42. Adam Raz, "A Brief History of the Netanyahu-Hamas Alliance," *Haaretz*, October 20, 2023, https://tinyurl.com/43j9bkrw.

43. Nicholas Kristof, "'We Are Overpaying the Price for a Sin We Didn't Commit,'" *New York Times*, October 28, 2023, https://tinyurl.com/59j4psjm.

44. Mehdi Hasan and Dina Sayedahmed, "Blowback: How Israel Went from Helping Create Hamas to Bombing It," *Intercept*, February 19, 2018, https://tinyurl.com/4un25mas; Andrew Higgins, "How Israel Helped to Spawn Hamas," *Wall Street Journal*, January 24, 2009, https://tinyurl.com/3evn7m33; Ishaan Tharoor, "How Israel Helped Create Hamas," *Washington Post*, July 30, 2014, https://tinyurl.com/2a62jrwd.

Would the West ever admit its complicity and role in the mess we find ourselves in, which has resulted in the death of thousands over the years?

Walk in Our Shoes

Throughout the last two chapters, I have aimed to set the context of October 7, namely, that of seventy-six years of settler colonialism, ethnic cleansing, apartheid, Zionism, and siege. This was by no means a comprehensive historical analysis. I could have said more about the intifadas, Oslo, and other episodes in our history. I could have said much more about the year 2023, wherein a record number of Palestinians were killed long before October 7.[45] There were also a number of violent incitements and invasions of Al-Aqsa Mosque in Jerusalem, which is why Hamas named its attacks on October 7 after Al-Aqsa—the Flood of Al-Aqsa. I could have said more about the violence enacted by Palestinians, for example, during the Second Intifada, or the missiles Gazans fired toward Israeli towns.

Explaining the context as I did does not mean that I believe that Palestinians are faultless. Nor is it an endorsement of Hamas or even armed resistance. To state the obvious, I do not support the ideology of Hamas, especially when it comes to creating a religious state. I cannot and would not deny the human rights abuses of Hamas before and during the war, just as I do not deny the corruption and abuses of freedom of expression within the Palestinian Authority. In explaining this context, I by no means intend to justify or endorse the events of October 7. As I have emphasized over and over, I cannot accept—to the contrary, I condemn—the killing and kidnapping of children and innocent civilians. Moreover, I am part of a broad Palestinian theology movement that believes in nonviolence and promotes nonviolent creative resistance.[46] But as we thirst and hunger for justice, we must tell the whole story.

45. "UN Agency Says 2023 'Deadliest Year on Record' for Palestinians in West Bank," *Anadolu*, December 29, 2023, https://tinyurl.com/2p8r9zes.
46. See, for example, the Kairos Document, section 4.2.3, which states:

The context I describe is the big picture. It explains the dynamic of power at play in Palestine. It challenges the myth of a "conflict" wherein the colonizer is defending itself from the colonized. Context matters, and ignoring it distorts the narrative and creates very harmful stereotypes of Palestinians, stereotypes that have tragically contributed to supporting and justifying a genocidal war against Palestinians in Gaza. Isolating October 7 and portraying it solely as a hateful act makes Israel's actions after October 7 appear to be self-defense, or even a war of survival. Rather, it is the Palestinians who have been struggling to survive over the years.

Palestinians are deeply troubled when the context of their oppression is ignored. One of the biggest hypocrisies of all is when Western governments and their citizens, who provide money for weapons around the world, pretend to be shocked by acts of resistance. Some years ago, Bethlehem Bible College hosted a well-known American evangelical speaker. The hall was packed to hear him speak. In a typical American evangelical manner, the speaker showed a captivated audience an exciting, sensational video that included the famous scene from the movie *Braveheart* when Scottish warrior William Wallace rushes toward his English oppressors during the First War of Scottish Independence shouting, "freedom!" At the time, I was sitting in the front row next to the founder and then president of the college, Dr. Bishara Awad. As we watched Wallace, played by actor Mel Gibson, lead an armed resistance, Dr. Awad leaned toward me and whispered: "If he had been a Palestinian, he would have been labeled a terrorist." This is sadly so true.

Westerners understand and even cherish stories of resistance when they portray a context that resonates with their own. The au-

---

"We say that our option as Christians in the face of the Israeli occupation is to resist. Resistance is a right and a duty for the Christian. But it is resistance with love as its logic. It is thus a creative resistance for it must find human ways that engage the humanity of the enemy. Seeing the image of God in the face of the enemy means taking up positions in the light of this vision of active resistance to stop the injustice and oblige the perpetrator to end his aggression and thus achieve the desired goal, which is getting back the land, freedom, dignity and independence." See https://tinyurl.com/2f87b2n6.

dience celebrates and acknowledges the courage of resistance as a noble struggle for liberation and justice. *Braveheart* won five Oscars, including Best Picture. Other award-winning films like *Dances with Wolves* and *There Will Be Blood* sold out theaters and became American classics. Yet when resistance is led by those bearing non-Western nationalities and darker skin colors, it is rarely celebrated or understood as a struggle for justice.

Wherever there is oppression, there is resistance against oppression. In fact, former Israeli Prime Minister Ehud Barak recently acknowledged in an interview, "If I were a Palestinian, I'd also join a terror group," while Ami Ayalon, the former head of the Israeli intelligence organization Shabak, stated that if he were Palestinian, he would have fought those who stole his land "without limits."[47] This is why it is important to explain the context that precedes such resistance. The world only sees one side—the response. It fixates on resistance to oppression, which is a minuscule fraction of the violence inflicted by the oppressor. This would be the equivalent of condemning the revolt Nat Turner led against the white slave owners in 1831, at the peak of slavery, as a hate crime. The revolt reportedly killed sixty white people in a brutal manner. Talking about the harsh and cruel realities of slavery to better understand this event is not necessarily an endorsement of the killing of women and children. But it safeguards against a narrow response that condemns the revolt as a hate crime against the white slave owners without understanding the larger context.[48]

For those who are quick to condemn the violence of Palestinians on October 7, I ask you to try walking in our shoes before lecturing us on how we should respond. Try living under the same circumstances, not for seventeen years, but for seventeen months—or even just sev-

---

47. Joseph Massad, "Why Israeli Leaders Admit If They Were Palestinian They Would Fight for Freedom," *Middle East Eye*, September 16, 2024, https://tinyurl.com/5bybkdhc.

48. This particular point of comparison was made by Jewish American scholar Norman Finkelstein in an interview with Candace Owens: "Israel vs. Palestine with Norman Finkelstein," YouTube, November 17, 2023, https://www.youtube.com/watch?v=lY63nlpVhUg.

enteen days—before saying how Gazans ought to respond to so many years of brutal mistreatment. For the majority of Gazans, the siege, which renders Gaza the world's biggest open-air prison, is the only reality they've known.

How should Palestinians respond to the ongoing Nakba, to seventy-six years and counting of military occupation? How ought we respond to the confiscation of our land? And what of the denial of our basic human rights, like having access to water, or uniting with a spouse? The perspectives of those who criticize Palestinians would shift radically if they understood the depth of the generational pain and the harsh daily oppression that Palestinians face.

Should we try nonviolence? In fact, in 2005, representatives of more than 170 organizations representing Palestinian civil society made a call to embrace a comprehensive nonviolent plan to resist the occupation using three main methods: boycott, divestment, and sanctions (BDS).[49] The goal was to put political and economic pressure on Israel to comply with international law. Yet how did the Western world respond? It vilified the BDS movement and launched a substantial political movement against it that has, in the United States, succeeded in excluding companies that boycott Israel from competition for government contracts in numerous states.[50] Palestinians are intimately familiar with the West's hypocrisy, which is thinly veiled by a professed allegiance to democracy and freedom.

Gazans, too, have tried nonviolence! In 2018–2019, Gazans conducted weekly nonviolent border protests known as the Great March of Return. Thousands of Gazans participated in organized demonstrations each Friday in the Gaza Strip near the Gaza-Israel border

49. The BDS website can be accessed at https://tinyurl.com/5884c4w9.

50. The states that have passed legislation making it illegal for state agencies to work with companies that boycott Israel include Texas, Ohio, Illinois, Indiana, Florida, Arizona, Georgia, Iowa, Pennsylvania, Michigan, Arkansas, Minnesota, Nevada, South Carolina, Tennessee, Alabama, Rhode Island, New Jersey, Oklahoma, Kansas, North Carolina, Utah, Missouri, Idaho, West Virginia, Colorado, Mississippi, and New Hampshire. Matthew Impelli, "Map Shows States Where Boycotting Israel Is Illegal," *Newsweek*, April 29, 2024, https://tinyurl.com/3m6b4tys.

from March 30, 2018, until December 27, 2019. They protested the blockade and demanded the realization of their right of return to their towns and villages. How did Israel respond? Israeli forces killed more than two hundred Palestinians (including close to forty children) and injured around thirty thousand. Most of the injuries Gazans received were in their legs, caused by the live ammunition that Israeli forces unleashed against nonviolent protesters. These injuries left a long-lasting impact on thousands of Gazans. According to Médecins sans Frontières (Doctors Without Borders), "The acute and complex injuries sustained by protestors vastly exceed the available capacity and capability of the authorities and the few organisations working on the ground. . . . The surgical needs are enormous; we have tripled our surgical capacity in Gaza since the beginning of 2018, but our teams are overwhelmed."[51]

How did the world respond? The siege continued. The denial of rights continued. And Palestinians were blamed, as always.

Should we try diplomacy? The United States is ready with its veto power, having vetoed UN Security Council resolutions critical of Israel fifty-three times as of February 2023.[52] Armed resistance? We will be called terrorists, yet again. The tragic irony is that we Palestinians are being lectured by our colonizers and their allies, deeply entrenched in their own histories of racism and violence, about nonviolence and diplomacy.

A Sermon in Response to October 7

I addressed my two congregations in Beit Sahour and Bethlehem in the Sunday service on October 8, and of course, the sermon was on Gaza. This was twenty-four hours after the attacks. The nature of the attacks, and the numbers killed, were not yet clear, including the full details of the attack on the music festival. The sermon was one

51. "Shattered Limbs, Shattered Lives," Médecins sans Frontières, accessed November 20, 2024, https://tinyurl.com/2yyzbz7h.

52. Alon Pinkas, "When Will the U.S. Get Tired of Helping Israel with UN Vetoes?" *Haaretz*, February 17, 2023, https://tinyurl.com/ycx2d6cp.

of lament—one in anticipation of war. It was a lament for Gaza. Here are parts of the sermon I preached on that day, which I hope will shed some light on how we as Palestinians felt the first day of the war:

We were all shocked by what happened yesterday. We were glued to our phones and televisions, following the events as they unfolded. We were shocked by the strength of the Palestinian man, who defied his siege. We remembered that in this land we live in a constant state of war. Think with me about how many wars and uprisings we have lived through. Today, what we fear is that we have begun a long-term war.

It is important to understand the events in their context. What is happening in Gaza is not an isolated or special case. What is happening is a result of the injustice that has befallen us as Palestinians since the Nakba until now. The majority of the people of Gaza are displaced refugees, and many of them were displaced two, three, or four times in their lives. Its youth, whom we saw yesterday, have only known the reality of the siege since 2007— that is, sixteen years ago—and they are living in the harshest conditions of life. It is "hell" on earth. Pressure generates explosion. Frankly, anyone following the events was not surprised by what happened yesterday.

Gaza today is evidence that humanity has lost its conscience. The world does not care about the people of Gaza. No one talks about Gaza except during wartime, and then we forget it again. One of the scenes that left an impression on my mind yesterday— and there are many scenes—is the scene of the Israeli youths who were celebrating a concert in the open fields, just outside the borders of Gaza, and how they escaped in horror.[53] What a great contradiction, between the besieged poor on the one hand, and the wealthy people celebrating as if there was nothing behind the wall.

53. At the time of this sermon, the nature of the attack on the festival was not clear, nor the fact that many participants in the festival were mercilessly killed by Hamas militants in the attack.

Gaza reveals the hypocrisy of the world. We follow the news and hear about Israel's right to exist and its defense of itself—but do the people of Gaza have the right to defend their freedom? Their existence? We hear about terrorism, but what about state terrorism? We hear about condemning the killing of civilians and their kidnapping. We do not justify or support the killing of civilians or the abuse of the corpses of prisoners. War is always ugly, but the hypocrisy of the world is something truly harmful.

Israel began preparing its response. Since yesterday, all the people of Gaza have been living in a state of terror 24 hours a day—in their big prison. I cannot even imagine being in their place. They are the victims of war!

America, Britain, and many countries have expressed their absolute support for Israel. There are reports of financial aid to Israel, in order to support its "revenge." Indeed, war is a business to some, especially those in the arms trade. Humans are the victims. Even Christian Zionists began raising money for Israel's security. Safety doesn't come through walls, weapons, and money. This matrix fell apart yesterday, and its failure has been proven. Power does not bring peace. Safety will only come with justice and equality. Peace is the key to security. We are two peoples on this land. Does Israel imagine that peace will come through the oppression of 7 million Palestinians? Or through blockading them? This mentality is the cause of destruction. Either we live together or we destroy each other.

Israel will return us to the spiral of violence. They say they want to eliminate Hamas, but they will create many times more militants, and we will continue this spiral. And we wonder, for how long?

Our call is not to lose our humanity. In our rejection of and resistance to evil, and in our self-defense, we must strive not to lose our humanity. There are things that happen in war that we cannot accept or be happy about. Human feelings rejoice in revenge, especially after years of oppression. But revenge and the culture of "an eye for an eye" and "a tooth for a tooth" can damage our soul, and this too leads to an endless cycle of violence. The real catastrophe in the logic of revenge occurs when the two sides are not equal in strength—and we see it today in our land. An eye for an eye has become an eye for ten eyes! In the logic of revenge, the weak always loses, and the victims are children and innocents. . . .

Today we are called first to pray. Pray for the war to stop. Pray for protection for the innocent. Every human being who dies is a human being created in the image of God. God does not rejoice in death, and we do not rejoice in death. Today we cry out to God and seek His mercy on our land. Lord have mercy. . . .

Today also in our prayers, we mourn death and injustice. God weeps before death, and we too should weep with him. As a church, we must rediscover the importance of lament in the Christian life.

4

Coloniality, Racism, and Empire Theology

On January 11, 2024, South Africa presented a case against Israel at the ICJ in The Hague. The eighty-four-page case claimed that Israel's actions "are genocidal in character because they are intended to bring about the destruction of a substantial part of the Palestinian national, racial and ethnical group"[1] in a direct violation of the 1948 Genocide Convention.[2]

During the deliberations, lawyers for South Africa showcased copious evidence that Israel is indeed committing genocide, and intentionally so, as demonstrated by statements made by Israeli leaders themselves. The court "has the benefit of the past thirteen weeks of evidence that shows incontrovertibly a pattern of conduct and related intention" that amounts to "a plausible claim of genocidal acts," South African lawyer Adila Hassim told the judges in The Hague.[3] "The intent to destroy Gaza has been nurtured at the high-

---

1. The South African brief is available here: https://tinyurl.com/yu aa3mcb. See also Mike Corder, "South Africa Says Israel's Campaign in Gaza Amounts to Genocide. What Can the UN Do About It?" Associated Press, January 11, 2014, https://tinyurl.com/3u9ja8hb.

2. Alexandra Sharp, "South Africa Presents Genocide Case Against Israel in Court," *Foreign Policy*, January 11, 2014, https://tinyurl.com/ufavs799.

3. Mike Corder and Raf Casert, "South Africa Tells Top UN Court Israel

est level of state," Tembeka Ngcukaitobi, another lawyer for South Africa, told the judges.[4]

On January 26, the ICJ ruled that it is "plausible" that Israel has committed acts that violate the Genocide Convention. In a provisional order, the court ordered that Israel must ensure "with immediate effect" that its forces not commit any of the acts prohibited by the convention.[5] The ruling was a clear rebuke of Israel's actions. At the time, its attack on Gaza had killed more than twenty-six thousand Palestinians, of whom around ten thousand were children, and had expelled nearly 85 percent of Gazans from their homes—a crime of ethnic cleansing.

How did the major Western nations respond? They did nothing! Israel condemned the allegations and called them "atrocious and preposterous," citing self-defense as justification.[6] White House National Security Communications advisor John Kirby's response carried tones of condescension and racism as he dismissed the South African case as "meritless, counterproductive, and completely without any basis in fact whatsoever."[7] Similarly, UK foreign secretary David Cameron claimed the case was "wrong" and "unhelpful," arguing that Israel was acting in "self-defense" and that accusations of genocide were "nonsense."[8] Germany even pledged to intervene on behalf of Israel in the ICJ.[9]

The day after the court's provisional order, the governments of the United States, Britain, Germany, Italy, the Netherlands, Switzer-

Is Committing Genocide in Gaza as Landmark Case Begins," Associated Press, January 12, 2014, https://tinyurl.com/y34jstup.

4. Sharp, "South Africa Presents Genocide Case Against Israel in Court."

5. Fatima Al-Kassab, "A Top U.N. Court Says Gaza Genocide Is 'Plausible' but Does Not Order Cease-Fire," NPR, January 26, 2024, https://tinyurl.com/46cd7f95.

6. Sharp, "South Africa Presents Genocide Case Against Israel in Court."

7. Andrew Feinberg, "White House Dismisses South Africa's Genocide Case Against Israel as 'Meritless,'" Independent, January 3, 2024, https://tinyurl.com/mv6janvn.

8. Jennifer Scott, "'Nonsense' for South Africa to Accuse Israel of Genocide, Says Foreign Secretary," Sky News, January 15, 2024, https://tinyurl.com/2pyrk6ne.

9. Rachel Fink, "Germany Announces Decision to Intervene on Israel's Behalf in ICJ Case," Haaretz, January 14, 2024, https://tinyurl.com/4xdafcdb.

land, Finland, Australia, and Canada responded swiftly and firmly. They did not sanction or even condemn Israel but rather decided to pause funding for UNRWA, the primary UN aid agency for Palestinian refugees. These nations made this decision in light of Israel's allegations that twelve UNRWA staff members took part in attacks on Israel on October 7. This decision was made even though these were unsubstantiated allegations against a staff that had already been checked and approved by Israeli security, and despite Israel's well-documented record of fabricating information.[10]

The amount of hypocrisy in this double standard is incomprehensible. The level of racism involved in this hypocrisy is appalling.

Western nations' contradictory responses to a court ruling that was based on thorough examination—as opposed to Israel's allegations—are indeed appalling and shameful. But it is not difficult to understand the ideologies that shape such contradictory engagement. Why would the United States, the United Kingdom, and other European countries continue to defend Israel's obvious and clear war crimes and genocide while punishing the main source for humanitarian support to the Palestinians? This can be explained, I would argue, by three intertwining factors: coloniality, racism, and empire theology. These three elements work hand in hand in the context of Palestine. Coloniality is based on racism—the belief that some people groups have less dignity and worth than others, to put it simply. Empire theology justifies and gives legitimacy to the sins of coloniality and racism. As I unpack each, it will become apparent that the three work together as a unit and are hard to separate.

Coloniality

In a major Christian gathering in 2004 in Accra, Ghana, the World Alliance of Reformed Churches (now the World Communion of Reformed Churches) completed a nine-year process of "recognition, education, and confession" (*processus confessionis*) that began as a

10. Julian Borger, "Israel Yet to Provide Evidence to Back UNRWA 7 October Attack Claims—UN," *Guardian*, March 1, 2024, https://tinyurl.com/2xbwexaf.

response to an "urgent call" from its southern African constituency regarding global economic injustice and ecological destruction.[11] The resulting Accra Confession is an important ecumenical document that explains the reality of empire today. Empires are alive today and take many different shapes. The Accra Confession defines empire as "the coming together of economic, cultural, political and military power that constitutes a system of domination led by powerful nations to protect and defend their own interests."[12] This is an important definition, as it shows the various dimensions of empire today, and how empires still exist in modern times, though they may not resemble those of the past. It also helps us see that the modern state of Israel is an expression of empire.

Let us not forget that, as I explained in chapter 2, Israel was established as a settler-colonial entity. The colonial history of western Europe and the United States is well known. And today Israel is part of the same colonial system: Israel serves the interests of the West. Economic support and arms sales are significant components of this relationship. Israel's utility for Western interests is seen in the long US history of regarding Israel as a critical "strategic ally" in the Middle East. During a July 2024 meeting with Israeli president Isaac Herzog, President Joe Biden repeated a line he first uttered in 1986. His words to Herzog were, "If there were not an Israel, we'd have to invent one," leaving unspoken the explanation that he gave in 1986: "Were there not an Israel, the United States would have to invent an Israel, *to protect her interest in the region*."[13] Biden was referring

11. "The Accra Confession," World Communion of Reformed Churches, accessed November 22, 2024, https://tinyurl.com/44ayrzza, paragraph 1.

12. "The Accra Confession," paragraph 11.

13. Muhannad Ayyash, "Biden Says the U.S. Would Have to Invent an Israel If It Didn't Exist. Why?" *Conversation*, July 24, 2024, https://tinyurl.com/2hfpam4d (emphasis added). For Biden's full remarks to Herzog, see the White House, "Remarks by President Biden and President Herzog of the State of Israel Before Bilateral Meeting," October 26, 2022, https://tinyurl.com/2p8et56. His 1986 remarks are available in a videorecording: "Senate Session," C-Span, June 5, 1986, https://tinyurl.com/yep2kk5d. A transcript of the relevant section is available here: "Did Biden Say If Israel Didn't Exist,

to what he had just called the "naked self-interest of the U.S." This American self-interest should always guide US Middle East policy.[14] This explains why the United States continues to provide Israel with the political cover it needs through US veto power in venues like the United Nations. According to the Israeli newspaper *Haaretz*, "Fifty-three times since 1972 the United States has cast a veto in the UN Security Council against anti-Israel resolutions or condemnations of Israel. This is the diplomatic shield with which Washington has covered its ally for decades."[15] This figure does *not* include the three times the United States vetoed cease-fire resolutions during the recent war on Gaza. This is also why international law does not apply, it seems, to Israel, in situations such as its attack on the Iranian consulate in Damascus.[16] Given that an attack on a diplomatic mission is a clear violation of the 1961 Vienna Convention on Diplomatic Relations, it is clear that Israel was emboldened by the knowledge that it would not be held accountable for its actions.[17]

The point is simple: Israel serves the interest of the United States. As a colonial entity, it operates like a military base for the United States. It protects one of the United States's largest investments: its military economy. This explains why Israel is one of the largest recipients of US military aid, which currently stands at $3.8 billion annually, including funding for advanced weaponry. This funding comes in the form of grants that can be used to purchase military equipment, weapons, and technology from US defense contractors. The defense industries of Israel and the United States collaborate extensively, and Israeli companies commonly partner with American

---

the US 'Would Have to Invent an Israel'?" Snopes, February 8, 2024, https://tinyurl.com/ycxan7ar.

14. Ayyash, "Biden Says the U.S. Would Have to Invent an Israel If It Didn't Exist. Why?"

15. Alon Pinkas, "When Will the U.S. Get Tired of Helping Israel with UN Vetoes?" *Haaretz*, February 17, 2023, https://tinyurl.com/ycx2d6cp.

16. "Israel Strikes Iran Consulate in Syria's Capital Damascus: What We Know," *Al Jazeera*, April 2, 2024, https://tinyurl.com/yzurytpp.

17. Daoud Kuttab, "Amid the Israel-Iran Escalation, It's Time for a Region-Wide Ceasefire," *Al Jazeera*, April 14, 2024, https://tinyurl.com/3hsp77f2.

defense contractors to develop and produce military technologies. Israel also regularly participates in joint military exercises with the United States, which involve the sharing of military strategies, tactics, and technologies—enhancing both countries' military capabilities and interoperability.

The United Kingdom has similar ties with Israel. According to Human Rights Watch, "since 2015, the UK has licensed at least £474 million worth of military exports to Israel, including components for combat aircrafts, missiles, tanks, technology, small arms and ammunition. The UK provides approximately 15 percent of the components in the F-35 stealth bomber aircraft currently being used in Gaza."[18] The information technology (IT) sector as well is part of this matrix. In 2022, British investment in Israeli tech soared to half a billion dollars a year, taking second place only to the United States.[19]

The details of Western nations' military and economic relationship to Israel make it easier to explain their double standard regarding Israel's actions. And when these policies translate into violence against other people—the colonized—the result is racist dismissal. Perhaps nothing highlights the connection between coloniality and racism better than the words of Jared Kushner, former President Donald Trump's son-in-law. Kushner served as a senior advisor to Trump and was tasked with preparing a peace plan for the Middle East in 2018. In an interview at Harvard University in February 2024, Kushner praised the "very valuable" potential of Gaza's "waterfront property" and suggested Israel should remove civilians while it "cleans up" the strip.[20] Kushner viewed the Gaza crisis as a business opportunity. He looked at the unfolding catastrophe—the genocide, destruction, and

18. Yasmine Ahmed, "Selling Weapons to Israel Could Make UK Complicit in War Crimes," Human Rights Watch, December 12, 2023, https://tinyurl.com/yeayfbwc.

19. Sharon Wrobel, "Investment in Israeli Tech Startups Plunged by Almost Half in 2022, Data Shows," *Times of Israel*, January 10, 2023, https://tinyurl.com/445rdrzm.

20. Patrick Wintour, "Jared Kushner Says Gaza's 'Waterfront Property Could Be Very Valuable,'" *Guardian*, March 19, 2024, https://tinyurl.com/5hy8ru2y.

starvation of Gaza—and saw a dollar sign. In order to capitalize on the war, he proposed that the area be "cleaned up":

> It's a little bit of an unfortunate situation there, but from Israel's perspective I would do my best to move the people out and then clean it up. . . . I would just bulldoze something in the Negev, I would try to move people in there. . . . I think that's a better option, so you can go in and finish the job. . . . I do think right now opening up the Negev, creating a secure area there, moving the civilians out, and then going in and finishing the job would be the right move.[21]

Kushner did not even try to disguise his racism or his call for ethnic cleansing. He had a business project in mind, and the lives and fate of the people of Gaza were the least of his concerns. He speaks of Palestinians as disposable humanity.

In short, the relationship between Israel and the great powers of the world is deeply rooted in joint economic and military interests that override concepts of fairness and justice, denying the human dignity of the colonized. In the logic of empire, might and power trump the human value and worth of those on the receiving end of colonialism. In this war of genocide, the United States and other Western countries have chosen to advance their interests in the Middle East by supporting their strategic ally, knowing all too well that Israel is committing war crimes. These Western nations should stop claiming that they are beacons of democracy and freedom in the world. They should stop pretending that they care about human rights or the lives of Palestinians. They do not.

The Colonial Narrative

One of the powerful tools of empire today is its control of the narrative. This war has served as a textbook example of how empires

---

21. Wintour, "Jared Kushner Says Gaza's 'Waterfront Property Could Be Very Valuable.'"

control and distort the narrative to protect their interests and images. This is evident in the way the media has covered the current events in Gaza. A clear bias perpetuates and normalizes the dehumanization of Palestinians. A British analysis of major news outlets in the United Kingdom and United States revealed systematic dehumanization of Palestinians, perpetuation of harmful narratives, and platforming of Israeli narratives that omits Israeli violations of international law.[22] It points to the headlines of major news outlets in the West covering deadly incidents, where Israelis are reported as being "killed" or "murdered" while Palestinians passively or spontaneously "die."[23]

During the war, the *Intercept* published an analysis of the coverage of the war on Gaza from October 7 to November 24 in the *New York Times*, the *Washington Post*, and the *Los Angeles Times*. The study showed that these major newspapers reserved terms like "slaughter," "massacre," and "horrific" almost exclusively for Israeli civilians killed by Palestinians, rather than for Palestinian civilians killed in Israeli attacks. It showed how in that period, the *New York Times* had described Israeli deaths as a "massacre" on fifty-three occasions and those of Palestinians just once. The ratio for the use of "slaughter" was 22 to 1, even as the documented number of Palestinians killed at the time reached fifteen thousand.[24]

Mehdi Hasan of media company Zeteo demonstrated that online BBC coverage of the war shows a systematic disparity: BBC describes Palestinian deaths in the passive voice, suggesting a natural or accidental occurrence, while Israeli deaths are described in the active voice, attributing direct responsibility. This disparity exists at a staggering ratio of 100 to 1. Hasan argued that Palestinians are often presented as mere statistics—faceless and nameless—whereas

22. Claire Lauterbach and Namir Shabibi, "Analysis: How the UK and US Media Dehumanise Palestinians," Declassified UK, November 22, 2023, https://tinyurl.com/3xhhr3x4.

23. Lauterbach and Shabibi, "Analysis."

24. Adam Johnson and Othman Ali, "Coverage of Gaza War in *The New York Times* and Other Major Newspapers Heavily Favored Israel, Analysis Shows," *Intercept*, January 9, 2024, https://tinyurl.com/2pcfpb22.

Israelis are humanized, referred to as mothers, brothers, and sisters. Television coverage shows that American guests are more than twice as likely to sympathize with Israelis, and Israeli guests outnumber Palestinian guests by a factor of ten.

The dehumanization extends to political discourse as well. Politicians often prioritize the suffering of Israelis over Palestinians, a form of racism that reflects and reinforces the Western media's biased portrayal of global news. Anti-Palestinian racism and bigotry in media and politics persists because so few have challenged it. Hasan has noted that despite this one-sided coverage, polls show that Americans still support a cease-fire. If the media regularly provided context, depicting Palestinians as human beings and as victims of decades of Israeli violence, public opinion would shift even further. To Hasan, the systematic disparity in media coverage prioritizes the suffering of one group over another, contributing to a skewed public perception of Palestine that is not just a failure of journalism but a deliberate act of racism and dehumanization.[25]

The colonial discourse about this war has totally disregarded the context for October 7, which I have explained in chapter 2. Throughout the war, reporters and politicians have fixated on demanding that Palestinians condemn Hamas. This insistence is meant, I would argue, to shape the narrative into one in which the war began on October 7. When we insist that this war did not start on October 7, we can then begin to examine the context of this war rather than continue to debate everything that happened on October 7. A question has circulated in various forms in Western media: "What is an appropriate response to what Hamas did on October 7?"[26] As a Palestinian, I ask: What is an appropriate response to seventy-six years of ethnic cleansing and oppression? Let us remember that 80 percent of Gazans are refugees from the 1948 Nakba who have not been granted

25. Mehdi Hasan, "'The Deliberate Dehumanization of the Palestinians': Mehdi Hasan Calls Out Media Bias on Gaza," Zeteo, April 17, 2024, https://tinyurl.com/23twrw5y.

26. Kelly Garrity, "Majority of Americans Say Israel's Response to Hamas Attack Is Justified, CNN Poll Finds," *Politico*, October 15, 2024, https://tinyurl.com/msnbccx3.

rights as Israeli citizens or any compensation for their displacement. Most media outlets frame the genocide in Gaza as a post–October 7 war rather than the continuation of the Nakba.

During the war, we have heard much talk about the humanitarian situation in Gaza deteriorating to the point where people have literally died from starvation. In our anger and frustration, we as Palestinians ask: Where was this anger for the last seventeen years, since the start of the blockade? Gaza was hell *before* October 7. Shortages of food, electricity, and water happened *before* October 7. The situation had been unbearable for years, leading to extremely high unemployment and increased suicide among youth. This was *before* October 7. For seventy-six years, Palestinians have endured displacement, settler violence, land theft, demolition of housing, segregation, aggressive settlement building, apartheid, and extreme right-wing governments. The Western media have largely ignored these effects of occupation and apartheid for decades, so it is not surprising that it has taken a genocide to ignite global concern about conditions in Gaza.

Israel is exercising its right of self-defense, we are told. This is probably the argument most commonly used to justify and normalize the genocide in Gaza. Everyone has used this line, from politicians to church leaders. Yet this seemingly logical assertion serves an illogical narrative. I ask:

How is the colonizer defending itself from the colonized?
How is the occupier defending itself from the occupied?
How is the besieger defending itself from the besieged?

And, I must also ask:

How is the killing of more than seventeen thousand children considered self-defense?

I don't condone violence. I believe in creative nonviolent resistance. I have always advocated for this. But again, no one is talking about *the Palestinians'* right to self-defense. *Do Palestinians have the right to defend themselves? Do the people of Gaza have the right to defend themselves? Why not?* The West Bank and Gaza are internationally rec-ognized as occupied territories. And as inhabitants of occupied terri-tories, under international law, Palestinians clearly have the right to defend themselves, as articulated by UN special rapporteur on Pal-estine Francesca Albanese.[27] Yet if Palestinians defend themselves against the Israeli military, they are labeled terrorists. The power of empire trumps international law, rendering international law inef-fective or inapplicable when it comes to empires and their allies.

Despite the seventy-six years of Israel's violence toward and eth-nic cleansing of Palestinians, Israel and its defenders repeatedly de-scribe its actions as self-defense. Israel continues to present itself as the victim, despite being the occupier.[28] In turn, before Palestinians are allowed to share their narrative, they are expected to begin every conversation by condemning Hamas, violence as a whole, and the evil of antisemitism. We are expected to defend our colonizer's right to exist as a precondition of being allowed to speak.

This narrative distortion has been an effective tool in the arse-nal of empire throughout modern history. Have we forgotten that the United States and its allies lied to the world about the Iraqi war, claiming first that it was about the "weapons of mass destruction" and then about "promoting freedom and democracy" in the Arab world? Two hundred thousand Iraqi civilians were killed in a war that was based on a lie, a war that served the interests of empire. Two hun-dred thousand precious lives. Was anyone ever held accountable?

The distortion of narrative in the war on Gaza is accompanied and aided by the constant dehumanizing and demonizing of the Palestin-ians. The people of Gaza have been subjected to an unprecedented campaign of dehumanization throughout this war, a campaign that goes so far as to reject the legitimacy of their accounts of attacks in Gaza. Award-winning American journalist Jeremy Scahill of the

27. "UN Special Rapporteur: Israel Can't Claim 'Right of Self-Defence,'" *Al Jazeera*, November 15, 2023, https://tinyurl.com/3hm8ecyb.

28. Ahmed Moor, "Gideon Levy in NYC: Israel Is 'the Only Occupier in History That's Completely Convinced of Its Own Present Ongoing Victim-hood,'" *Mondoweiss*, October 5, 2010, https://tinyurl.com/cjtpn9fx.

Intercept wrote: "At the center of Israel's information warfare campaign is a tactical mission to dehumanize Palestinians and to flood the public discourse with a stream of false, unsubstantiated, and unverifiable allegations."[29]

The most infamous lie Israel told in the beginning of the war was its claim that Hamas militants beheaded forty Israeli children. Let us be clear: this was not a rumor that came from conspiracy-theory social media accounts. This was a lie that came directly from Israeli *and American* officials. Israeli news channel i24 claimed it had received confirmation from soldiers that babies' heads were cut off.[30] Spokespersons for the IDF and Israeli prime minister Benjamin Netanyahu spoke to major news sources, reporting that soldiers had found decapitated babies.[31] US president Joe Biden even announced that he had seen "confirmed pictures of terrorists beheading children."[32] The White House later walked back this claim.[33]

This lie spread quickly over the Internet and was shared by many politicians. A day after i24 made the first claim on X, that post alone showed 44 million impressions, 300,000 likes, and over 100,000 reposts.[34] Imagine how deeply this lie shaped the world's response to October 7 and the world's perception of Palestinians.

29. Jeremy Scahill, "Netanyahu's War on Truth: Israel's Ruthless Propaganda Campaign to Dehumanize Palestinians," *Intercept*, February 7, 2024, https://tinyurl.com/yc78nahf.

30. i24NEWS English (@i24NEWS_EN), X, October 10, 2023, https://tinyurl.com/26942nkn.

31. Lauren Izso and Mostafa Salem, "Babies and Toddlers Were Found with 'Heads Decapitated' in Kfar Aza, Netanyahu Spokesperson Says," *CNN*, October 11, 2023, https://tinyurl.com/2nzcwrtr; Joshua Nelken-Zitser and Rebecca Cohen, "IDF Says Hamas Decapitated Babies in Israel," *Business Insider*, October 10, 2023, https://tinyurl.com/wn7vtwm2.

32. Jacob Magid, "Meeting with Jewish Leaders, Biden Confirms Reports That Hamas Beheaded Israeli Children," *Times of Israel*, October 12, 2023, https://tinyurl.com/3pnsdsht.

33. "White House Walks Back Biden's Claim He Saw Children Beheaded by Hamas," *Al Jazeera*, October 12, 2023, https://tinyurl.com/yxy8jwtz.

34. Marc Owen Jones (@marcowenjones), X, October 11, 2023, https://tinyurl.com/49edkha3.

The lie about the forty babies was not an isolated fabrication. The US secretary of state, Antony Blinken, repeated a story about a family of four being butchered at the breakfast table: "The father's eye was gouged out in front of his two children, aged eight and six. The mother's breast was cut off. The girl's foot was amputated, and the boy's fingers cut off, before they were all executed. The executioners then sat down and had a meal next to their victims."[35] According to Israeli newspapers and other reports, these things did not actually happen.[36] There was Israel's claim that Al-Shifa Hospital was used as a compound for Hamas and that the kidnapped Israelis were held there. There were allegations against UNRWA, that some of its staff took part in the October 7 attacks. There was the controversial claim by the *New York Times* that Hamas weaponized sexual violence on October 7,[37] which has since been widely disputed.[38] Cases of sexual assault and violence by Hamas fighters on October 7 have been documented, and a UN report finds convincing information that hostages in Gaza were raped, and this is abhorrent and evil.[39] But false claims that such acts were widespread and systematic are transparent attempts to demonize Palestinians.

35. Jonathan Cook, "War on Gaza: We Were Lied into Genocide. Al Jazeera Has Shown Us How," *Middle East Eye*, March 28, 2024, https://tinyurl.com/5n8aunfu.

36. Arun Gupta, "American Media Keep Citing Zaka—Though Its October 7 Atrocity Stories Are Discredited in Israel," *Intercept*, February 27, 2024, https://tinyurl.com/2s8vxazv; Aaron Rabinowitz, "Death and Donations: Did the Israeli Volunteer Group Handling the Dead of October 7 Exploit Its Role?" *Haaretz*, January 31, 2024, https://tinyurl.com/2v4wb7fc.

37. Jeffrey Gettleman, Anat Schwartz, and Adam Sella, "'Screams Without Words': How Hamas Weaponized Sexual Violence on Oct. 7," *New York Times*, updated March 25, 2024, https://tinyurl.com/bdz2fczz.

38. Jeremy Scahill, Ryan Grim, and Daniel Boguslaw, "'Between the Hammer and the Anvil': The Story Behind the *New York Times* October 7 Exposé," *Intercept*, February 28, 2024, https://tinyurl.com/3t7zff5r; David Folkenflik, "Newsroom at 'New York Times' Fractures over Story on Hamas Attacks," *NPR*, March 6, 2024, https://tinyurl.com/4y7ysxyv.

39. Kareem Khadder, Lucas Lilieholm, and Nadeen Ebrahim, "Hamas-Led Groups Committed 'Numerous War Crimes' on October 7, Rights Group Says," *CNN*, July 18, 2024, https://tinyurl.com/54vyjun5.

The lies generated during this war at the expense of Palestinians are abhorrent. It is despicable to fabricate stories of horrific killings of Israeli babies in order to justify the actual killing of Palestinian babies. October 7 was horrifying enough. Many innocent Israelis, including thirty-six children, were brutally killed on that day. This is tragic in itself. But for a nation not far removed from the horrors of the Holocaust to fabricate events or exaggerate details in this manner is indeed appalling. It raises questions about the credibility of Israeli media and officials more broadly. According to a poll conducted during the early stages of the war, only 4 percent of *Israeli Jews* find Netanyahu a reliable source on the Gaza war,[40] yet Western media, members of Congress, and church leaders take his word as infallible and never dare question the Israeli sources.

One must question the real motivation behind these fabrications. On the one hand, they serve only to portray Palestinians as barbarians or animals. On the other, they provide the pretext and justification for a genocide. Scahill's comments are important:

> These stories are a set of audacious lies weaponized to generate the type of collective rage used to justify the unjustifiable.... Propaganda and weaponized lies can only obscure the dead bodies, the forced starvation, the mass killing of children, and the utter destruction of an entire society for so long.[41]

The tragic irony is that Palestinian children have been killed over the years by the Israeli military in brutal ways—more than sixteen thousand in this war alone—and we have seen little outrage or sympathy from the global community. Palestinian children are commonly held in Israeli prisons with no charges—they are kidnapped—and we see no outrage from Western governments. Reports, even videos, of sex-

40. "Poll: Less Than 4% of Jewish Israelis Believe Netanyahu Is Reliable Source of Info on War," *Times of Israel*, November 15, 2023, https://tinyurl.com/5cfywe4d.
41. Scahill, "Netanyahu's War on Truth."

ual violence against Palestinian women and men in Israeli jails are widely published, and yet Israel is not held accountable.[42]

Narrative is a very powerful tool in the hands of empire; it can even be abused to casually cover up obvious war crimes. In the months following October 7, Israel kidnapped and tortured (some to death) close to nine thousand Palestinians, including children. How is such systematic violence justified? It is simple. Once terminology is deployed that dehumanizes Palestinians, representing them as barbarians or animals, the world can justify their erasure much more easily. When Palestinians are designated as "terrorists," they are no longer "kidnapped" but "arrested" in service of self-defense and terrorism prevention. There is no need for proof. No trial is needed. No evidence is needed. The narrative that Israel has told of Palestinians is sufficiently powerful and authoritative to justify even the killing and torture of Palestinian doctors, as in the case of Dr. Adnan Al Bursh, the renowned Palestinian orthopedic surgeon and head of the orthopedic department at Al-Shifa Hospital in Gaza, who was killed through torture after nearly four months in Israeli detention.[43]

One important aspect of Israel's control of narrative is the weaponization of "antisemitism," an accusation used to silence any criticism of Israel. If you express sympathy for the children of Gaza, you risk being accused of being a Hamas supporter and an antisemite. The fear of being labeled antisemitic has silenced many Westerners, including church leaders who have personally admitted this to me. Trepidation keeps leaders and international organizations from speaking out against Israel, even when it is clear that Israel is committing war crimes in Gaza. Israel and its allies have an army of media outlets that are ready to smear any critic of Israel, and the charge of antisemitism is the first weapon in their arsenal.

---

42. "Israel/oPt: UN Experts Appalled by Reported Human Rights Violations Against Palestinian Women and Girls," OHCHR, February 19, 2024, https://tinyurl.com/55xwpjfv; Aurora Almendral, "U.S. Decries Reported Sexual Abuse of Palestinian Prisoners After Graphic Video Aired on Israeli TV," *NBC News*, August 10, 2024, https://tinyurl.com/yumnv9jp.

43. "UN Expert Horrified by Death of Gazan Orthopedic Surgeon in Israeli Detention," OHCHR, May 16, 2024, https://tinyurl.com/2hsj69eu.

The weaponization of the charge of antisemitism was evident during the student-led protests at American and European universities. Many vilified these protests as motivated by hatred of Jews, whereas in fact Jewish students led many of these demonstrations. In one incident in Germany, police who cracked down on a demonstration that one German official labeled antisemitic arrested Jews who were leading the demonstration![44] Israeli historian Raz Segal, who is associate professor of Holocaust and genocide studies at Stockton University in the United States, wrote an important piece for *Time* warning against weaponizing the charge of antisemitism:

> As Gaza solidarity encampments take root at dozens of campuses across the U.S., many Democratic and Republican lawmakers— in addition to President Joe Biden—have accused protestors and colleges of rampant antisemitism.
>
> That's woefully misguided—and dangerous. Indeed, the blanket assertion by pro-Israel advocates is intended as a political cudgel: weaponizing antisemitism to shield Israel from criticism of its attack on Gaza, which has left at least 35,000 Palestinians dead in the wake of the Oct. 7 Hamas attack, wounded tens of thousands more, and forcibly displaced nearly 2 million Palestinians who now face famine conditions. The conditions in Gaza are such that many scholars have said that the situation amounts to a genocide.
>
> Ultimately, the weaponization of antisemitism intensifies the discrimination and exclusion against vulnerable communities in the U.S.—including Jews.
>
> Indeed, those accusing protesters of antisemitism do not appear to consider the many Jews among the protestors in the encampments as Jews, arguing in effect that Jews can only be Jews if they support Israel or do not express pro-Palestinian sentiment.[45]

44. James Jackson, "'We Jews Are Just Arrested; Palestinians Are Beaten': Protesters in Germany," *Al Jazeera*, April 1, 2024, https://tinyurl.com/3b387b5w.
45. Raz Segal, "How Weaponizing Antisemitism Puts Jews at Risk," *Time*, May 14, 2024, https://tinyurl.com/2u5rmdej.

As a Palestinian Christian leader and activist, I have experienced this weaponization firsthand over the years and during this war. It is shameful to use this label in such a casual way. Antisemitism is real. It is dangerous and evil. It should not, however, be confused with advocating for the rights of Palestinians or criticizing Israel. If Israel has committed war crimes, I will speak out against them. As people of faith, our integrity and credibility are at stake here.

This is the power of empire. These are the mechanisms of coloniality. Israel is immune. It can rely on the United States to veto any resolution against it. It can rely on the West to continue to provide it with weapons with no accountability. It can rely on politicians and the media to continue to defend it and to promote the distorted imperial narrative that justifies its action and provides it with the necessary legal cover. It can rely on the US Congress, the European Union, and the UK Parliament for political, financial, and military support with no strings attached. This is the principle of "might makes right" at its worst. Just as the United States and the United Kingdom defended and supported apartheid in South Africa to the very end, resisting and blocking global campaigns for economic sanctions against South Africa, today they resist and block global movements to boycott and sanction Israel. And just as in the 1980s both Reagan and Thatcher condemned Mandela and the African National Congress as communists and terrorists at a time when the apartheid government promoted itself as a Cold War ally against communism, the superpowers of our day, led by the United States, condemn Palestinians as terrorists while the apartheid Israeli regime promotes itself as an ally in the "axis of good" against Iran and Islamic terrorism.[46]

Racism

This war has convinced us Palestinians that many in the Western world, and certainly their leaders, do not see Palestinians as equals. We are less human, it seems, less deserving of human rights and dignity: this is what I mean by the word "racism." Throughout this

46. Becky Little, "Key Steps That Led to End of Apartheid," History, updated August 22, 2023, https://tinyurl.com/yj2prpm2.

war, we have witnessed an unprecedented level of dehumanization, which has enabled Israel to continue its war of genocide for so long with sustained severity.

During this war, Western colonial narratives have employed the racialized paradigm of good versus evil, describing Hamas as "brutal," "inhuman," and "animals." One member of the US Congress went so far as to claim that all Gazans are Nazis and therefore that there are no innocent Gazans.[47]

Indeed, this war has showcased the systematic dehumanization of Palestinians. Israel's defense minister, Yoav Gallant, declared on October 9 that Israel is "fighting human animals and will act accordingly." This racist ideology was his rationale for total war on the Gaza Strip, motivating him to assert: "There will be no electricity, no food, no fuel, everything is closed."[48] Gallant does not view Palestinians as humans, and his racist beliefs are far from unique.

Prime Minister Netanyahu claimed that Israel is fighting on behalf of the "civilized world" against the "barbarians."[49] In a phone call on October 11, Netanyahu told President Biden: "We were struck Saturday by an attack whose savagery I can say we have not seen since the Holocaust. . . . They took dozens of children, bound them up, burned them and executed them. . . . We have never seen such savagery in the history of the state. They're even worse than ISIS and we need to treat them as such."[50] (Note the repeated use of "savagery": this is how European colonizers have always described indigenous peoples.)

The violent and racist views of Israel's leaders are further exem-

47. Akela Lacy, "GOP Representative Denies Existence of 'Innocent Palestinian Civilians' and Tries to Hobble Aid to Gaza," *Intercept*, November 1, 2023, https://tinyurl.com/3xcvxvbd.

48. Emanuel Fabian, "Defense Minister Announces 'Complete Siege' of Gaza: No Power, Food or Fuel," *Times of Israel*, October 9, 2023, https://tinyurl.com/4utv9fy5.

49. David Isaac, "Netanyahu Calls Civilized World to Arms Against 'Forces of Barbarism,'" Jewish News Syndicate, October 30, 2023, https://tinyurl.com/222f3dks.

50. Scahill, "Netanyahu's War on Truth."

plified in their references to the biblical Amalekites, which amount to implicit calls for the annihilation of the people of Gaza. "You must remember what Amalek has done to you, says our Holy Bible," Netanyahu said in a speech to the Israeli public, echoing the words of Deuteronomy 15. The full biblical reference says:

> Remember what Amalek did to you on your journey out of Egypt, how he attacked you on the way, when you were faint and weary, and struck down all who lagged behind you; he did not fear God. Therefore, when the LORD your God has given you rest from all your enemies on every hand, in the land that the LORD your God is giving you as an inheritance to possess, *you shall blot out the remembrance of Amalek from under heaven; do not forget.* (Deut. 25:17–19)

In 1 Samuel 15:3, God tells Samuel to instruct King Saul, "Now go and attack Amalek, and utterly destroy all that they have; do not spare them, but kill both man and woman, child and infant, ox and sheep, camel and donkey." Boaz Bismuth, an Israeli Knesset member from the Likud party, also invoked the image of Amalek and called for no mercy against the people of Gaza, arguing, "It is forbidden to take mercy on the cruel, there's no place for any humanitarian gestures. . . . The memory of Amalek must be erased."[51]

These references to Amalek carry clear connotations of ethnic cleansing and aim to justify a similar campaign of mass murder in Gaza. This way of using Scripture should give us pause, not only because it endorses violence but also because it correlates modern Israel with the Israel of the Bible and the Palestinians of today with the biblical nations that stood in the way of Israel's obtaining the land. This kind of reading implies that Israel is retaking the land God gave it thousands of years ago, and that in the process, the enemies of God must be completely annihilated. Such a twisted vision of biblical

---

51. Emma Graham-Harrison and Quique Kierszenbaum, "Israeli Public Figures Accuse Judiciary of Ignoring Incitement to Genocide in Gaza," *Guardian*, January 3, 2024, https://tinyurl.com/2ha9etfb.

conquest and annihilation is precisely what Israel sought to enact following October 7. The goal was to erase Gaza as we knew it, leaving little possibility of its ever being rebuilt.

The demonization of the people of Gaza has been an important tool in enabling this genocide. To Netanyahu, this war "is a struggle between the children of light and the children of darkness."[52] By this logic, the people of Gaza are the enemies of God's people and of God. Like the Amalekites, they must be "utterly destroyed," "their remembrance blotted out from under heaven." Palestinian scholar Nadera Shalhoub Kevorkian made an important observation about the impact of the weaponization of biblical Amalek by Israeli politicians:

> Framing Palestinians as Amalekites [deprives] us of life, of homes, of neighborhoods, of hospitals, of schools and cities. . . . Such religious claims with their method of elimination and techniques of policing and governing against . . . the Amalekite means that anyone that meets Palestinians can kill them, even as babies in incubators.[53]

The worthlessness of Palestinian lives in the eyes of the Western world is on full display in the difference between how the world reacted to war crimes against Ukrainians and how it reacted to war crimes against Palestinians. A number of global leaders, including Ursula von der Leyen, the president of the European Commission, have expressed this racist double standard. While she labeled the Russian attacks on Ukrainian civilian infrastructure—water, electricity, and heating—as "war crimes" and acts of "terror," she described the very same actions of Israel in its war on Gaza as "self-defense."[54]

52. "Excerpt from PM Netanyahu's Remarks at the Opening of the Winter Assembly of the 25th Knesset's Second Session," [Israeli] Ministry of Foreign Affairs, October 16, 2023, https://tinyurl.com/2ay2wr7n.

53. Nadera Shalhoub Kevorkian, paper on theology of empire presented at Genocide in Gaza: World Academic Forum for Palestine, Scholars Against the War on Palestine, April 7, 2024 Houston, https://tinyurl.com/56df7vyh.

54. "EU Chief von der Leyen Slammed for 'Double Standards' on

Similarly, Secretary of State Blinken called out Russia for using food as a weapon of war,[55] labeling such a tactic "unjustified" and "unconscionable,"[56] but never condemned or rebuked Israel for using the same warfare methods in harsher ways; he only urged (but did not force) Israel to do a better job of allowing food and aid to enter Gaza.[57] In contrast, the United States to date has neither halted military aid to Israel nor made it conditional in response to the war. Only after seven *international* aid workers from the World Central Kitchen were killed in an Israeli strike did thirty Democratic members of the House of Representatives call for President Biden to halt the weapon supply to Israel.[58] Such demands, however, were not met. The killings of nearly two hundred Palestinian aid workers[59] and tens of thousands of Palestinians were not enough to prompt such a demand, it seems.

We Palestinians are collateral damage. Global leaders speak of us as if we are boxes in homes: "Where do we take these Palestinians?" "Why doesn't Egypt open the borders?" I have already mentioned Jared Kushner's appalling statement that Gaza must be "cleaned up" so that Israelis can develop its real estate. In a similarly racist and condescending tone, then presidential candidate Nikki Haley called for the ethnic cleansing of Gaza, arguing that Palestinians should relocate to "pro-Hamas" countries. She added:

War-Hit Ukraine and Gaza," *New Arab*, October 13, 2023, https://tinyurl.com/3vd782xd.

55. Kevin Shalvey, "Blinken Warns Russia to Stop Using 'Food as Weapon of War' in Ukraine," *ABC News*, August 3, 2023, https://tinyurl.com/y23trxjz.

56. Margaret Besheer, "Blinken Criticizes Russia for Impact of War on Global Hunger," *VOA News*, August 3, 2023, https://tinyurl.com/yc25n8t9.

57. Tom Bateman, "Gaza's Entire Population Facing Acute Food Insecurity, Blinken Warns," *BBC News*, March 19, 2024, https://tinyurl.com/9rf26f75.

58. "Pelosi Joins US Democrats Call for Biden to Halt Arms Transfer to Israel," *Al Jazeera*, April 6, 2024, https://tinyurl.com/4nkhfpjv.

59. Claudia Williams, "Almost 200 Humanitarian Workers Have Been Killed in Gaza. This Is What Organisations Do to Try to Keep Staff Safe," *ABC News Australia*, April 2, 2024, https://tinyurl.com/ycksysjz.

Why won't Egypt take them? Because they don't trust which ones are terrorists and which ones aren't? It's a sad state of affairs, but the reality of that evil is very clear in Arab countries too.[60]

Calls for Arab countries to receive Palestinian refugees are essentially calls for ethnic cleansing. We cannot be fooled by their pretended humanitarian concern. Such calls ignore Palestinians' rootedness in the land and their national identity; such calls are not in the interest of Gazans. Why don't Nikki Haley and others who make such calls instead ask why the United States or western European countries don't open their borders to take in Israeli Jews? The idea that Palestinians are mere numbers that can be moved from one place to another while Israelis take more and more Palestinian land embraces the logic of ethnic cleansing, dehumanizes Palestinians, and denies their right to self-determination in their homeland.

Other instances of the racist logic that has dominated imperial discourse about the war in Gaza can be seen in the discourse surrounding human shields and hostages. The Israeli army first claimed that Hamas uses civilians as human shields without providing any evidence, and the West has repeated the charge at length. Even if this claim were true, would it justify the killing of children sheltering in a school or families in a hospital? If a serial killer were to escape police custody in Dallas, for example, and take a hundred children as hostages while hiding out in a school, would the United States argue for bombing the school to kill this serial killer?

Civilians, even if used as human shields, are entitled to protection. Yet Palestinians are not deemed worthy of such protection.

When Israel liberated four Israeli hostages in June 2024, the world rejoiced and celebrated.[61] The release and safety of these hostages should certainly be celebrated, but at what price? As the Western me-

60. Jacob Magid, "Nikki Haley: 'Pro-Hamas Countries' Qatar, Iran and Turkey Should Take in Palestinians Fleeing War," *Times of Israel*, December 21, 2023, https://tinyurl.com/5n8wpm8t.

61. Emanuel Fabian, "IDF Rescues 4 Hostages Alive in Stunning Operation in Central Gaza," *Times of Israel*, June 8, 2024, https://tinyurl.com/32dtyvkf.

dia celebrated their release, no mention was made of the hundreds of Gazans who were killed as collateral damage in that operation. And if the disproportionate nature of this attack was raised, Hamas alone was blamed. Here again we see total disregard for Palestinian lives. The world responded with great sympathy and empathy to the killing of nearly 1,200 Israelis on October 7, projecting the Israeli flag onto their monuments and government buildings. More than forty thousand Palestinian lives later, we are still waiting to see the Palestinian flag on a monument.

Again, the anti-Palestinian racism displayed in Western media is also found in the mouths of the most powerful Western public officials. Responding to a question about the high number of Gazan civilians killed by Israeli airstrikes, US president Joe Biden said that he had "no confidence in the number that the Palestinians are using."[62] This remark, which can be characterized as racist, minimizes the scale of death of Palestinians in Gaza and discredits the ability for Palestinians to report on the scale of catastrophe they are experiencing.

Biden described Israel's military response in Gaza as "over the top," which raises the question of how many deaths would be deemed justifiable.[63] If five thousand children were killed, would this be within reason? What about ten thousand or even thirteen thousand? At what point do we consider the murder of children and innocent civilians to have gone too far? By Biden's understanding, only when destruction threatens an entire population can it be described as "over the top." This is racism at its worst.

Biden is commonly referred to as a man of empathy, and he does seem to show empathy to those of his own clan. The Palestinians of Gaza, however, did not qualify for his empathy. Any words of "sympathy" regarding Palestinians that he has offered fall flat given his continuous unconditional military support to Israel.

62. "Biden Says He Has 'No Confidence' in Palestinian Death Count," *Reuters*, October 25, 2023, https://tinyurl.com/3xh8vsar.

63. Kevin Liptak, "Biden Calls Israel's Response in Gaza over the Top," *CNN*, February 8, 2024, https://tinyurl.com/yj4k4438.

Jon Finer, a deputy national security advisor in the Biden adminis-
tration, remarked in a meeting with Arab Democrats in Michigan that
Israel's response to the attacks of October 7 included "missteps."[64]
The genocide of tens of thousands of Palestinians is a "misstep"!
Consider this language with me for a moment.

A misstep is when you take the wrong turn on the highway. A misstep is when you bypass an instruction manual and assemble a piece
of furniture incorrectly. The killing of tens of thousands of children
is not a misstep. It is a war crime. It is a genocide.

This attitude brings to mind how the West viewed the Iraq War.
This is a war that cost approximately $728 billion and resulted in
the killing of 200,000 Iraqi civilians. Yet a staggering 45 percent of
Americans said in 2003 that removing Saddam Hussein from power
was worth the casualties and cost.[65] The West's devaluation of Arab
lives, and its willingness to accept their deaths as collateral damage,
are not new.

Such a stance reflects a racist mentality, one arguably driven
by the West's shameful history of antisemitism, which was not
addressed at a foundational level after World War II. Instead, the
Western powers exported their racism to Palestine, sacrificing the
Palestinians to atone for their own sin, without confronting their own
prejudice, sense of superiority, and white supremacy. The West's
unquestioned support for Zionism, an exclusivist ideology that has
now constructed a system of apartheid in Palestine, is a response
to and avoidance of their own historical antisemitism and racism.
Racism persists in the West, and Arabs, Muslims and Palestinians,
including Palestinian Christians, have become the main targets of
these attitudes.

64. Margaret Brennan et al., "Biden Aide Acknowledges Missteps on
Gaza and Regrets Failure to Express Concern over Loss of Palestinian Life,"
CBS News, February 11, 2024, https://tinyurl.com/bc5jr56w.

65. Nicholas Anastacio and Mark Murray, "The Iraq War—by the Numbers," *Meet the Press Blog*, March 20, 2023, https://tinyurl.com/5n7k4yyx.

Theology

Upon his election as the US House Speaker in late October 2023, Mike Johnson delivered a troubling address to the Republican Jewish Coalition. In it he remarked that, "as a Christian, we believe the Bible teaches very clearly that we're to stand with Israel, that God will bless the nation that blesses Israel."[66] Without any reference to history or context, Johnson, an evangelical Christian with strong ties to Israel, affirmed the United States's unconditional support of Israel for the simple reason that "the Bible teaches that Christians must support Israel." Without even asking whether "Israel" in this or that biblical text can be identified with the modern State of Israel, he simply assumes it can. To Johnson, it doesn't matter what the State of Israel has done, even though, according to many human rights organizations, Israel is committing war crimes in Gaza. "The Bible teaches that Christians must support Israel." Period.

This sentiment reflects a long tradition of American and European support for Israel that is embedded in a narrow vein of biblical interpretation and theological tradition. Since October 2023, many American politicians and officials have echoed this sentiment. In three separate interviews with journalist Lee Fang, GOP members of Congress said:

> This entire matter [support to Israel] is based upon faith in our creator . . . faith of a chosen people. (Pete Sessions)

> There have been two nations created to glorify God: Israel and the USA. (Lauren Boebert)

> Those who bless Israel will be blessed. (Tim Burchett)[67]

66. Marc Rod, "'We Are Going to Stand like a Rock with Our Friend and Our Ally Israel,' New House Speaker tells RJC," *Jewish Insider*, October 30, 2023, https://tinyurl.com/becwxj5v.

67. Lee Fang (@lhfang), X, October 25, 2023, https://tinyurl.com/2s2tjr6y.

As a Bible scholar and a theologian, I can affirm wholeheartedly that this is bad theology. The stories in the Bible do not speak about a secular state in the twenty-first century. The God of the Bible is not a God who shows favoritism. In the Bible, we do not find a God who takes sides based on nationality or ethnicity. Biblical chosenness is not about privilege, superiority, and supremacy. It is about the calling to be a messenger for God and a means of blessing to the nations of the world. God's promises to Israel that appear in Scripture do not implicate a sense of entitlement, and they certainly do not entail political support of contemporary nation-states! All people were created equal in God's likeness, the *imago Dei*, and God does not bless people on the basis of their allegiance to any secular state.

Boebert's words are most telling. They give theological language to American-Israeli exceptionalism. The United States and Israel have a special bond both horizontally with one another and vertically with God. Here the theology of empire is clearly in play: God is on the side of empire. This gives legitimacy for even acts of violence. And it makes all those who oppose the United States and Israel enemies of God. This attitude was fully displayed during a congressional hearing about the encampments set up on numerous US university campuses in protest against the war. Representative Rick Allen from Georgia asked the president of Columbia University, Nemat Shafik, if she was familiar with Genesis 12:3. Allen proceeded:

> Well, it's pretty clear, it was a covenant that God made with Abraham. And that covenant was really clear: If you bless Israel, I will bless you. If you curse Israel, I will curse you. And then in the New Testament, it was confirmed that all nations will be blessed through you.

Allen then used this as a pretext to intimidate and even bully Shafik in a shocking and aggressive manner:

> Do you consider that a serious issue? Do you want Columbia University to be cursed by [the] God of the Bible?[68]

68. "US Congressman Rick Allen: 'Do You Want Columbia University to Be Cursed by God of the Bible?'" Middle East Eye YouTube Channel, April 24, 2024, https://tinyurl.com/2n7ntvr9.

This is a member of Congress citing a biblical text to pressure a university president to ban demonstrations against Israel on her campus so that God won't curse her. Let us put aside the fact that Allen's exegesis completely butchers the biblical text. Can you imagine for a moment if Ilhan Omar, a Muslim member of Congress, used texts from the Qur'an to warn others in a congressional session to support Palestine lest Allah curse the United States? All hell would break loose. Allen is not a marginal pastor in a remote church in the South preaching to a handful of evangelicals. This is a member of the most powerful legislature in the world.

Palestinian American evangelical leader Fares Abraham commented on this confrontation:

> When political Christians like Allen claim divine approval for their ideologies or views, they engage in what can be described as spiritual terrorism, using biblical texts to instill fear among non-Christians. This fundamentally contradicts our Christian faith.[69]

Abraham is spot-on in his choice of words. This is spiritual terrorism. Abraham then rightly points out that this is a misuse of Genesis 12:3. As a Christian, he argues that the blessings promised to Abraham are fulfilled through the sacrifice of Jesus, who, according to Galatians 3:16, is the one and true seed of Abraham, and who embodies the ultimate realization of these blessings. "To enjoy the Abrahamic blessings, we abide in Christ's redemptive work, rather than blindly support geopolitical strategies."[70]

Palestinian Christians find it deeply disturbing when the Bible is misinterpreted to justify our oppression. It is hard to contain our anger and frustration in response to such claims, especially as we witness the ongoing brutal war against Gaza. We wish that those

---

69. Fares Abraham, "Christians Must Confront the Weaponization of a Sacred Promise," *Religion News Service*, April 23, 2024, https://tinyurl.com/2rd7yt89.

70. Abraham, "Christians Must Confront the Weaponization of a Sacred Promise."

who reflect such views would listen to us and see our experience as worthy of consideration. We yearn for Western Christians to realize the damage they inflict on us Palestinian Christians and on believers throughout the Middle East by their conflation of politics and theology. For us Palestinian Christians, the United States's unconditional support of Israel continues to be a significant cause of our pain, anguish, and suffering.

Palestinian theologian Mitri Raheb refers to the ideologies that enable Israel to continue its occupation and oppression of Palestinians as the "software of empire":

> Israel does not occupy the land of Palestine purely with the military hardware (hard power) provided by the United States and several European countries, but the State of Israel, Zionist Jews, and their many Christian Zionist allies weaponize the Bible to provide the occupation with the needed software, that is, soft power.[71]

The war on Gaza has spotlighted the Western church's complicity in perpetuating this software. It has displayed the strong affinity between Western Christians and Israel. The ties between them manifest most poignantly in Christian Zionism, a pro-Israeli theologized ideology that manifests not only among evangelical Christians but across the spectrum of Christian traditions.

Christian Zionism can be defined as Christian support of Zionism on Christian biblical and theological grounds. Christian Zionism actually predates the modern movement of secular Jewish Zionism.[72] Protestant theologians have long been obsessed with the question of

71. Mitri Raheb, *Decolonizing Palestine: The Land, the People, the Bible* (Orbis Books, 2023), 125.

72. See Raheb, *Decolonizing Palestine*, 32–38; Nur Masalha, *The Bible and Zionism: Invented Traditions, Archaeology, and Post-Colonialism in Palestine-Israel* (Zed, 2007); Robert O. Smith, *More Desired Than Our Owne Salvation* (Oxford University Press, 2013); Donald M. Lewis, *A Short History of Christian Zionism: From the Reformation to the Twenty-First Century* (InterVarsity, 2021).

the fate of the Jews. Historically, British Puritan Christians believed that the "restoration" of the Jewish people (their embrace of Jesus as Messiah, understood as a necessary step in the unfolding of the end times) depended upon their presence in the land of Palestine. This belief gained popularity among Protestant Christians over time and was fueled by growing antisemitism in Europe throughout the nineteenth and twentieth centuries. Jewish emigration to Palestine coupled with the creation of a Zionist state served a threefold goal for imperial-Christian Great Britain: catalyzing the restoration of the Jews, solving the "Jewish problem" in Europe (which was a direct result of widespread antisemitism), and extending the British Empire into Palestine, a region previously controlled by the Ottoman Empire.

Today, far higher percentages of Christians than of Jews around the world express support for Zionism. This dynamic manifests acutely in the United States, where a 2013 survey showed that more white evangelicals than Jews said God gave Israel to the Jewish people.[73] And with the growth of the evangelical movement worldwide, support for Israel has grown globally as well.

Support for Israel among Christians, however, is not confined to evangelicals. Although many Christians in mainline churches do not agree with the articulation of Christian Zionism that centers on end-time prophecy fulfillment, they nonetheless support Israel, even if for different theological or political reasons. Many mainline Christians who tend to hold more progressive theological and political views emphasize the Jewish connectedness to the land on the grounds of the Abrahamic covenant. The post-Holocaust theology and Christian-Jewish dialogue movements in the Western church, centrally motivated by a desire to make amends for the horrors of the Holocaust, have fostered strong support of Israel, often accompanied by Islamophobic and anti-Palestinian sentiment.[74]

73. "For example, twice as many white evangelical Protestants as Jews say that Israel was given to the Jewish people by God (82% vs. 40%)." Michael Lipka, "More White Evangelicals Than American Jews Say God Gave Israel to the Jewish People," Pew Research Center, October 3, 2013, https://tinyurl.com/yc8sftr3.

74. Raheb, *Decolonizing Palestine*, 38–45.

Evangelical Christian Zionism has become the scapegoat of many progressive mainline Christians. Pointing to the often extreme views of evangelical Christian Zionists is an easy way to make mainline Christians look more peace-loving and less colonial in comparison. Let us remember that probably the most influential Christian Zionist today is not John Hagee or Mike Johnson but Joe Biden, a committed Catholic and self-confessing Zionist, who for ideological reasons supported and funded a genocide.[75] If this war has taught us anything, it is that the theological commitments of these two groups do not produce significantly different results: both mainliners and evangelicals actively defend and support the modern State of Israel. This is why Mitri Raheb focuses his analysis of Christian Zionism on the actions that result from it: what Christian Zionists *do*, not what they *believe*. Raheb provides a fresh perspective of the phenomenon by defining Christian Zionism as a *lobbying* group:

> Christian Zionism should be defined as a *Christian lobby* that supports the Jewish settler colonialism of Palestinian land by using biblical/theological constructs within a metanarrative while taking glocal considerations into account. This definition is less focused on the biblical discourse of Christian Zionists, which can vary considerably from literalists to post-Holocaust theologians, from very conservative to liberal. In fact, the biblical/theological rationale espoused by the majority of Christian Zionists is vague and based on a few varied verses from the Bible. The emphasis of my proposed definition is on the lobbying aspect of Christian Zionism: not on what people *believe* but what they *do* based on that belief. It is naïve to think that a few biblical passages power Christian Zionism.[76]

75. Matt Spetalnick et al., "'I Am a Zionist': How Joe Biden's Lifelong Bond with Israel Shapes War Policy," Reuters, October 21, 2023, https://tiny url.com/4wrvb2v7.

76. Raheb, *Decolonizing Palestine*, 54.

In 1948, Western churches provided Israel with the theology needed to colonize Palestine. For seventy-six years, Christian Zionists have provided the cover for Israel to continue the occupation and displacement of Palestinians. For seventy-six years, Western churches have ignored Palestinian Christians' numerous calls and pleas to intervene. Churches that have ignored our requests to call out Israeli policies as apartheid are complicit in the suffering of the Palestinians.[77] Christians, in their justification of this war and their failure to call for an immediate cease-fire, are complicit in this genocide. This charge, this lament, was articulated in a letter signed by twelve leading Palestinian Christian organizations: "We say it with a broken heart, we hold Western church leaders and theologians who rally behind Israel's wars accountable for their theological and political complicity in the Israeli crimes against the Palestinians, which have been committed over the last seventy-five years."[78]

I wish those who use the Bible to justify their support of Israel and to defend the right of Jews to possess the land would pay closer attention to what they are in reality telling us Palestinians. In essence, they are imposing their religious beliefs on millions of Palestinians and Arabs. Christian Zionists want Palestinians and Arabs to accept the notion that God gave the land to the Jews and simply surrender to their conviction of what the will of God is. Forget international law. Forget history, recent and ancient. Forget the fact that Palestinians have been living in and farming their lands for centuries. For Palestinians, the claim that this is Palestinian land is not a political one; rather, when Palestinians say this is our land, they mean that this is land that we and our ancestors inherited and farmed for generations. Yet Christian Zionists want us to accept that a Jew born in Brooklyn, New York, by virtue of being Jewish, is entitled to settle in Palestine

---

77. "World Council of Churches Refuses to Call Israel an Apartheid State," *Christian Network Europe News*, September 12, 2022, https://tinyurl.com/5axbkctf.

78. "A Call for Repentance: An Open Letter from Palestinian Christians to Western Church Leaders and Theologians," Kairos Palestine, October 20, 2023, https://tinyurl.com/47djev3e.

and enjoy more rights than Palestinians, even displacing Palestinians if necessary, because "the Bible says so."

We must then ask: Should the Bible be the reference point for solving this political dispute and determining to whom the land belongs? Should we not refer to laws and frameworks that are accepted by the international community? The alternative is not just chaos but each side having their own subjective notion of what is right and wrong. The international law is not perfect. But it is what we have. Human rights conventions are not perfect, but they exist for a reason, and they serve as a reference point that we all agree on. The reference point cannot be religious texts, for these texts are particular to certain religious communities and do not have universal consensus. If your side of the argument is "my God told me so," or "God gave the land to our ancestors as an eternal possession," then how can I argue or respond? And if I impose my own religious beliefs on you, we then make it a war between the gods. This is why I say that I wish Christian Zionists would listen carefully to what they are telling us! If religious texts are to be used, it is to promote faith values of justice, dignity of human lives, equality, and protection of the vulnerable. The tragic irony for Palestinians is that our human rights are abused by religious texts, the very same texts that are supposed to protect these rights.

The Truth Is Evident

In November 2023, I traveled to the US capital to advocate for a cease-fire. I had meetings with officials at the White House, the State Department, and throughout Capitol Hill. This was not the first time I had traveled to DC to advocate for the rights of Palestinians. Every time I've done so, I have left with a sense of hopelessness. The problem with politicians is not that they do not know the facts or the right and moral thing to do. In fact, this is precisely the problem: They do indeed know, but for the reasons I've explained above, they are rarely willing to act.

While in DC in November 2023, I gave a sermon at a vigil for Gaza at St. Mark's Episcopal Church on Capitol Hill. I used the words of

Jesus from Luke 19:1–8 to encourage the faithful who gathered to pray without ceasing. The parable talks about a widow who kept pleading for justice in front of "a judge who neither feared God nor had respect for people." And I said:

> We are now in DC. We had many meetings. It feels like speaking to a judge who "neither feared God, nor had respect for people!" How can such atrocities be justified?! How is the killing of more than five thousand children in less than two months accepted? How is the destruction of more than forty-six thousand homes, and the displacement of more than 1.7 million people, who themselves are descendants of Nakba survivors—how is that accepted? Where is justice? Can the horrific events of October 7 justify this? Is this indeed a response to October 7?

A judge that "neither feared God nor had respect for people!"

Meeting with foreign political leaders reminds me that the truth about what is happening in Gaza is already evident. We do not have to explain the realities or their implications, whether we are talking about before or after October 7, 2023. In fact, Israel's leaders repeatedly declared their intention to wipe out Gaza and recolonize it. Yet somehow international courts are still deliberating whether what is happening is a war of genocide or not, and the world is still debating whether there needs to be a cease-fire or not! This is not a matter of "If they only knew." The fact that this war has continued for as long as it has is a result of these three factors: coloniality, racism, and theology. And as Gazan theologian Yousef AlKhoury argued, this all began with the framing of Palestine as a land without people:

> Genocide against the Palestinian people did not start in 2023 but rather has been ongoing for more than a hundred years. Genocide, after all, is a story, a narrative, before it is executed. It is an ideology that began in the minds of proto-Zionist Christians, Zionists, and orientalists who claimed that Palestine was a land without people.[79]

79. Yousef AlKhouri, "Theologizing and [de]Un-theologizing Genocide,"

Coloniality, racism, and theology all meet in this framework of "land without people," or as the evangelical politician Lord Shaftesbury put it in 1875, "a country without a people."[80] It is not as if the evangelical theologians in England who made such claims in the nineteenth century did not know that the land had people. They knew this too well. But in a typical colonial mentality, people on the receiving end of colonialism are less human, and the desires and interests of the empire crush their rights and even humanity. And if there is a need to justify such violent acts and ideology, sacred texts can help. The empire will always find theologians to write and promote imperial theologies.

Future historians will record that in the years 2023–2024, a genocide took place in Gaza. They will record that it was the tragic result of politicians who "neither feared God nor had respect for people," and whose actions and inactions were fueled by coloniality, racism, and empire theology.

---

paper presented at the Christ at the Checkpoint conference in Bethlehem in May 2024. A video of the lecture is available at https://tinyurl.com/4jkwf64h.
80. Smith, *More Desired Than Our Owne Salvation*, 164.

5

Theology of Genocide

The first few days of this war were very difficult for all involved. We were filled with shock, anger, fear, and uncertainty. Palestinians in Bethlehem were shocked as the events of October 7 unfolded. We were glued to our screens—we could not believe what we were witnessing. We were gripped by fear, as we knew that Israel's response would be swift and strong. In the following days, we watched with horror as Israel began its massive bombardment of Gaza. We watched, paralyzed, as Israel dropped roughly six thousand bombs on Gaza in six days, an amount that nearly matches the number of bombs the United States used in Afghanistan over an entire year.[1] We were concerned for our loved ones in Gaza and feared that the war would eventually reach us in the West Bank. We prayed a lot. We pleaded for mercy.

Yet for American pastor Greg Locke, it was an entirely different story. Locke, founder and pastor of Global Vision Bible Church in Tennessee,[2] preached in the early days of October 2023 on how this war created in him a sense of "hope"—hope that it would "usher in

---

1. "Israel Says 6,000 Bombs Dropped on Gaza as War with Hamas Nears a Week," *Al Jazeera*, October 12, 2023, https://tinyurl.com/ms9er48y.
2. See the church's website at https://tinyurl.com/mpj9zkdb.

the coming of Jesus." He also called for Israel to "make the Gaza Strip a parking lot by this time next week."[3]

Can you imagine how Palestinian Christians felt when we saw this widely circulated story? Can you fathom the damage it did to the gospel witness of Arab Christians in our land and region? What if the Christians seeking refuge in the two churches in Gaza read this story? Can you imagine them grappling with how a "brother in Christ," a "Christian" leader, could call for their annihilation?

It is really hard for us Middle Eastern Christians to understand American evangelicals who are obsessed with war and violence.

Locke's attitude, which is devoid of mercy and compassion, is clearly unbiblical—but it is by no means his alone. He reflects the wider phenomenon in American, and more broadly Western, Christianity of unconditional support for Israel, even to the extent of condoning grotesque violence against Palestinians. Over the years, Christian Zionist groups have supported Israel heavily through financial backing and political lobbying. This phenomenon is well documented.[4] For decades, organizations like Christians United for Israel have promoted Zionist narratives among popular audiences and political leaders. This war, however, has taken this support to a different level.

This was a painful chapter to write. For us Palestinian Christians, the attitudes of many Christians around the world at the beginning of the war, and throughout, have been beyond troubling. The hurtful views voiced by our fellow Christians have been demoralizing and painful. They have added to our suffering and misery, like salt in our fresh wounds. It stings when your siblings in Christ do not rush to help and comfort you when you most need it. Yet it hurts ten thousand times more when these siblings justify and support the

3. Matthew Impelli, "Pro-Trump Pastor Hopes Israel War Sparks Jesus' Return," *Newsweek*, updated October 16, 2023, https://tinyurl.com/ycddrjnd.

4. The International Fellowship of Christians and Jews raises about $130 million a year; see Marcy Oster, "After Death of Rabbi Yechiel Eckstein, Daughter Inherits Billion-Dollar Charity," *Times of Israel*, February 27, 2019, https://tinyurl.com/5n967j65. More broadly, see now Ilan Pappe, *Lobbying for Zionism on Both Sides of the Atlantic* (OneWorld, 2024).

violence that causes your suffering. This chapter was written out of this agony.

My argument is simple: a genocide took place in Gaza, and many Western Christians and churches have been complicit in it, whether by supporting and justifying it or by remaining silent.

Supporting a Genocide

In the early days of the war, Israeli prime minister Benjamin Netanyahu invoked the biblical image of the Amalekites,[5] a reference we have already examined, in order to suggest that Palestinians should be wiped from the face of the earth. Using Scripture to call for a genocide is despicable for anyone, regardless of religious affiliation. It is worth mentioning that the International Christian Embassy in Jerusalem (ICEJ), which is a leading international Christian Zionist organization, used the same reference before Netanyahu did, which leaves one wondering if Netanyahu got it from them.[6] In a troubling article, David Parsons, the ICEJ vice president and senior spokesperson, defined the spirit of Amalek as "a spirit of undying envy and hostility towards Israel. . . . This jealous spirit refuses to acknowledge God's unique, enduring election over [*sic*] Israel for the purpose of world redemption, their distinct blessing, and their sole inheritance of the Land of Israel."[7]

It is important to emphasize that for Parsons and the ICEJ, like most Christian Zionists, the Israel of the Bible is the same as the State of Israel of today. In other words, not accepting Israel's *sole* inheritance of the land today, as guided by a certain reading of the biblical promise, is the spirit of Amalek, and merits annihilation. Parsons then engages in a shameful discourse that demonizes Islam, which he claims "also has been infected with the Spirit of Amalek from its

---

5. "Netanyahu's References to Violent Biblical Passages Raise Alarm Among Critics," *NPR*, November 7, 2023, https://tinyurl.com/4tyymzt3.

6. David Parsons, "Israel, Hamas and the Spirit of Amalek," ICEJ, October 26, 2023, https://tinyurl.com/3w7s56bw.

7. Parsons, "Israel, Hamas and the Spirit of Amalek."

inception. . . . We can clearly see the envious Spirit of Amalek at work in the religion of Islam from its very beginnings, refusing to acknowledge Israel's election."

This Zionist rhetoric is immensely dangerous. It frames the conflict as a religious campaign that is supported, even required, by biblical texts. This is precisely the issue that many Palestinians have with the discourse *emanating from Hamas,* which renders the conflict as religious rather than political. When the conflict is portrayed as a religious one, it becomes a battle of religions, and even worse, of gods! Violence becomes holy violence. This sort of sanctified violence is evident in the words of Southern Baptist senator Lindsey Graham,[8] who declared, "We're in a religious war here. I am with Israel. . . . Do whatever the hell you have to do to defend yourself. Level the place."[9]

The dehumanizing rhetoric of Amalek was repeated by several evangelical leaders. In a conversation with American Jewish Zionist commentator Ben Shapiro, prominent pastor John MacArthur explained:

> This is like the modern version of Amalek. And until they are wiped out, this is just gonna go on, and on, and on. . . . I don't want to be callous about things, but God has in his sovereignty made a decision for the preservation of Israel into the future, into the kingdom of Messiah. . . . You can be a part of that by coming to the Messiah and a part of his kingdom. . . . But if you are trying to destroy the very people that are the heart and soul of God's plan, then you come under the judgment of God.[10]

8. "Biography," Lindsey Graham, accessed November 22, 2024, https://tinyurl.com/yc8zdzaa.

9. Ja'han Jones, "Republicans Deploy Dangerous Rhetoric Around Israel-Hamas," *ReidOut Blog, MSNBC,* October 12, 2023, https://tinyurl.com/yc5zxxpp.

10. "The Religious Decline of the West: John MacArthur," Ben Shapiro YouTube Channel, June 9, 2024, https://tinyurl.com/2ptupnft. The quotation is from around 47:14.

Not only did MacArthur call for wiping out the Palestinians in Gaza; he advocated for viewing the Jewish people primarily as they function in his own "Christian" eschatology, which one could argue is a form of antisemitism. Ben Shapiro and countless others are willing to accept this form of antisemitism as long as it advances their Zionist vision. In fact, MacArthur has openly taught from his pulpit that current Israel is under "divine judgment," and that "they are not a righteous people. They have not acknowledged their Messiah. They are not obedient to the Word of God. They are under a divine curse from God. . . . As an entity, there could be another disaster happen [*sic*]. There could be another holocaust. There could be another form of judgment that could come from Iran [or] some other source."[11] Not only are MacArthur and others wrong when they allege that anti-Zionism is necessarily antisemitic. Ironically, MacArthur clearly demonstrates that some Christian rationalizations of Zionism are antisemitic: they subordinate Jewish people to violent "Christian" fantasies. MacArthur participates in an old and long-running strain of antisemitism that declares Israel to be under a curse and deserving of divine condemnation.

Representative Tim Walberg, a Republican from Michigan, served as an evangelical pastor prior to his political career. He holds degrees from both Moody Bible Institute and Wheaton College. In a town hall meeting during the height of the humanitarian crisis in Gaza, *more than five months after the war began*, he made shocking remarks suggesting that bombs should be dropped on Gaza "like Nagasaki and Hiroshima" to "get it over quick."

When asked whether the United States should send humanitarian aid to Gaza, Walberg replied: "I don't think we should. . . . We shouldn't be spending a dime on humanitarian aid." Walberg said this at a time when the UN warned that famine was imminent in parts of Gaza and that 70 percent of the population was already suffering from catastrophic levels of hunger.

---

11. "Bible Questions and Answers," part 56, Grace to You, April 4, 2010, https://tinyurl.com/3je26pz5.

Walberg later tried to walk back his statement, claiming that he was speaking "metaphorically." But he did not apologize. He did not repent. He danced around it.[12]

This is an American evangelical politician—an ordained minister—supporting the continued starvation of Gazans and calling for a complete annihilation of Gaza. With his flippant comments, Walberg was calling for the genocide of my people and our families. When I first saw this, I was shocked, like many other Palestinian Christians. Fares Abraham, an American Palestinian evangelical leader, provided an insightful critique of Walberg's rhetoric. Abraham, whose wife's family lives in Gaza and were among the many Christians who have taken refuge in the two churches in Gaza throughout the war, expressed his distress and shock in response to Walberg's words:

> Walberg's suggestion that Gaza should be treated akin to Hiroshima and Nagasaki in 1945 is not only repulsive but also fundamentally devoid of Christian values. Furthermore, his callous desire to cut off food and aid to 2.2 million innocent Gazans, who are already on the brink of famine, is nothing short of reprehensible. . . . Walberg's statements aren't merely poisonous words; their implications hold the potential to bring unimaginable suffering for Gazans and, more personally, for my wife's family, who are presently seeking refuge within the ancient walls of Gaza's historic churches. In times as dire as these, where the lives of innocents hang in the balance and the very essence of humanity is under siege, the imperative to denounce such vile rhetoric could not be more urgent. It falls upon voices of conscience to rise against ideologies—and misguided theologies, I should add—that threaten to tear apart the fabric of compassion and decency, sparing neither thought nor action to protect the innocent women and children of Gaza.[13]

12. Sam Fossum, "GOP Congressman Appears to Suggest Dropping Bombs on Gaza to End Conflict Quickly, Referring to 'Nagasaki and Hiroshima,'" *CNN*, March 31, 2024, https://tinyurl.com/mrxdf288.

13. Fares Abraham, "Who Is This 'Godly' Man Calling for Gaza's Nuclear Incineration?" *Newsweek*, updated April 4, 2024, https://tinyurl.com/4urakywn.

These were not the only remarks from American members of Congress that lacked any empathy or compassion.[14] However, what grieves me most is that Walberg is a professing Christian and an ordained minister with degrees from respected evangelical institutions. His remarks are enraging and deeply disappointing. They not only incite violence against innocent people but tarnish the credibility and integrity of our Christian witness. Lord, have mercy!

Sometimes I wonder whether Walberg and Locke are reading the same Gospels as I am. Didn't Jesus say: "Blessed are the merciful"? Didn't he say, "Love your enemies"? Is their way the way of Jesus? Religion aside, should politics be devoid of mercy, compassion, and empathy? Further, should Christians simply forget everything Jesus said and taught when it comes to warfare?

Walberg's invocation of Nagasaki and Hiroshima should horrify us. What is even more scary is that this does not seem like a farfetched suggestion. Israel bombed Gaza intensely for a year, destroying it completely, and the world has remained largely unfazed. Within the first month of bombing, Israel dropped more tons of explosive on Gaza than the two nuclear bombs the United States dropped on Nagasaki and Hiroshima, but has any nation held them accountable?[15] Leaders like Walberg and Locke embolden Israel's actions, affirming that it can count on Western Christian leaders to defend such acts, justifying them both politically and theologically.

This attitude of Locke and Walberg is reminiscent of a story from the Gospel of Luke, in which the disciples, reacting to a Samaritan town that did not welcome Jesus, suggest: "Lord, do you want us to tell fire to come down from heaven and consume them?"

Let fire come down and consume them. The disciples' suggestion to respond with all-consuming violence is echoed by Walberg and Locke today. Yet in the gospel, Jesus *rebukes* the disciples for even

14. Matt Shuham, "Babies Killed in Gaza Are 'Not Innocent Palestinian Civilians,' House Republican Says," *Huffington Post*, February 1, 2024, https://tinyurl.com/yxc5zuud.

15. "Israel Hits Gaza Strip with the Equivalent of Two Nuclear Bombs," Euro-Med Human Rights Monitor, November 2, 2023, https://tinyurl.com/363kmf4j.

suggesting such a response. Jesus came to save, modeling a nonviolent way of love and compassion. His way was not one of political naivete but rather a countercultural and subversive model. To call for the genocide of two million people is a betrayal of the politics of love and justice that Jesus embodied and a betrayal of the Way that Christians commit to living out. As Palestinian theologian Anton Deik has emphasized, the fact that Western Christians seem to ignore the ethics of Jesus when it comes to warfare continues to baffle Palestinian Christians:

> For Palestinian Christians, "love your neighbor" and "love your enemy" are community markers. I'm not saying that we're a perfect community. But, for us, Jesus's ethic of love is what makes a Christian, Christian! This is what sets us apart from the rest! So, it is extremely hard for us to understand how some Western Christians can follow Jesus and yet not take his teachings and ethics with utmost seriousness.[16]

Justifying a Genocide

In an article published in *Christianity Today* on the day of the October 7 attacks, prominent evangelical ethicist Russell Moore pleaded with Christians to support Israel in its retaliatory war against Hamas. The assertive title of Moore's short article, "American Christians Should Stand with Israel Under Attack," is revealing. The title suggests that Israel alone is under attack and that the only way for Christians to respond is to stand by their country's ally unquestioningly. Moore's arguments are a good illustration of a common mode of support for Israel among progressive evangelicals who distance themselves from the dispensational prophecy-focused mode of support for Israel.

Moore first argues that Christians should, with moral clarity, recognize Israel's right and duty to defend itself. States have not only the

---

16. Tony Deik, "Missiology After Gaza: Christian Zionism, God's Image, and the Gospel," unpublished paper, Christ at the Checkpoint conference, Bethlehem, May 2024, https://tinyurl.com/2um36tjm. The quotation is from around 18:19.

right but the responsibility to protect themselves and the lives of their citizens. Moore then, using Romans 13 as a pretext, employs just war theory, "which holds that war is always awful, but—under certain, very limited circumstances—can be morally justified." There is no moral confusion in this case, Moore argues, as he maintains the right of Israel to protect its citizens, given that Hamas has attacked innocent civilians before. He then details "the unique circumstances that led to the formation of the Jewish state," namely, antisemitism and Jewish persecution in Europe. Moore argues that Americans should stand with Israel because of its positionality as "a fellow liberal democracy" in the Middle East, surrounded by extremist authoritarian nations. Christians, though, he believes, should further be keenly aware of violence enacted against Israel "just as they would pay special attention to a violent attack on a member of our extended family, because Christians are grafted on to the promise made to Abraham." Jesus was a Jewish person from the region, and any attack against Jewish people is an attack against him. Moore concludes:

> No one wanted to wake up to war in what was already a tinderbox of the world order. But war has come, and we should recognize terrorism for what it is. *We should also recognize the justice of a forceful response to that terrorism.* However we read the prophecy passages of the Bible, and however we disagree on world politics, American Christians ought to stand together with Israel now.[17]

This "forceful response" quickly became a war of genocide and starvation that killed more than forty thousand people and displaced nearly two million. Further, this "forceful response" was directed not simply against Hamas but against children and innocent families, including relatives of my church community who were brutally killed in this "moral and just forceful response." These individuals are a part of large numbers of Gazan Christians murdered amid Israel's

---

17. Russell Moore, "American Christians Should Stand with Israel under Attack," *Christianity Today*, October 7, 2023, https://tinyurl.com/bf6h9at2 (emphasis added).

retaliation, all of whom are Moore's siblings in Christ as well. In his short article, Moore—an evangelical ethicist—gave a theological justification for a genocide, including the murder of Gazan Christians, calling it a moral and just response to October 7.

I have addressed many of Moore's arguments in the previous chapters, most of which are representative of racism, coloniality, and empire theology. The "self-defense argument" that appears in Moore's article is widely used by prominent evangelical leaders. That argument, as I've explained, is meant to hide the history of seventy-six years of colonialism, ethnic cleansing, and apartheid, substituting a narrative of Islamic terrorism at war with a peaceful and democratic state.

Moore references Europe's shameful history of antisemitism but deflects the blame for this history onto Palestinians. He describes the founding of Israel in 1948 as a response to Nazism and the Holocaust yet fails to say anything about the Nakba. This displays Moore's willful ignorance and total disregard for Palestinian suffering and tragedy.[18] A letter signed by more than sixty evangelical leaders, including Moore himself, conflates the modern State of Israel with the Jewish people and actually suggests that Jews are attacked because "God called them as His people."[19] In other words, this is not about apartheid, the siege on Gaza, or even Israel's settler colonization of Palestine. Palestinians attacked "the Jews" because "God called them as His people." This charge of antisemitism is meant to give authority to a narrative wherein Palestinian resistance against its occupier is configured solely as hateful violence against an ethno-religious people. In reality, however, Palestinians do not engage in resistance against Israel—whether violent or nonviolent—because they hate the Jews. *Palestinians have an issue with Zionism, not Judaism.* Arguments that caricature Palestinian resistance against Israel as racist, antisemitic, and violent demonize Palestinians and rob us of the right to tell our own story. We lament the fact that Western nations—and their churches—have dealt with their

18. It was Palestinian theologian Daniel Bannoura who pointed out this point to me in a private conversation.

19. "Evangelical Statement in Support of Israel," Ethics and Religious Liberty Commission, October 11, 2023, https://tinyurl.com/mrxc2jh7.

own antisemitism at the expense of Palestinians, offering our land and people as an atonement for what they did on their land.

Further, Moore's reference to Israel as a liberal democracy comes across as naive and offensive. In light of the significant criticism Moore received regarding this article, I hope he spends time carefully reading and studying the reports that classify Israel as an apartheid state. I invite any who espouse the kinds of views Moore articulates in his writing to imagine walking in the shoes of Palestinians living under discrimination and forcible displacement. Are these beliefs rooted in genuine ignorance, or is it dismissive arrogance? As I've wrestled with these questions in the wake of many Christian responses like Moore's to October 7, I am reminded that such defenses of imperial violence are nothing new in the Western church. After all, did not many in the white American church defend apartheid in South Africa and Jim Crow in the United States?

The use of just war theory is actually a new tool in the arsenal of Christian Zionists. It was also employed in the aforementioned letter penned by evangelical leaders. This theory was elaborated within Christian empires in different times and contexts. While originally intended to place moral limits on the conduct of war, it has been used over time to justify wars waged by the powerful and give them a "just" character. This theory has been applied throughout history, bearing horrific consequences. Palestinian Christians have commented on this:

> We are aware of the Western Christian legacy of Just War Theory that was used to justify dropping atomic bombs over innocent civilians in Japan during World War II, the destruction of Iraq and the decimation of its Christian population during the latest American war on Iraq, as well as the unwavering and uncritical support for Israel against the Palestinians in the name of moral-supremacy and "self-defense." Regrettably, many Western Christians across wide denominational and theological spectra adopt Zionist theologies and interpretations that justify war, making them complicit in Israel's violence and oppression.[20]

20. "A Call for Repentance: An Open Letter from Palestinian Christians

Anton Deik has criticized Moore's use of Romans 13 to promote just war theory as hermeneutically naive, arguing that in the Palestinian context, the use of Romans 13 is inapplicable. Deik highlights that Moore wrongly matched the civil authorities to whom Paul encourages Roman Christians to submit with the modern State of Israel, and comments:

> That Romans 13 is inapplicable to oppressive systems, such as settler-colonial apartheid, is indicated by the context of the text. This is how Paul argues his case in Romans 13:3–4: "Rulers are not a terror to good conduct, but to bad. Do you wish to have no fear of the authority? Then do what is good, and you will receive its approval; for it is God's servant for your good." Our lived experience as Palestinians and the facts on the ground completely invalidate Moore's application of Romans 13 to the Palestinian context. The Israeli authorities, unlike what Paul is talking about, are a *terror* to good conduct.[21]

Another Palestinian theologian, Daniel Bannoura, highlighted the hypocrisy and double standards in Moore:

> Mind you this is the same Russell who wrote in 2023 *Losing Our Religion: An Altar Call for Evangelical America* where he bemoaned that American evangelical Christianity has lost its way, that its witness is diminished beyond recognition, congregations are torn apart over Donald Trump, Christian nationalism, racial injustice, and sexual predation. And there, he recounted his conversations with MAGA folks who were fighting whatever culture war the media has thrown at them. And when Russell attempted to remind them about the Sermon on the Mount, those MAGA people told him, "No we can't believe in that. The Sermon on the Mount is too

---

to Western Church Leaders and Theologians," Kairos Palestine, October 20, 2023, https://tinyurl.com/47djev3e.

21. Deik, "Missiology After Gaza."

weak." Now as it happens, Russell himself didn't quote the Sermon on the Mount when he wrote his article defending Israel's war.[22]

It is sad to see this support of a brutal war as *the* means of solving conflict. This, I argue, is a distinctly American notion. Americans have operated by this logic for decades, war after war. We might question what the Vietnam, Iraq, and Afghanistan wars actually achieved. Did they resolve international conflict, create peace, or ensure the reign of "liberal democracy" in these nations, as they purported to do? Did a technical application of the principles of just war theory justify the killing of more than 200,000 civilians in Hiroshima and Nagasaki?

Yet perhaps Moore's most dangerous and appalling argument is his last one. Because Jesus was and is Jewish, Moore argued that "rage against the Jewish people" is rage against Jesus, and, because Christians are in Jesus, against Christians. By that logic, for myself as a Palestinian living under apartheid and occupation, rage against my occupier and oppressor is rage against Jesus himself! Here Moore creates a very dangerous religious polemic, binding Zionist Christians and Zionist Jews in an unbreakable bond and pitting them against anyone who challenges the violence enacted by the Israeli state. Our world, and especially my region, does not need any of this toxic ideology.

Moore's argument is different from seeing Jesus's image in my adversary—as born in God's image and worthy of life—something I believe and call for. What Moore argues, rather, is that the Jewish people are distinct in such a way that opposing them amounts to opposing Jesus, regardless of the circumstances! This is Jewish exceptionalism par excellence. And in the context of this war, it is better characterized as *Israeli* exceptionalism, influenced naturally by white American exceptionalism.

22. Daniel Bannoura, "A Call to Repentance," unpublished paper, Christ at the Checkpoint conference, Bethlehem, May 2024, https://tinyurl.com/2xx6zzj7.

I mourn Moore's article most due to his lack of compassion and empathy as a Christian ethicist. He writes from a noticeable distance, and from a place not just of comfort but of superiority and power. His immediate response to the attacks on October 7 was in a forceful voice of revenge and retaliation. Is this the way of Jesus or the way of empire? Moore's employment of just war theory meant that by describing Israel's war on Gaza as *just*, he asserts "that ethnic cleansing and apartheid are part and parcel of God's conception of justice."[23]

As the time passed, and as the killing intensified, Moore remained silent. It was a very loud silence. This disgraceful silence was later echoed by Moore's own denomination, the Southern Baptist Convention (SBC), in their annual gathering in June 2024 and the resolution "On Justice and Peace in the Aftermath of the October 7 Attack on Israel."[24] This is a meeting of representatives of the largest US Protestant denomination, containing around thirteen million members. This is a gathering that took place almost eight months after October 7, when at least thirty-five thousand Palestinians had been killed, including fifteen thousand children, and around two million had been displaced. While these realities had been well publicized worldwide, the resolution mentioned nothing, and I mean NOTHING, about any Palestinians killed or displaced in the war. The resolution only mentions the Israelis who were killed. The Palestinians killed in the war are not even worthy of consideration:

> RESOLVED, That the messengers to the Southern Baptist Convention meeting in Indianapolis, Indiana, June 11–12, 2024, condemn Hamas' terrorist attacks of October 7, commit to standing with the Jewish people and those suffering in the region, and oppose all forms of antisemitism; and be it further

23. Deik, "Missiology After Gaza."
24. "On Justice and Peace in the Aftermath of the October 7 Attack on Israel," Southern Baptist Convention, June 12, 2024, https://tinyurl.com/mrf6busr.

RESOLVED, That we deny assertions of moral equivalence between Israel and Hamas; and be it further

RESOLVED, That we are appalled by anti-Israel and pro-Hamas activities on university campuses, within professional associations, and in the culture at large; and be it further

RESOLVED, That we commit to supporting biblical solutions to the conflict, advocating for principles of justice, mercy, and humility in all actions taken by Israel in its pursuit of a just peace (Micah 6:8); and be it further

RESOLVED, That we oppose calls for the nation of Israel to lay down its arms, repudiating any calls for a permanent ceasefire that do not also result in the immediate release of all hostages; and be it further

RESOLVED, That we call for the international community to redouble its efforts to support the nation of Israel toward a just and lasting peace, addressing underlying issues such as terrorism, human rights violations, and regional instability, consistent with biblical calls to defend the oppressed and promote justice, especially among non-combatants and civilians (Psalm 82:3-4; Isaiah 1:17); and be it further

RESOLVED, That we recognize the dignity and personhood of all people living in the Middle East and affirm God's love and offer of salvation to them through Jesus Christ, honoring the difficult ministry of Jewish and Palestinian believers who labor for the gospel as we pray for their protection and ministry; and be it finally

RESOLVED, That we encourage Southern Baptists to pray diligently for a peaceful resolution to the war and all affected by warfare, petitioning God for wisdom, protection, and the ultimate blessing of a just and lasting peace among nations (1 Timothy 2:1-2).

I have read this statement several times, seeking to find any mention of the thousands of Palestinians killed in the war. It is an intentional omission that stems from an ideology that perceives Palestinians as less worthy of life. There is no other explanation. With this statement, the SBC cannot even pretend that they are concerned or troubled by the killing of Palestinians. One would have expected that they would, at a minimum, mention the "deaths" of Palestinians, perhaps blaming Hamas's actions for those retaliatory deaths. Yet the resolution communicates no desire to consider the value of lost Palestinian lives. The resolution even boldly opposes a cease-fire and affirms Israel's right to deploy its arms against Palestinians—a tactic that it somehow finds to be in "pursuit of a just peace."

This resolution manifests appalling racism. It is reminiscent of the settler-colonial discourses that erased the indigenous communities. It dishonors the gospel message that it pretends to proclaim. Ironically, the resolution expresses interest in reaching Palestinians with the gospel, but the course of action endorsed by the resolution would leave no Palestinians alive to be evangelized.

Church Diplomacy and Complicity

Churches posted numerous statements following the attacks of October 7—statements that condemned the attacks while simultaneously claiming solidarity with Israel. Many of these statements bear similar characteristics. On the most basic level, they condemn Hamas's actions on October 7 and affirm Israel's right to defend itself against such acts of terrorism. These statements typically also include a call for the release of Israeli hostages, and if the atrocities Palestinians experienced are mentioned, Israel is not condemned for committing them.

The Church of England in the early stages of the war exemplified these positions in its statements. Justin Welby, the archbishop of Canterbury, affirmed before making a trip to Jerusalem in the very first days of the war that "the evil and heinous terror attacks by Hamas on people in Israel were crimes against God and humanity." Moreover, Welby asserted that "Israel has a legitimate right and duty to defend itself, and to pursue a proportionate and discriminate response to establish its security."[25] In an official statement, he stated:

> I join with the US Secretary of State and others in urging the Israeli government to exercise their right of defense with the wisdom that might break the cycles of violence under which generations have struggled. Amidst the chaos and confusion of war, and as much as is possible, I join the calls for Israel's military response to be proportional and to discriminate between civilians and Hamas.[26]

A week after the war began, Welby reiterated: "I want to make clear that there is no equivalence between the atrocities of Hamas against Israeli civilians, and the right and duty of Israel to defend itself."[27] By emphasizing Israel's right to self-defense, Welby joined the political leaders of the superpowers who endorsed this war. When it comes to Israel and Palestine, Western churches tend to parrot Western empire.

While in Jerusalem, Welby participated in several interviews. When asked about grieving Palestinians, he said that it was not the time to point fingers. He then immediately qualified his statement by affirming that he actually does point a finger at Hamas, claiming that "this is terrorism at its most extreme and most evil." Placing blame on Israel, however, is "not useful" and "makes everything worse."[28]

I believe that Welby's intentions in visiting Jerusalem were good. He truly wanted to be present in times of suffering. But his thinking

---

25. "Palestinian Christians Slam Archbishop of Canterbury for 'Relegating' Their Plight," *Arab News*, October 25, 2023, https://tinyurl.com/2bu724p6.

26. "Archbishop of Canterbury Statement on Israel and Gaza," The Archbishop of Canterbury, October 13, 2023, https://tinyurl.com/5ckc3j69.

27. "Presidential Address to Synod from the Archbishop of Canterbury," The Church of England, November 13, 2023, https://tinyurl.com/3vjmcj7k.

28. "Israel Vows to Intensify Bombing as Second Convoy Arrives in Gaza," Channel 4 News YouTube Channel, October 22, 2023, https://tinyurl.com/2nb7269h.

and his statements nevertheless reflected an attitude that Palestinian Christians hear frustratingly often from the global church. Our frustration is well articulated in a letter to Welby written by Palestinian Anglicans from the parishes of Ramallah and Birzeit in response to his visit and statements. The letter does not mince words in its criticism. It is filled with raw anger and frustration. I encourage you to sit with the emotions present in these excerpts:

> We do not remember a single statement from our church referring to the well-documented crimes of the Israeli occupation as "evil and heinous crimes," even when Anglicans have been affected.
>
> We are utterly perplexed by the public statements coming out from your office on the current situation in Palestine. It has become clear to us that our voices as Palestinian Anglicans are not being heard in Canterbury and our interests are being relegated.
>
> We are afraid that domestic British ecumenical and political considerations are more relevant in your decision-making process than the accurate recognition and implementation of the inalienable rights of the Palestinian people in general, and of the Anglican Palestinian community in particular.
>
> Our position unequivocally opposes all attacks against civilians regardless of national, ethnic or religious identity and calls for the full implementation of international humanitarian law.
>
> What we would expect from our church is to fully condemn the systematic denial of our rights and calls to annihilate our people, especially as these are being publicly expressed by the current fascist Israeli government, rather than attempting to create a balance between the oppressed and the oppressor.[29]

The letter's mention of domestic British ecumenical and political considerations is important, as I discovered firsthand during my visit to the United Kingdom in early 2024 to advocate for a cease-fire. By then, Archbishop Welby and the Church of England were calling

---

29. "Palestinian Christians Slam Archbishop of Canterbury for 'Relegating' Their Plight."

for a cease-fire, and they repeated this call multiple times. Almost a month after the war began, Welby made a passionate cry that "the killing must stop," adding that the call for a cease-fire was a "moral cry,"[30] something he repeated over and over throughout the war. So my friends in the United Kingdom had arranged for me to meet the archbishop himself, and a meeting was scheduled. But then the archbishop's office discovered that I would also be speaking at a major national protest in London.

These London protests drew hundreds of thousands of demonstrators. The archbishop had sparked controversy when, asked about the large crowds in London, he answered that these people demonstrating and naming Israel's actions as genocide have "no understanding of what [they] are saying."[31] This answer dismissed the anger of the millions, not just in the UK but around the world, who had witnessed the decades of injustice suffered by the Palestinians. Of course, Palestinians did understand what they were saying; it was the Church of England that needed to listen and learn more, not the other way around. To his credit, as the war progressed, the archbishop met several times with Palestinians, myself included, and listened carefully and pastorally to the plight of Palestinians, and his position shifted gradually, as I will highlight.

But during my UK visit in early 2024, when the archbishop's office realized that I would be speaking at the protest, we heard back from the archbishop's office that they had an issue with my sharing the stage with Jeremy Corbyn, a member of the UK Parliament representing the Labor Party. Corbyn, a strong supporter of Palestinian rights and a critic of the policies of Israel, had been the target of a strong smear campaign by the UK Zionist lobby, who (of course) accused him of antisemitism, a charge he unequivocally denied. In fact, Corbyn had strong support from many Jews in the United Kingdom,

30. Harriet Sherwood, "Archbishop of Canterbury Makes 'Moral Cry' for Israel-Hamas Ceasefire," *Guardian*, November 13, 2023, https://tinyurl.com/ys72zusy.

31. "Israel Vows to Intensify Bombing as Second Convoy Arrives in Gaza." This remark comes at 7:40 in the video.

within the Labor Party and beyond. But given the political environment, the archbishop's office seemingly decided that it would be too controversial for them to host someone who shared the stage with Corbyn. They preferred not to step into any potential controversy. So, they asked me to make a decision: either speak at the protest or cancel the meeting with the archbishop.

To put things in simple terms: the archbishop's office chose to maintain the curated political image of the Church of England rather than meet with a Palestinian pastor pleading for a cease-fire in a genocide against his people, in the midst of one of the bloodiest and most brutal wars in recent history.

To be honest, I was not surprised. I have experienced this before. I wrote extensively about this kind of silencing from the Western church in my book *The Other Side of the Wall*. For far too long, Palestinian Christians have been ignored, dehumanized, and even demonized by our fellow Christians. Often our experiences are discredited and our presence excluded simply because we are Palestinians.

I, too, had a choice. I could have canceled my speaking engagement at the protest. However, in the end, it was an easy choice. I chose to speak to the people on the streets. I chose to represent the values I stand for rather than negotiate my commitment to standing up for my church and my people. I ended up speaking to around 250,000 people in London. I represented my community, my church, and my faith. I called for a cease-fire as a follower of Christ. The voice of the church must be heard, and it must be heard loudly. And the opportunity to bring Christian witness to the streets, advocating for a cease-fire, is an opportunity we shouldn't have to bargain for.

My intent is not to shame the Church of England or the archbishop himself, who has become a friend; he has encouraged and prayed for me and my ministry. Rather, my critique is of a wider phenomenon I call "church diplomacy," in which the church seeks to be neutral, avoid controversy, and not offend any of its vested interests. By the logic of church diplomacy, the Palestinians are always the first to be sacrificed.

During my visit to the United Kingdom, a British journalist asked me whether I was planning to meet with the archbishop during my time in London. In my response, I explained what had transpired with the archbishop's office, not knowing the backlash and controversy it would spark on social media.[32] To his credit, and in a testimony to his humility, the archbishop later publicly apologized, and his apology, I believe, was genuine. He said in a statement on X:

> Recently I declined to meet with Rev Dr @MuntherIsaac during his UK visit. I apologise for and deeply regret this decision, and the hurt, anger, and confusion it caused. I was wrong not to meet with my brother in Christ from the Holy Land, especially at this time of profound suffering for our Palestinian Christian brothers and sisters. I look forward to speaking and praying with him next week.[33]

Later, we had a fifty-minute Zoom call, just the two of us. And our meeting was grace-filled. We spoke as brothers in Christ, and he listened to the plight and frustrations of my people. I explained my decision, that I prefer to speak in front of 250,000 and share from my faith why this war must end immediately, a sentiment the archbishop shared with me at that time. I shared stories from Gaza. I asked for the Church of England to express a stronger position simply from the standpoint that the war had not ended. I suggested that the archbishop travel again to Jerusalem with other faith leaders to call for a cease-fire. I emphasized the urgency. The archbishop kindly prayed for me and my ministry.

As noted above, the archbishop had been an early advocate of a cease-fire. Moreover, the Church of England maintains a very strong relationship with the Anglican Diocese of Jerusalem and has supported the Palestinian church for years. It is because of their longstanding support that I write these words. My goal is to humbly point at the serious shortcomings in the global church, even if these short-

---

32. Patrick Wintour, "Pastor Says Welby Would Not Meet Him If He Spoke at Palestine Rally with Corbyn," *Guardian*, February 21, 2024, https://tinyurl.com/ycyskmmw.

33. Archbishop of Canterbury, X, February 29, 2024, https://tinyurl.com/2jhy9jfn.

comings stem from good intentions. It is essential to highlight the strong support of Zionism among many Western churches today. It is often an unquestioning support. These churches might claim otherwise, but in practice, they remain supportive of Zionism. The Church of England, like countless other churches, has adopted the Zionist narrative while ignoring the colonial reality of Zionism and its racism. It has continued to provide theological legitimacy for Zionism, as reflected in its responses to the war in the early stages, which endorsed what proved to be a brutal genocide.

The statement of the bishops of the Church of Sweden almost a month after this war began is another example of how church statements seemingly endorse and justify a genocide. The statement, issued on November 6, begins with words of sympathy and peace. It then comments on the actions of Hamas on October 7:

> Hamas has indiscriminately and brutally killed children and civilians, desecrated their bodies, ruthlessly taken hostages and fired thousands of rockets at civilian targets in Israel. We condemn the Hamas attack. Hamas is also holding its own people hostage by hiding among the people of Gaza and using them as human shields. All these actions are reprehensible and in violation of international law.[34]

The actions of Hamas are condemned. They are described as indiscriminate, brutal, and ruthless. The statement highlights the desecration of bodies and the targeting of civilians. The statement also adopts the Zionist narrative that Hamas is using civilians as human shields, which, as I have already mentioned, is an argument that dehumanizes Palestinians.[35] It concludes that all these actions are reprehensible and in violation of international law. They must be condemned.

34. "Bishops of the Church of Sweden: 'We Plead for Peace,'" The Church of Sweden, November 6, 2023, https://tinyurl.com/2fbau3fw. English translation via Google Translate.

35. Israel has not documented its accusations that Hamas uses human shields, but Israeli use of human shields is well documented. See Yaniv Kubovich and Michael Hauser Tov, "Haaretz Investigation: Israeli Army

When it comes to the actions of Israel, the statement first emphasizes Israel's "self-evident right to defend itself against the violence and terror directed against its population." (I have never seen a church statement recognizing that Palestinians have the right to defend themselves against Israeli violence and terror.) The statement then shifts into a narrative mode to explain what happened after October 7, making no moral judgments about the actions of Israel:

> In all wars, international humanitarian law applies: civilians must be protected and both the precautionary principle and the principle of proportionality must be applied. But for almost a month, thousands of civilians in Gaza, including many children, have been killed in Israeli airstrikes in violation of these principles. In the Gaza Strip, there is a human tragedy and humanitarian catastrophe with enormous suffering. Hundreds of thousands of people have fled from the north to the south. There is an acute shortage of water and electricity is largely knocked out. The healthcare system is overwhelmed, medicines and medical equipment are lacking. The humanitarian convoys that have been allowed into Gaza so far are totally inadequate.

Israel is not condemned. War crimes are not called out. The actions of Israel are not described as indiscriminate, brutal, and ruthless. There is nothing about the desecration of thousands of children's bodies by bombs. These genocidal acts are a "human tragedy" that deserves sympathy—but they somehow remain legitimate acts of self-defense by Israel.

The statement then moves into the "appeal" part, which did not even call for a cease-fire, but mere "humanitarian pauses." It calls for the following to take place:

Uses Palestinian Civilians to Inspect Potentially Booby-Trapped Tunnels in Gaza," *Haaretz*, August 13, 2024, https://tinyurl.com/5yyf5k56; "'Human Shielding in Action': Israeli Forces Strap Palestinian Man to Jeep," *Al Jazeera*, June 23, 2024, https://tinyurl.com/4yynxb54; "Israeli Soldiers Use a Palestinian Man, 'Abd a-Rahim Gheith, as Human Shield During Clashes in Jericho," B'Tselem, April 9, 2018, https://tinyurl.com/bde8h5pm.

- That all sides in the conflict abide by international humanitarian law in the event of war.
- That Hamas immediately release all hostages.
- That Hamas stop firing rockets at civilians in Israel.
- That Israel's military response take into account the safety of civilians.
- That humanitarian pauses in the war be created and safe corridors be established so that water, food, medicine and other necessities can reach the civilian population in Gaza.
- That the states of the world, after the war, work for a sustainable and just peace in Israel and Palestine.[36]

The appeal calls for Hamas to release all hostages, but nothing is mentioned about the thousands of Palestinian prisoners, which include hundreds of children, who are often held without a trial. The Palestinian prisoners are deemed terrorists, it seems, and are not worthy of being released. Hamas must stop firing rockets at civilians in Israel, but Israel can continue firing missiles at Gaza; Israel is asked only to take into account the safety of civilians—something Israel has never shown any sign of caring about in its actual conduct.

The statement does not mention Israel's destruction of entire neighborhoods, or the attacks on churches, mosques, and hospitals. Israel can continue to carry out these kinds of attacks, it seems, from the appeal's silence on this. The bishops advocated for humanitarian pauses but not for a cease-fire! In other words, Israel should ensure that Palestinians are fed before continuing with its mass killing campaign of the very same Palestinians!

On February 28, 2024, the five main Lutheran churches in Nordic countries sent a letter of solidarity to the Evangelical Lutheran Church in Jordan and the Holy Land (ELCJHL) (my church) to show their support and solidarity with us during the difficult circumstance our land was going through.[37] The letter was sent almost five months

36. "Bishops of the Church of Sweden."
37. The letter can be viewed at the Facebook Page of the ELCJHL, March 1, 2024, https://tinyurl.com/2v28xjhk.

after the war began—after five months of our advocacy. Israel had killed thirty thousand Palestinians by then, including thirteen thousand children. Close to two million were displaced. The letter acknowledges this, but it makes no moral judgment against Israel, and it does not name Israel's acts war crimes. Its writers refer to the horrors in Gaza and how they watch them unfolding with heavy hearts. They talk about indescribable suffering and painful reports. They mention the lack of food, water, and medicine—not forced starvation, which is a war crime, but "lack of food." In short, no one is held accountable.

This letter of "solidarity" did not even call or pray for a cease-fire! The letter mentioned praying for the children, men, and women of Gaza, and the Christian community there, yet it said nothing about the end of the war. However, it did speak of praying for the immediate release of all hostages held by Hamas! At the end of the letter, the writers make a general statement about how they pray for violence to end and peace to prevail in the Holy Land.

This was supposed to be a letter of solidarity. It was a letter of solidarity that dehumanized Palestinians by not calling for an end to their genocide, while only calling for concrete action with regard to the Israeli hostages. I still cannot believe how after five months these five churches failed to call for a cease-fire! Forget about calling what was happening a genocide. Forget about calling out obvious war crimes. Forget about condemning the method of starvation. Forget about calling for aid to enter immediately. Nothing. They were merely concerned. They had heavy hearts.

In a call with the leaders of one of these five churches a few days after we received it, I communicated with them how I felt about this letter. I said it was an insult to us.

As the war has progressed, and the death toll, destruction, and starvation have increased, the frustration of Palestinian Christians with the global church has only grown. On the one hand, we were pleading, even begging, for a cease-fire (not just a humanitarian pause). Some churches did actually call for a cease-fire, but their calls often lacked the urgency and force required by the situation. They came across as empty calls for peace, and in some cases, they were too late. We were also frustrated that these churches did not admit their own guilt. If you label Israel's actions justified self-defense, you are complicit in this genocide (even if indirectly).

Weeks passed, then months, and the evidence of what was already happening—a textbook case of genocide—was there for all to see.[38] Not only was there no admission of guilt, but there was hardly any condemnation of Israel. The whole world rushed to condemn Hamas and Palestinians on day one—and demanded that all Palestinians do so as well. Yet all we heard regarding Israel's crimes were diluted "calls for peace." The very same churches that have lectured us for years on human rights and international law stood silent as the South African judges exhibited to the world the case for genocide.

Calling for a Cease-Fire

Christians are called to be peacemakers. Jesus famously said: "Blessed are the peacemakers, for they shall be called children of God." Peace*making* is important. It is different, however, from calling for peace. The church can be really good when it comes to *calling* for peace. Many church statements and positions in this war have called for peace. I cannot and do not intend to cast any doubt that these calls were genuine and carried good intentions. I wonder, however, what these statements mean or achieve for people enduring a genocide, especially when the statements are not coupled with actions.

Throughout this war, there have been genuine calls for a cease-fire from churches and church leaders, most notably from the heads of churches in Jerusalem. They released several statements warning that violence and war would only make things worse, and that innocent civilians would suffer. They called for addressing the root causes of issues, while condemning the killing of all civilians. They continuously called for aid to enter Gaza. Strong language was used

---

38. Raz Segal, "A Textbook Case of Genocide," *Jewish Currents*, October 13, 2023, https://tinyurl.com/32pum2n5; "Public Statement: Scholars Warn of Potential Genocide in Gaza," *Third World Approaches to International Law Review*, October 17, 2023, https://tinyurl.com/2s4xejck.

particularly when churches were targeted.³⁹ Sadly, those calls fell on deaf ears.

The World Council of Churches was among the first church bodies to call for a cease-fire. It made a statement in the very early days of the war that said: "The World Council of Churches appeals urgently for an immediate cessation of this deadly violence, for Hamas to cease their attacks and ask both parties for de-escalation of the situation."⁴⁰ The leaders of the church of Norway made an appeal—"Is Humanity Failing?"—for aid to enter Gaza and for a stop to the warfare, stating that "an immediate ceasefire is essential."⁴¹ The Lutheran World Federation and the Church of England also demanded a cease-fire.⁴²

I have already mentioned that, through the course of the war, Archbishop Welby's tone has shifted when he speaks of Gaza. As the war progressed, he emphasized that it must stop, asserting that there is no moral justification for the devastating loss of civilian life in Gaza.⁴³ After one of our meetings, he posted on X: "I condemn the killing of Palestinian civilians, the destruction of homes and neighborhoods, and pushing people to the brink of starvation—there is no moral justification for this."⁴⁴ Had this kind of strong, prophetic lan-

39. Numerous statements may be found at the website of the Latin Patriarchate of Jerusalem: https://tinyurl.com/25497ufs. Note, for example, the October 13 "Statement on the Escalating Humanitarian Crisis in Gaza" and the statement of October 17, "Mourning Civilian Victims of the Massacre in Gaza and Extending Solidarity to the Episcopal Diocese of Jerusalem."

40. "WCC Urgently Appeals for Immediate Ceasefire in Israel and Palestine," World Council of Churches, October 7, 2023, https://tinyurl.com/3f8tr9yw.

41. Olav Fykse Tveit and Einar Tjelle, "Is Humanity Failing?" The Church of Norway, December 8, 2023, https://tinyurl.com/mseu3uhd.

42. "LWF Calls for Ceasefire and Humanitarian Access to All Those in Need," Lutheran World Federation, November 6, 2023, https://tinyurl.com/3u4j4pbp.

43. Sherwood, "Archbishop of Canterbury Makes 'Moral Cry' for Israel-Hamas Ceasefire."

44. Archbishop of Canterbury, X, March 7, 2024, https://tinyurl.com/yn4pyw36.

guage been used earlier in the war, and had other prominent church leaders used it as well, I wonder if this would have made a difference. It could have at least shaped the opinions of the faithful toward more righteous anger.

Pope Francis made headlines for his several passionate appeals to end the war. In November, after meeting with Israelis and Palestinians, he said: "I heard how both sides suffer, and this is what wars do, but here we've gone beyond war. . . . This is terrorism. Please, let us move forward to peace. Pray for peace."[45] In a later statement, he called for an end to the "terrorism" of war and condemned an Israeli military attack on Gaza's Holy Family Catholic Parish.[46] In a reported call with the Israeli president at the end of November, he said: "It is forbidden to respond to terror with terror."[47] And throughout the war, he continued to appeal to the conscience of world leaders: "Enough! Stop! Please, put an end to the clash of arms and think of the children, all the children, as you do your own children. They need homes, parks and schools, not tombs and mass graves."[48]

These calls to end the war were passionate and genuine, and, moving beyond words, they encouraged acts of generous giving and support to relief efforts. These churches' actions demonstrate a desire to embody the heart of God when it comes to compassion and mercy. They seek to mobilize people to pray for peace and for an end to the war. I can't help but wonder, however, if more could have been done with regard to practical steps on the ground. Jesus created a movement that made an everlasting difference in our broken

45. Steve Hendrix et al., "After Israel-Hamas Deal, the Agonizing Wait for the Release of Captives," *Washington Post*, November 22, 2023, https://tinyurl.com/24trnzkp.

46. Devin Watkins, "Pope Condemns Attacks on Civilians in Gaza: 'It Is War; It Is Terrorism,'" *Vatican News*, December 17, 2023, https://tinyurl.com/5n6n2m3n.

47. Anthony Faiola, Stefano Pitrelli, and Louisa Loveluck, "In Undisclosed Call, Pope Francis Warned Israel Against Committing 'Terror,'" *Washington Post*, November 30, 2023, https://tinyurl.com/42kvjp3h.

48. "Gaza: Stop War, I Suffer Greatly—Pope," *Vanguard*, April 12, 2024, https://tinyurl.com/5f69y6wa.

world. He was a mobilizer. He was about action. He called people to sacrifice and give, and he modeled that himself. When a genocide takes place and stretches on for months, for the whole world to see, we need more than prayers and statements.

Even the more passionate statements lacked the clarity and tenacity needed to respond to war crimes. They felt tepid. This is what a South African friend once described to me as "toothless Christianity." This is particularly true when the church shies away from speaking truth to power and calling things by their name. The thing that was lacking the most in most of these "calls for peace" was a call to hold Israel accountable, to investigate war crimes, and to take measures such as boycotting and halting the sending of weapons to Israel. Many people read these statements and leave with a sense of emptiness when it comes to what can be done. Prayer is important. It is truly needed, and it can and does make a difference. But it makes all the more difference when coupled with action. Prayer should set our *agenda*, that is, the list of actions that we know we must take. Prayer should mobilize people to act and make a difference.

"Pray for the peace of Jerusalem!" Christians commonly use this phrase with regard to our land whenever there is violence. But such a call for prayer is not enough when a genocide is unfolding. I believe in prayer, and I have led several prayer services for Gaza throughout this genocide. I genuinely value and appreciate the good intentions and sincerity that arise during these times of prayer.

But good intentions are not enough.

In his Sermon on the Mount, Jesus didn't say, "Blessed are the peace prayers." He said, "Blessed are the peace*makers*" (Matt. 5:9). Peacemakers of every faith pray—and in their prayer they discern what's really happening, an awareness that then urges them to call things by their names and speak truth to power.[49] Acts of truth telling almost always lead to action. In a letter I helped write to churches around the world urging for a cease-fire, we encouraged the faithful to speak out, join demonstrations, mobilize within their commu-

49. Munther Isaac, "An Open Letter to U.S. Christians from a Palestinian Pastor," *Sojourners*, May 20, 2021, https://tinyurl.com/mvcr3pdb.

nity, put pressure on their political leaders through calls and written correspondence, and organize nonviolent direct-action campaigns and sit-ins. "Whatever it takes to compel your government and decision-makers to take action" is what is required of us in a time of genocide.[50]

State Theology, Church Theology, and Christian Zionism

During the era of apartheid in South Africa, the South African Kairos Document introduced the global church to the concepts of "state theology" and "church theology." The document was written and promoted by grassroots church activists and leaders from the anti-apartheid movement. It played an important role in challenging the church in South Africa, and around the world, to bring an end to the apartheid system in South Africa.

The document defined state theology as

> The theological justification of the status quo with its racism, capitalism and totalitarianism. It blesses injustice, canonizes the will of the powerful and reduces the poor to passivity, obedience and apathy.... It does it by misusing theological concepts and biblical texts for its own political purposes.[51]

This articulation of state theology could easily be mistaken for an articulation of Christian Zionism! Though written in 1985 in reference to the South African context, these words are extremely relevant today in the Palestinian context. Christian Zionism is state theology in its support and justification of Israeli apartheid and genocide in Gaza. The State of Israel weaponizes theological concepts and biblical texts in order to justify and sustain its settler-colonial project.

50. "Palestinian Christian Appeal: Immediate Ceasefire in Gaza," Change, November 11, 2023, https://tinyurl.com/2bsa4dux.
51. "The South Africa Kairos Document 1985," Kairos Southern Africa, accessed November 27, 2024, https://tinyurl.com/4nj9uw2t.

The South African Kairos Document also talks about "church theology," a theology that speaks of reconciliation, justice, and non-violence. According to the document:

> "Church Theology" takes "reconciliation" as the key to problem resolution. . . . "Church Theology" often describes the Christian stance in the following way: "We must be fair. We must listen to both sides of the story. If the two sides can only meet to talk and negotiate, they will sort out their differences and misunderstandings, and the conflict will be resolved." On the face of it this may sound very Christian.

The writers of the document challenge this concept of reconciliation—a notion that appears to be very Christian but, in reality, lacks justice. It states:

> In our situation in South Africa today it would be totally unChristian to plead for reconciliation and peace before the present injustices have been removed. Any such plea plays into the hands of the oppressor by trying to persuade those of us who are oppressed to accept our oppression and to become reconciled to the intolerable crimes that are committed against us. That is not Christian reconciliation, it is sin. It is asking us to become accomplices in our own oppression, to become servants of the devil. No reconciliation is possible in South Africa *without justice*.

These South African church leaders could have been talking about Palestine. They could have been describing the many churches that preach to Palestinians about peace and reconciliation without any appeal to justice. They could have been portraying the countless churches that prayed for the end of this war in Gaza without any reference to historical context, accountability, and action.

The document then goes on to challenge the top-down approach to justice common in the church, one that presumes that power lies within the oppressor. The authors question,

Why then does "Church Theology" appeal to the top rather than to the people who are suffering? Why does this theology not demand that the oppressed stand up for their rights and wage a struggle against their oppressors? Why does it not tell them that it is their duty to work for justice and to change the unjust structures? Perhaps the answer to these questions is that appeals from the "top" in the Church tend very easily to be appeals to the "top" in society. An appeal to the conscience of those who perpetuate the system of injustice must be made. But real change and true justice can only come from below, from the people—most of whom are Christians.

Finally, the document challenges the concept of neutrality in church theology in the way it addresses the issue of violence. It argues:

> In practice what one calls "violence" and what one calls "self-defense" seems to depend upon which side one is on. To call all physical force "violence" is to try to be neutral and to refuse to make a judgment about who is right and who is wrong. The attempt to remain neutral in this kind of conflict is futile. Neutrality enables the status quo of oppression (and therefore violence) to continue. It is a way of giving tacit support to the oppressor.[52]

Again, the words of this statement resonate strongly with Palestinian Christians and our observance of the global church's neutrality when it comes to the realities on the ground. And when the response to an unfolding genocide is neutrality, something is inherently wrong with our theology.

Theology of a Genocide

What the South African document describes as state theology and church theology is what Palestinian theologian Mitri Raheb calls

52. "The South Africa Kairos Document 1985."

the software of empire, which we have discussed in chapter 4.[53] In Gaza, the theologies of state and church have become a theology of genocide. But is there such a thing as a theology of a genocide— as the title of this chapter suggests? Does the Bible, under any circumstance, portray God as endorsing, accepting, even supporting a genocide? For Gazan theologian Yousef AlKhouri, the answer is an emphatic NO.

> Genocide cannot be theologized. Theology according to the various Christian traditions is the study of a god who revealed God's self in and through Christ. There is no "Theo" in a "logy" that endorses and justifies a genocide and colonialism, but an ideology that does not glorify God nor acknowledges the humanity of those created in the image of God.[54]

Theoretically, AlKhouri is right. He is right in the same way that it is right to say that the Bible cannot be used to support slavery, colonialism, or apartheid. But it was so used. In this war, the Bible has even been used to justify a genocide. Such a use of the Bible calls for lament, weeping, and radical reversal. It calls for repentance. We should be outraged by the weaponization of the Bible. We should be ashamed by this violent brand of Christianity that is so far from the teachings of Jesus.

About two years ago I took part in a webinar under the title "How Strong Is the Biblical Basis for Christian Zionism?"[55] In it, I gave a

---

53. Mitri Raheb, *Decolonizing Palestine: The Land, the People, the Bible* (Orbis Books, 2023), 125.

54. Yousef AlKhouri, "Theologizing and [de]Un-theologizing Genocide," unpublished paper, Christ at the Checkpoint conference, Bethlehem, May 2024, Christ at the Checkpoint YouTube Channel, https://tinyurl.com/3bb3t6nk.

55. "How Strong Is the Biblical Basis for Christian Zionism?" Churches for Middle East YouTube Channel, https://tinyurl.com/3dfs6a7f. I presented my remarks in part 4, July 13, 2022, https://tinyurl.com/t4bmhk2t, beginning at 21:00.

critical analysis of this movement as a Bible scholar and a Palestinian Christian. I concluded by saying, given that Zionism today is an exclusive, oppressive ideology that is engaged in occupation and apartheid, that the biblical basis for Christian Zionism is as strong as the biblical basis for injustice and apartheid.

Following the unfolding of the horrific events since October 7, I can add that the biblical basis for Christian Zionism is as strong as the biblical basis for justifying, defending, and endorsing a genocide.

6

A Call to Repentance

Almost a week after the war on Gaza began, three of my closest friends and colleagues at the Bethlehem Bible College, Yousef AlKhouri, Anton Deik, and Daniel Bannoura, asked that we pray together and figure out how to respond to what was happening in Gaza. For one of those friends, Yousef, it was deeply personal. He is from Gaza, and his parents and his sister's family live there. At the time, he was in the Netherlands working on his PhD while his family was seeking shelter in the Orthodox church in Gaza. He was deeply concerned for their safety, and his family barely survived the attack on the very same church his parents were sheltering in, which killed eighteen innocent Palestinian Christians. While dealing with this tremendous trauma, he, like many other Palestinian Christians, could not help being distracted and disturbed by hearing his "siblings in Christ" calling for the killing of his family. Anton and Daniel were also outside of Palestine working on their PhDs, but for Anton, leaving Palestine was the result of a forced displacement. Anton's wife is from Latin America, and Israel denied her the visa to come and live in Bethlehem with her husband, forcing the family to relocate outside of Palestine, just in order to be united as a family. It is one of those cruel laws of apartheid. The four of us talked and prayed a lot in those early days of the war.

My friends insisted that we as Palestinian Christians must speak up—not just regarding what is happening in our land, but mostly about the response of churches in the West and around the globe. Because of our commitments as followers of Christ, we cannot be silent. For us Palestinian Christians, it was hard to contain the frustration and anger that we felt from the Western church's response to the unfolding war on Gaza. The first few weeks were acutely difficult, as one statement and article after another was released defending and attempting to justify this war. We were troubled by the one-sidedness of these responses and by their lack of understanding, compassion, and mercy. As Palestinians, we saw clearly how the demonization of our people was normalized across cultures and religious traditions. As Christians, we were truly concerned for the credibility of the gospel witness, given the responses we saw from Christian leaders and churches.

After much prayer and deliberation, we decided to issue a call to church leaders and theologians in the West who were supporting this war. My friends made a draft, and then we worked together on it and quickly mobilized support for it from twelve leading Palestinian Christian organizations and movements. Those groups made suggestions and edits to the draft, and we published it collectively on October 20, 2023.[1]

The letter was a call to *repentance*. I vividly remember the conversation between us about the title and the nature of the call. Given the intensity of Israel's bombing of Gaza in the first few days of the war, and the complicity of many in the West in it, this was not the time for diplomacy. We did not call for "dialogue" or "reconciliation." A genocide was beginning to unfold in front of the world's eyes, and

---

1. The organizations that collectively made this call were: Kairos Palestine; Christ at the Checkpoint; Bethlehem Bible College; Sabeel Ecumenical Center for Liberation Theology; Dar al-Kalima University; Al-Liqa Center for Religious, Heritage, and Cultural Studies in the Holy Land; the East Jerusalem YMCA; the YWCA of Palestine; Arab Orthodox Society, Jerusalem; Arab Orthodox Club, Jerusalem; The Department of Service to Palestinian Refugees of the Middle East Council of Churches; and Arab Education Institute Pax Christi, Bethlehem.

the position of many church leaders was to defend and justify it. We felt they were complicit, and we called them to repent.

I now share the main parts of the call, a call that echoes even stronger today, with the magnitude of the devastation of this war. Tragically, we saw what was coming when we made this call. The call was published less than two weeks after October 7, so the numbers and events mentioned reflect what had unfolded at that point in time. Although many Christians around the world supported this call, we were left wishing that far more would listen and respond.

A Call for Repentance: An Open Letter from Palestinian Christians to Western Church Leaders and Theologians

"Learn to do right; seek justice; defend the oppressed" (Isa 1:17).

We, at the undersigned Palestinian Christian institutions and grassroots movements, grieve and lament the renewed cycle of violence in our land. As we were about to publish this open letter, some of us lost dear friends and family members on October 19, 2023, in the atrocious Israeli bombardment of innocent civilians, Christians included, who were taking refuge in the historical Greek Orthodox Church of Saint Porphyrius in Gaza. Words fail to express our shock and horror with regard to the ongoing war in our land. We deeply mourn the death and suffering of all people because it is our firm conviction that all humans are made in God's image. We are also profoundly troubled when the name of God is invoked to promote violence and religious national ideologies.

Further, we watch with horror the way many Western Christians are offering unwavering support to Israel's war against the people of Palestine. While we recognize the numerous voices that have spoken and continue to speak for the cause of truth and justice in our land, we write to challenge Western theologians and church leaders who have voiced uncritical support for Israel and to call them to repent and change. Sadly, the actions and double standards of some Christian leaders have gravely hurt their Christian witness—and have severely distorted their moral judgment with regards to the situation in our land.

We come alongside fellow Christians in condemning all attacks on civilians, especially defenseless families and children. Yet, we are disturbed by the silence of many church leaders and theologians when it is Palestinian civilians who are killed. We are also horrified by the refusal of some Western Christians to condemn the ongoing Israeli occupation of Palestine, and, in some instances, their justification of and support for the occupation. Further, we are appalled by how some Christians have legitimized Israel's ongoing indiscriminate attacks on Gaza, which have, so far, claimed the lives of more than 3,700 Palestinians, the majority of whom are women and children. These attacks have resulted in the wholesale destruction of entire neighborhoods and the forced displacement of over one million Palestinians. The Israeli military has utilized tactics that target civilians such as the use of white phosphorus, the cutting off of water, fuel, and electricity, and the bombardment of schools, hospitals, and places of worship—including the heinous massacre at Al-Ahli Anglican-Baptist Hospital and the bombardment of the Greek Orthodox Church of Saint Porphyrius which wiped out entire Palestinian Christian families.

Moreover, we categorically reject the myopic and distorted Christian responses that ignore the wider context and the root causes of this war: Israel's systemic oppression of the Palestinians over the seventy-five years since the Nakba, the ongoing ethnic cleansing of Palestine, and the oppressive and racist military occupation that constitutes the crime of apartheid. This is precisely the horrific context of oppression that many Western Christian theologians and leaders have persistently ignored, and even worse, have occasionally legitimized using a wide range of Zionist theologies and interpretations. Moreover, Israel's cruel blockade of Gaza for the last seventeen years has turned the 365-square-kilometer Strip into an open-air prison for more than two million Palestinians—70 percent of whom belong to families displaced during the Nakba—who are denied their basic human rights. The brutal and hopeless living conditions in Gaza under Israel's iron fist have regrettably emboldened extreme voices of some Palestinian groups to resort to militancy and violence as a response to oppression and despair. Sadly, Palestinian nonviolent resistance, to which we remain wholeheartedly committed, is met with rejection, with some Western Christian leaders even prohibiting the discussion of Israeli apartheid as reported by Human Rights Watch, Amnesty International, and B'Tselem and as long asserted by both Palestinians and South Africans.

Time and again, we are reminded that Western attitudes towards Palestine-Israel suffer from a glaring double standard that humanizes Israeli Jews while insisting on dehumanizing Palestinians and whitewashing their suffering. This is evident in general attitudes towards the recent Israeli attack on the Gaza Strip that killed thousands of Palestinians, the apathy towards the murder of the Palestinian-American Christian journalist Shireen Abu Akleh in 2022, and the killing of more than three hundred Palestinians, including thirty-eight children in the West Bank this year, before this recent escalation.

It seems to us that this double standard reflects an entrenched colonial discourse that has weaponized the Bible to justify the ethnic cleansing of indigenous peoples in the Americas, Oceania, and elsewhere, the slavery of Africans and the transatlantic slave trade, and decades of apartheid in South Africa. Colonial theologies are not *passé*; they continue in wide-ranging Zionist theologies and interpretations that have legitimized the ethnic cleansing of Palestine and the vilification and dehumanization of Palestinians—Christians included—living under systemic settler-colonial apartheid. Further, we are aware of the Western Christian legacy of Just War Theory that was used to justify dropping atomic bombs over innocent civilians in Japan during World War II, the destruction of Iraq and the decimation of its Christian population during the latest American war on Iraq, as well as the unwavering and uncritical support for Israel against the Palestinians in the name of moral supremacy and "self-defense." Regrettably, many Western Christians across wide denominational and theological spectra adopt Zionist theologies and interpretations that justify war, making them complicit in Israel's violence and oppression. Some are also complicit in the rise of the anti-Palestinian hate speech, which we are witnessing in numerous Western countries and media outlets today.

Although many Christians in the West do not have a problem with the theological legitimization of war, the vast majority of Palestinian Christians do not condone violence—not even by the powerless and occupied. Instead, Palestinian Christians are fully committed to the way of Jesus in creative nonviolent resistance (Kairos Palestine, §4.2.3), which uses "the logic of love and draw[s] on all energies to make peace" (§4.2.5). Crucially, we reject all theologies and interpretations that legitimize the wars of the powerful. We strongly urge Western Christians to come alongside us in this. We also remind ourselves and fellow Christians that God is the God of the downtrodden and the oppressed, and that Jesus rebuked the powerful and lifted up the marginalized. This is at the heart of God's conception of justice. Therefore, we are deeply troubled by the failure of some Western Christian leaders and theologians to acknowledge the biblical tradition of justice and mercy, as first proclaimed by Moses (Deut 10:18; 16:18-20; 32:4) and the prophets (Isa 1:17; 61:8; Mic 2:1-3; 6:8; Amos 5:10-24), and as exemplified and embodied in Christ (Matt 25:34-46; Luke 1:51-53; 4:16-21).

Finally, and we say it with a broken heart, we hold Western church leaders and theologians who rally behind Israel's wars accountable for their theological and political complicity in the Israeli crimes against the Palestinians, which have been committed over the last seventy-five years. We call upon them to reexamine their positions and to change their direction, remembering that God "will judge the world in justice" (Acts 17:31).[2]

---

2. "A Call for Repentance: An Open Letter from Palestinian Christians to Western Church Leaders and Theologians," Kairos Palestine, October 20, 2023, https://tinyurl.com/2ryv57r2.

Once our call was published, God only knows how many webinars and discussions we took part in to reflect on and further emphasize the urgency of the call. Along with my colleagues, I channeled my anger and grief into acts of advocacy and raising awareness. We felt compelled to speak on behalf of the people of Gaza, who were truly living in hell on earth. We also led many prayer services, in person and virtually around the world.

The call made an impact. We are grateful that some have listened and responded to the call. More than twenty-two thousand people signed the call on our petition website. A special session was held at the annual meeting of the American Academy of Religion featuring our voices, and positive responses were offered by Jewish and Christian scholars. Christ at the Checkpoint hosted a webinar about the statement, with responses from Shane Claiborne and Frank Chikane from South Africa, and it was attended by hundreds. The Latin American Theological Fraternity, which is the largest network of Latin American theologians, also held a seminar about the call. There was a powerful response from prominent evangelical leaders that I will highlight later in the book.

All of this was not enough, however, as the war continued.

I find myself coming back again and again to this call, marveling at the fact that it was written less than two weeks after the war began. We, as Palestinians, realized from the beginning the seriousness and severity of the situation. We felt the urgency of the matter. As months passed by, we were left broken and traumatized by the war's long duration and by the continual repetition by many Christians of the same lines of argument.

Calling Out Politicians and the World

As the war progressed, I felt compelled to use my platform as a pastor in Bethlehem, and with Christmas approaching, to advocate for a cease-fire. And so, in November 2023, as we were about to enter the season of Advent, I traveled to the United States to urge politicians to advocate for a cease-fire. I carried with me a letter from the clergy of Bethlehem, calling for peace and a cease-fire. We held several meetings in Washington, DC, including meetings in the White House and at the State Department. I pleaded for *peace* as I shared the following words in a speech at the White House:

We have come all the way from Bethlehem carrying a letter signed by the main historic churches in Bethlehem and addressed to President Biden. As we begin our Advent season, we have one ask: a constant and comprehensive ceasefire.

This war has been so brutal. Thousands have been killed, the majority of whom are children and women. We are hearing and seeing horror stories. It is hell on earth in Gaza. This war, if it continues, has the potential to drive the whole region into chaos. Extremism and support for violence have already increased. Young people are driven to despair. There must be other ways.

What is happening has gone way beyond a response to the horrific events of October 7. As we say in the letter, we lament the death of all peoples, Palestinians and Israelis. We pray for freedom for all. We affirm that every human being is created in the image of God and is worthy of living a dignified life. But I ask today: How is the displacement of 1.7 million people a response to October 7? How is the killing of more than five thousand children a response to October 7? When we use words like "genocide" to describe what is happening in Gaza, we are only echoing the declared intentions of Israeli politicians about this war and describing what we see taking place in Gaza.

We lament that this could have been avoided. We are sorry to say: we have seen this coming. This is the natural result of no peace process, and extremists taking power and enforcing unchecked extreme policies.

In the letter we say: "There can be no peace and security without justice and equality. There can be no peace and security without equal rights for all. Siege, violence, and war cannot bring peace and security. A comprehensive and just peace is the only hope for Palestinians and Israelis alike."

Justice for Palestinians is long overdue. Freedom and self-determination for Palestinians are long overdue.

So please allow me to read our simple request that we present in the letter: "We are writing to plead with you to help stop this war. All we want this Christmas is a constant and comprehensive ceasefire. Enough death. Enough destruction. This is a moral obligation. There must be other ways. This is our call and prayer this Christmas."

We hope and pray that President Biden will receive this letter, signed by the main historic churches in Bethlehem; a letter that asks that there will be an immediate and constant ceasefire, and we hope and pray that the President takes this plea into consideration.

This was only one of many calls that fell on deaf ears.

Upon returning from the United States, I continued my advocacy. In our church, the Evangelical Lutheran Christmas Church in Bethlehem, we created a special manger display from rubble. We placed baby Jesus in the midst of the rubble, resembling the images that we have been witnessing on a daily basis of children being pulled out from under the rubble. The manger scene was meant to be pastoral in nature, yet when we shared it on our social media, it went viral and received much attention from all over the world. It became iconic! I was consumed with requests from different media outlets. The manger scene was featured in stories from major news outlets around the world. My face appeared in so many articles and TV interviews. Sundays during Advent were particularly awkward, as our church was crowded with TV crews wanting to film the manger display and talk to me and our congregants after the service. I used this media attention to point to the harsh realities in Gaza. I remember looking at the TV cameras while preaching on a Sunday and urging them: Why are you here? The headlines are in Gaza, not here! Throughout this period, I repeated over and over to the journalists who flooded our church to photograph this manger scene that we wanted it to point to the genocide in Gaza. I repeated: "This is what Christmas looks like in Palestine this year: houses destroyed, families displaced, and children killed."

But the war continued. And all of our efforts felt as if they were in vain.

Calling Out the Church

When Christmas Eve came in 2023, I delivered a special sermon as a part of a Christmas vigil for Gaza. The sermon was part of a joint initiative between Palestinian and international Christian organizations who broadcast the vigil live on their social media outlets, hoping to draw a large number of viewers. I was asked to preach and address the Western church regarding the ongoing war on Gaza. This was the genesis of the "Christ in the Rubble" sermon.

I poured myself into this sermon. I spoke from a place of authentic anger and brokenness. I put aside any language of diplomacy. We were in immense pain and distress, and I felt compelled to call out the church; I felt compelled to call out the world. I did not call for peace or reconciliation. Instead, I called out the church for its complicity. I challenged the listeners to reflect, repent, and act.

The result was a sermon that received great attention globally. Tens of millions watched and shared it. It moved the world, and, I believe, it challenged people's hearts. In it, I said:[3]

> We are angry . . .
>
> We are broken . . .
>
> This should have been a time of joy; instead, we are mourning. We are fearful.
>
> More than twenty thousand killed. Thousands are still under the rubble. Close to nine thousand children killed in the most brutal ways, day after day after day. Around 1.9 million displaced. Hundreds of thousands of homes destroyed. Gaza as we know it no longer exists. This is an annihilation. This is a genocide.
>
> The world is watching; Churches are watching. Gazans are sending live images of their own execution. Maybe the world cares? But it goes on. . . .
>
> We are asking, could this be our fate in Bethlehem? In Ramallah? In Jenin? Is this our destiny too?

3. For the full text of the sermon, see "Christ in the Rubble: A Liturgy of Lament," Red Letter Christians, December 23, 2023, https://tinyurl.com/yxb74nch.

We are tormented by the silence of the world. Leaders of the so-called "free" lined up one after the other to give the green light for this genocide against a captive population. They gave the cover. Not only did they make sure to pay the bill in advance, they veiled the truth and the context, providing the political cover. And yet another layer has been added: the theological cover, with the Western Church stepping into the spotlight.

Our dear friends in South Africa taught us the concept of "state theology," defined as "the theological justification of the status quo with its racism, capitalism and totalitarianism. . . . It does so by misusing theological concepts and biblical texts for its own political purposes."

Here in Palestine, the Bible is weaponized against us. Our very own sacred text. In our terminology in Palestine, we speak of the empire. Here we confront the theology of the empire. A disguise for superiority, supremacy, "chosenness," and entitlement. It is sometimes given a nice cover using words like mission and evangelism, fulfillment of prophecy, and spreading freedom and liberty. The theology of empire becomes a powerful tool to mask oppression under the cloak of divine sanction. It divides people into "us" and "them." It dehumanizes and demonizes. It speaks of land without people even when they know the land has people—and not just any people. It calls for emptying Gaza, just like it called the ethnic cleansing in 1948 "a divine miracle." It calls for us Palestinians to go to Egypt, maybe Jordan, or why not just the sea?

I think of the words of the disciples to Jesus when he was about to enter Samaria: "Lord, do you want us to command fire to come down from heaven and consume them?" they said of the Samaritans. This is the theology of empire. This is what they are saying about us today.

This war has confirmed to us that the world does not see us as equal. Maybe it is the color of our skin. Maybe it is because we are on the wrong side of a political equation. Even our kinship in Christ did not shield us. So, they say, if it takes killing a hundred Palestinians to get a single "Hamas militant" then so be it! We are not humans in their eyes. But in God's eyes . . . no one can tell us we are not!

The hypocrisy and racism of the Western world is transparent and appalling! They always take the words of Palestinians with suspicion and qualification. No, we are not treated equally. Yet, on the other side, despite a clear track record of misinformation and lies, their words are almost always deemed infallible!

To our European friends, I never ever want to hear you lecture us on human rights or international law again—and I mean this. We are not white, I guess, so it does not apply to us according to your own logic.

In this war, the many Christians in the Western world made sure the empire had the theology needed. It is self-defense, we were told! And I continue to ask: how is the killing of nine thousand children self-defense? How is the displacement of 1.9 million Palestinians self-defense?

In the shadow of the empire, they turned the colonizer into the victim, and the colonized into the aggressor. Have we forgotten that the state was built on the ruins of the towns and villages of those very same Gazans?

We are outraged by the complicity of the church. Let it be clear: silence is complicity. And empty calls for peace without a ceasefire and an end to occupation, and shallow words of empathy without direct action, are all under the banner of complicity. So here is my message: Gaza today has become the moral compass of the world. Gaza was hell on earth before October 7, and the world was silent. Should we be surprised that they are silent now?

If you are not appalled by what is happening in Gaza, if you are not shaken to your core—there is something wrong with your humanity. If we, as Christians, are not outraged by this genocide—by the weaponizing of the Bible to justify it—there is something wrong with our Christian witness, and we are compromising the credibility of our gospel message!

If you fail to call this a genocide, it is on you. It is a sin and a darkness you willingly embrace.

Some have not called for a ceasefire; I am talking about churches.

I feel sorry for you. We will be okay. Despite the immense blow we have endured, we will recover. We will rise. We will stand up again from the midst of destruction as we have always done as Palestinians, although this is by far the biggest blow we have received in a long time. But we will be okay.

But again, for those who are complicit, I feel sorry for you. Will you ever recover from this?

Your charity, your words of shock AFTER the genocide, won't make a difference. And I know these words of shock are coming, and I know people will give generously for charity. But your words won't make a difference. Words of regret will not suffice for you. And let me say this: We will not accept your apology after the genocide. What has been done, has been done. I want you to look at the mirror, and ask: where was I when Gaza was going through a genocide?

This was literally a sermon heard around the world. It had unprecedented reach in a short period of time—with tens of millions of views within two weeks. It was immediately translated into several languages by social media activists. It was shared by world leaders, politicians, diplomats—by Muslims, Jews, Christians, and Buddhists—and featured on many news outlets. Queen Rania of Jordan urged people to listen to the sermon, calling it "moving."[4] Francesca Albanese, the UN Special Rapporteur for the Occupied Palestinian Territories, called it "one of the most profound liturgies" she had heard.[5] Evangelical pastor Bob Roberts Jr. claimed that it "will be most listened to Christmas sermon in 20 yrs," adding that the sermon "demands your listening—represents not just Gaza but how Global church sees Western Church—they resent our loudness when we're so broken ignorant apathetic deaf of their various con-

---

4. Rania Al Abdullah @QueenRania, X, December 25, 2023, https://tiny url.com/mr3m7fa8.

5. Francesca Albanese, UN Special Rapporteur oPt, @FranceskAlbs, X, December 25, 2023, https://tinyurl.com/4tafj3fh.

texts."[6] It was even quoted by the South African lawyers in their case against Israel in the ICJ.

The sermon moved hearts, evident by the thousands of interactions it received on social media. I believe that it set Gaza as the moral compass of the world. It also showed the power of our prophetic witness in the midst of the unfolding genocide, and the need for the church to speak out with courage and conviction. This was not the time to be silent. I spoke for Gaza, and in doing so, I spoke for humanity.

A Lenten Call to the Church

In February 2024, I went to the UK to advocate for a cease-fire. I had meetings at Parliament and with the press. I also led a vigil for Gaza at the beginning of the Lenten season. It took place at the famous Bloomsbury Central Baptist Church in London, where Martin Luther King preached his first sermon in the UK. The church was packed, and I delivered a sermon that, again, called the church to repent. I used these words of the prophet Isaiah about fasting as my foundation:

> Is not this the fast that I choose:
>   to loose the bonds of injustice,
>   to undo the straps of the yoke,
>   to let the oppressed go free,
>   and to break every yoke? (Isa. 58:6)

The sermon was a challenge to the church and an expression of Palestinian Christians' frustration with the global (mainly Western) church's response to the genocide in Gaza. In it, I said:

What happened to the conscience of the world leaders; I say world leaders, and lords of wars, because the voices in the street

6. Bob Roberts Jr. @bobrobertsjr, X, December 26, 2023, https://tinyurl.com/3rdt5284.

are speaking loud and clear: stop this genocide. But will the warlords listen?

The International Court of Justice was clear in its description of what is happening and its rebuke of Israel and those complicit in it, yet even the ruling of the ICJ was not enough to stop this genocide. And now we fear that Israel will assault Rafah! Could it get even worse?

The people of Gaza broadcast to us scenes of their genocide, and the war leaders have declared to us and to the world their intention to wipe out Gaza and recolonize it. And the world is still debating and deliberating whether what is happening is a war of genocide or not.

Israeli soldiers are posting mocking videos of the destruction of an entire civilization, while the world still debates and deliberates!

Friends, truth is evident for all to see. There is nothing to debate. Apartheid is clear. Genocide is clear. We don't need to explain anymore. Truth is evident for all to see. World leaders know the truth. They are denying it. In fact, they have been denying it for seventy-six years. How many delegations did we receive? How many lectures did we give? How many times did we explain things?

Meanwhile, Israel alleges that some members from UNRWA were involved in the attacks on October 7, and support to UNRWA stops directly from countries around the world. The amount of hypocrisy is incomprehensible. The level of racism involved in such hypocrisy is appalling. I cannot get beyond this!

Some world leaders and church leaders are beginning to change their stance. It is too late! You showed up to Jerusalem to show support; you provided the theological and political cover, you described it as self-defense and as such gave a green light. You even paid the bill, and now you are showing concern? I am sorry. You cannot undo what happened. You cannot change history. You cannot wash the blood from your hands.

Indeed, the conscience of the world is dead. They have grown numb. World leaders are obsessed with their thrones. They are intoxicated with power. They are literally autographing the missiles! They love war. They don't care for the victims. In fact, they already labeled them as terrorists, animals, and evil.

Don't tell me it is not racism! Those complicit in this genocide do not see us as equals, as humans. How else do you explain this lack of empathy for human lives? For children dying, pulled from under the rubble, for babies found decomposed in Gaza hospitals?

We are tired of sharing these stories; we are tired of sharing about the killing of our people. We have been pleading "Lord have mercy!" for more than 130 days, indeed, for seventy-six years.

As Palestinians, we find comfort in our faith. We find hope in the Word of God. This Sunday is the first in the season of Lent. As we journey towards the cross, may we reflect on the meaning of this season:

- It is a time of repentance.
- It is a time of fasting, and as such, a time to reflect on the meaning of true piety.
- It is a time to reflect on the mystery of suffering and how the road to glory goes through the Cross.

All three have profound meaning and message for what is happening in Gaza today.

Repentance: Oh, how our world needs to repent today from apathy, numbness to suffering, and normalizing and justifying a genocide.

When world leaders watch a genocide and ethnic cleansing unfold live on TV and social media, yet continue to explain it away, while only raising concern over the death of innocent civilians—our collective humanity is at stake.

When churches justify a genocide or are silent watching from a distance, making carefully crafted balanced statements—the credibility of the gospel is at stake.

We need to repent of our racism, superiority, and bigotry. This war has confirmed to me that the world does not look at us as equals. They describe a genocide as a "misstep" or something that is "over the top." We need to repent from the sin of apartheid—the idea that certain people are more entitled than others.

In this Lenten season, we are also called to reflect on our religious practices. God's message to us through fasting: Piety that does not produce compassion and mercy is false piety! Piety that does not lead to hunger for justice is false piety.

"Is not this the fast that I choose: to loose the bonds of injustice, to undo the straps of the yoke, to let the oppressed go free, and to break every yoke?"

Our world is full of false piety; A piety that lacks mercy, justice, and truth. Today's reading from Isaiah is as if it were talking about today.

Friends, these words from Isaiah go beyond "charity." This is about taking a stance and active participation to bring justice and liberation (not make a statement!).

Jesus did not say: I was hungry, and you prayed for me and made a statement! Jesus said: I was a prisoner and you came to me!

This is not about "praying for peace," "raising concern," and sending support. Piety, says Isaiah, means active participation in loosing the bonds of injustice, undoing the straps of yoke, letting the oppressed go free, and breaking every yoke. This is active solidarity; this is about action.

I ask: Is this what the church is doing today? Let us be honest with ourselves! Do you see why I have been crying out—where is the church? The question when we face injustice and suffering should not always be "Where is God?" Many times the question is "Where is the church?"

We are occupied by religious practices, and theological discussions.

Moreover, today I feel the thing we lack the most is courage. We know the truth. But we are not speaking. We fear the consequences. We fear the backlash!

The church wants to avoid controversy. Can you imagine if Jesus had walked on earth avoiding controversy! Can you imagine if, when he was asked a question, he had crafted a balanced statement that aimed at appealing to the Pharisees and the Sadducees and the disciples and the Romans (and if possible his heavenly father!)?

The way church statements dance around the issue of "cease-fire" or (God forbid) condemning Israel is indeed amazing. They write long statements that basically say nothing other than unequivocally condemning Hamas!

Honestly, we should not be surprised. As Palestinian Christians, how many times have we experienced rejection by the church? How many times have invitations sent to us to speak in global venues been canceled? For fear of controversy. There are church leaders who are willing to sacrifice us for the sake of avoiding the hustle of having to explain to outsiders why they are meeting with Palestinian Christians! They sacrifice us for comfort. Jesus sat with sinners, right? So, I say, consider me a sinner, and sit with me. It is indeed appalling.

They sacrifice us for comfort, the same way they offered us as an atonement sacrifice for their own racism and anti-racism—repenting on our land over a sin they committed in their land!

All of this while we claim to follow a crucified savior, who sacrificed everything, endured pain and rejection for the sake of those he loved!

When the church does not want to lose its comfort, something is seriously wrong with our Christian witness.

When the church sacrifices truth for the sake of conformity and avoiding controversy, something is seriously wrong with our Christian witness.

So thirdly, this is a season in which we reflect on the mystery of Christ's suffering and consider our identity in the cross and as followers of a crucified yet risen savior. We need to think of the meaning of costly solidarity.

Jesus said: "If any wish to come after me, let them deny themselves and take up their cross and follow me. For those who want to save their life will lose it, and those who lose their life for my sake, and for the sake of the gospel, will save it. For what will it profit them to gain the whole world and forfeit their life? Indeed, what can they give in return for their life?"

Jesus here tells us what it means to be a Christian: a follower of a crucified savior. Jesus says that a Christian is one who denies himself, who carries his cross, and who loses himself for the sake of Christ and the Gospel! He is the one who understands that if he wins the whole world, it has no value without saving himself.

Christianity without sacrifice is not Christianity. The first and most important thing we sacrifice is our "self/ego"—the "I." This is the logic of Jesus himself, and this is how he lived. He was the one who denied himself for us, and he was the one who was crucified for us humans. He wants the same from his followers.

Jesus' logic is sacrifice for the other; denying oneself for the sake of another; the logic of love that sacrifices for, and does not seek what is for itself, but rather what is for others. The love that says: The other is before me, and I am here for the other.

Here we come to the famous saying of Jesus: "For what does it profit a man if he gains the whole world and loses his own soul?"

Oh God, when I think about the amount of wisdom hidden in this phrase! How many people have lost themselves and sold their values in pursuit of glory and power, and in some cases, comfort? I am not just talking about political leaders.

How many nations lost their soul and their values when they took the same approach, the approach of colonialism, genocide and exploitation. The approach of force and tyranny. How many leaders and nations chose silence in the face of genocide in order to win the world? To gain the world! But in reality they lost their soul. What the world needs today is sacrifice and courage to speak the truth! There are political and religious leaders we know who have been bought off and lack the courage to speak the truth. Is this how we follow Christ? They won the world, and lost themselves.

I know influential church leaders who changed their stance completely when they received political power.

I am fed up with church leaders who share with me behind closed doors in confidentiality that they support us 100 percent, but that they are confined in what they can say! I hear this all the time, from church leaders and diplomats! You know how frustrating it is? Leaders in their comfort zone lack the courage to speak up, while the honorable people of Gaza risk everything for the sake of freedom and dignity. They have more honor and dignity than those politicians or faith leaders.

Friends: The followers of Jesus risk all to speak truth to power.

In Palestine, we do not only talk about solidarity; we talk about costly solidarity.

This war has shaken our faith—in humanity and even God. We continue to search for God.

Dear friends: Gaza is indeed today the moral compass of the world. This war, I truly believe, has clearly divided the world; and maybe this is a good thing. Gaza is the moral compass of the world. Either you side with power and ruthlessness, with the lords of war, and with those who justify and rationalize the killing of children; or you side with the victims of oppression and injustice, and those who are besieged and dehumanized by the forces of empire and colonization. It is really a simple choice: you either support a genocide, turn a blind eye or justify a genocide, or you cry out: No! Not in our name.

I call the church in the United Kingdom: as churches that seek justice and righteousness, in obedience to the commandment of Christ, we must have the courage to speak out and call things by name! This is not a conflict; Israel is not exercising its right of self-defense. Rather, Israel is the colonizer; Israel is a settler-colonial entity. We live under apartheid. What is happening in Gaza is a genocide and ethnic cleansing. Continuing to repeat the empire's narrative only serves to empower the aggressors.

On the basis of the foregoing, we must no longer speak in our churches of "peace," or even of the resolution of conflict—but of an end to tyranny and injustice. Vocabulary is important. We are not talking about a struggle between equal forces. This is not simply about a ceasefire; but putting an end to seventy-six years of ethnic cleansing. And today, ending a genocide in Gaza.

This is a time to act: to loose the bonds of injustice, to undo the straps of the yoke, to let the oppressed go free, and to break every yoke. . . .

It is time for the church to be the church!

How the churches of the world deal with injustice in our land will reveal a great deal about these churches. We do not exaggerate when we say that the credibility of the churches—our Christian witness—is at stake.[7]

Outcast Prophets

My short visit to the United Kingdom in February 2024 was filled with memorable moments. There was the protest in which I spoke to about 250,000 people in the streets of London. The vigil for Gaza at Bloomsbury was incredibly special and affirmed so much for me regarding grassroots solidarity with Palestinians. I also had the opportunity to meet leaders of the Palestinian diaspora community in London. Yet perhaps the moment that stuck with me the most happened during a small prayer meeting for Gaza I took part in that was organized by Christian Aid UK. I had just finished my meetings in the British Parliament, organized by the Palestinian ambassador to the United Kingdom, when we went to that prayer. There were close to twenty participants in the meeting, most of whom were clergy from different Christian traditions who had spent time and energy throughout the war to advocate for a cease-fire. We met in an outdoor space in London, outside of the Parliament building and opposite Westminster Abbey. We met in the dark, and it was getting a bit chilly. We all lit candles, read prayers for Gaza, and spent time in silent prayer.

As we were praying in silence, I was struck by the symbolism of the moment, by virtue of the place of the meeting. Standing outside of the Abbey and the Parliament, I felt like we were a group of outcast prophets, challenging both the empire and its religious institutions. This was also shortly after Canterbury had canceled my meeting with the archbishop. And here we were, a group of Christians motivated by our radical obedience to Christ to work for peace—lighting

7. For full text and video, see "Christ Under the Rubble: A Vigil for Gaza with The Revd Dr Munther Isaac," Bloomsbury Central Baptist Church, February 18, 2024, https://tinyurl.com/2s3bue63.

candles for Gaza and praying in silence for a cease-fire—outside, in the margins. The buildings that surrounded us were reminders of our failed systems. One building was responsible for arming Israel with the weapons used in this genocide; the other was involved in religious diplomacy that, at the time, I felt did not do enough to stop the genocide. As we were praying, brokenhearted, my phone beeped with breaking news—another missile had killed many people in Gaza. We continued to pray.

I was then asked to address the group, and I spoke about the urgency of the moment, reaffirming our commitment to the cause of advocating and working for a cease-fire. It felt then as if all of our efforts were in vain. I reminded those I was gathered with of Jesus's parable about the widow who kept persisting and demanding justice from an unjust ruler until she received what she asked for. It is a parable about persistence in prayer. I saw in that woman the resilience of the people of Gaza. My message to the group was simply that we cannot give up, stop our work, and give in to despair. We owe it to the people of Gaza. We owe it to their heroic sacrifices. We owe it to the doctors and nurses of Gaza, the first responders, and to the journalists who have sacrificed their lives to tell the stories of Gaza. We have to keep pressing on. Quitting is not an option. Quitting would cast serious doubt on everything we say we believe in. If evil, tyranny, injustice, and war will ultimately win, then something is seriously wrong with our Christian message. We have nothing to live for, and we cannot or should not do any good, because it is not worth it if injustice wins. But we cannot and should not accept this. If we give up, we communicate that injustice inevitably wins.

I reminded this group of faithful, persistent radicals that if we stop demonstrating and speaking about Gaza, then there is something wrong with our humanity, as it means that we have grown numb to suffering, death, and ultimately, genocide. We should not just "change the channel" and pretend that we no longer see or know. If we stop praying and persisting, then we accept that suffering from injustice is normal, and we normalize not only injustice but also genocide.

I urged the group that we must continue resisting the normalization of this violence, boldly declaring that we as Christians reject this degradation of humans bearing God's image. We must pray, advocate, and act. This is why in my Easter sermon two months later, with the war still going on, I lamented that the genocide had become normalized:

> Friends, a genocide has been normalized. As people of faith, if we truly claim to follow a crucified savior, we can never be ok with this. We should never accept the normalization of a genocide. We should never be ok with children dying from starvation, not because of famine, but because of a man-made catastrophe! Because of tyranny.
>
> A genocide has been normalized just as apartheid was normalized in Palestine, and before that in South Africa. Just as slavery and caste were normalized. It has been firmly established to us that the leaders of the world's superpowers, and those who benefit from this modern colonialism, do not look at us as equals. They created a narrative to normalize genocide. They have a theology for it. A genocide has been normalized. This is racism at its worst.[8]

For Such a Time like This

Throughout the war, I, alongside many Palestinian Christians, have been perceived to be harsh in our message to the global church. Some have raised concerns to me that I am not actually helping the church by continuing to publicly call it out in such a manner. Some have told me in private that I am shaming the church, that this is wrong, and I must stop.

I must admit that I actually gave serious consideration to these accusations. I did not dismiss them easily. I asked myself many times if I was being too harsh in my critique of the global church. I am also

---

8. For full text and video, see "Easter Vigil for Gaza, Bethlehem, March 30th, 2024, Rev. Dr. Munther Isaac," Red Letter Christians, April 2, 2024, https://tinyurl.com/mn53jvmh.

aware that many from other faith traditions have used my words to shame the church and score points against it, so to speak. Moreover, many Arab and Muslim leaders also failed to speak out, so why single out the church?

So, am I wrong in calling out the church in such a manner?

When a genocide of tens of thousands of people is normalized and accepted as a "necessary" evil, no, I do not believe I have been too harsh. When a genocide is largely accepted on a global scale, it means we have not done our job as people of faith to enact love and justice in our world. It means we have failed. After much prayer and discernment, I have come to understand that I have not been too harsh. In fact, I might not be harsh enough and honest enough in my witness.

One of the few bright spots during this war has been the solidarity movement that formed around the world for Gaza. I have made many precious new friends—people who are equally passionate, and maybe even more passionate than me, for the cause of Gaza. While in the United Kingdom, I met Ugandan theologian and activist bishop Dr. Zac Niringiye, who shared so much of his wisdom with me and was a source of comfort and encouragement. While having breakfast together in a pub in Oxford, I shared with him my doubts about whether or not I was shaming the church. Bishop Zac answered by pointing me to the calling of the Hebrew prophet Jeremiah. God gave Jeremiah this message:

> "Behold, I have put my words in your mouth.
> See, I have set you this day over nations and over
>   kingdoms,
> *to pluck up and to break* down,
> to *destroy and to overthrow,*
> to build and to plant." (Jer. 1:9–10 RSV)

Bishop Zac's understanding of the role of our witness is simple. There are times when we need to pluck up, break down, destroy, and overthrow *before* we build and plant. The Bible used four words to describe the *un*doing, and two words to describe the doing.

When genocide is normalized, we are called to pluck up and to break down, to destroy and to overthrow. This is a time in which we are called to challenge and dismantle colonial theologies of power, superiority, and racism. This is a time to call out the apathy and numbness of many in the Christian world. If not now, when?

It is also a time to challenge the church to rediscover the core of its calling: namely, to be a community marked with radical love of God and neighbor. During my visit to South Africa, preaching in the packed sanctuary of the famous Cape Town Cathedral (the seat of the late Archbishop Tutu), I said that the opposite of the theologies and ideologies of apartheid and Zionism is love:

> Racism in essence is the failure to love the neighbor the way God intended for us to do. It is the failure to see others as created in the image and likeness of God. Christian Zionism and apartheid theologies have so much in common: they are both racist and colonial ideologies that use biblical texts as a tool. They both fail at the most important calling: that of love. The opposite of Christian Zionism and apartheid is love.[9]

I love the church. I am a pastor. I have devoted my life to serving God and the church. The church is the bride of Christ, and I want to see her without any blemish. I want the church to be the church—fully devoted to love, mercy, justice, and righteousness, and healed of the sins of coloniality and racism. In such a time, when genocide has been normalized, we need a *kairos* moment—a moment of truth. A genocide normalized is a time in which we must call out the church for repentance.

9. The full sermon can be viewed at "Munther Isaac at St. George Cathedral in Cape Town—May 2024," Munther Isaac YouTube Channel, May 5, 2024, https://tinyurl.com/3ms7extu.

7

Christ Is in the Rubble in Gaza

It was a heartbreaking image: eighteen dead bodies, including those of nine children, wrapped in white plastic bags and laid out before the door of St. Porphyrius Church in Gaza.[1] The Orthodox priest was leading funeral prayers from an elevated staircase. People were surrounding this makeshift funeral, mourning.

For the two weeks leading up to the attack on St. Porphyrius Church on October 20, I watched in horror with my community in Bethlehem as Israel bombarded Gaza with an unprecedented number of bombs, killing and injuring thousands. We watched in agony as children and entire families were pulled from under the rubble. Yet this particular incident hit harder for many of us in Bethlehem—this was about family and friends. As a pastor of churches in the West Bank, I have always led communities living under apartheid. But pastoring people in the midst of genocide has been unspeakably challenging.

When the war began, many people fled from the northern and central areas of Gaza and headed south. The majority of the Chris-

---

1. See Emma Graham-Harrison, "'Destruction Chased Them': Funeral Held for Those Killed in Gaza Church Airstrike," *Guardian*, October 20, 2023, https://tinyurl.com/5aeapwjc.

tian community in Gaza lives in the central areas in Gaza City. Collectively, they decided not to head south but instead to take refuge in the two main churches in Gaza, one Catholic and the other Orthodox. As one friend there told me over the phone, "We'd rather die in the church, in the house of God, than head to the unknown and become refugees in Rafah or in the desert in Egypt." This evoked painful memories for many from the Christian community in Gaza, who, like most Gazans, are refugees from the 1948 Nakba. They have seen this before. They have lived it. And they chose to stay in the church with the hope that they would return to their homes. Little did they know that this war would nearly destroy Gaza entirely, including their homes. More tragically, they could not have known that the church was not a safe refuge.

The Orthodox and Catholic church campuses in Gaza are in very close proximity to one another, as well as to the Al-Ahli Baptist Hospital (which is in fact run by the Episcopal Diocese in Jerusalem). Around nine hundred people packed their essential belongings and took refuge in the two churches. They thought this would be a short stay. They slept on mattresses in the sanctuary, church halls, and school classrooms. They thought they would be safe on the church campus, close to one of the main hospitals in Gaza. Tragically, they were wrong.

On October 20, the day of the attack, I attended an ecumenical prayer service in Bethlehem in which we prayed and pleaded for the end of the war. We prayed for the protection of our loved ones and all innocent people impacted by this war. God did not listen, it seems. God did not protect those beloved people in the ways that we prayed.

Later that night, a missile hit a building directly adjacent to the church hall of the Orthodox church, causing the hall to collapse on those in it.[2] This was the hall the refugees in the church had designated for families with small children. The result was tragic. Eighteen people were killed, including nine children. We were shocked. Gazan Christians have relatives in Bethlehem and the rest of the

---

2. Ylenia Gostoli and Abdelhakim Abu Riash, "'We Were Baptised Here and We Will Die Here': Gaza's Oldest Church Bombed," *Al Jazeera*, October 20, 2023, https://tinyurl.com/5a35x2z3.

West Bank who panicked upon hearing about the attack. Because of the darkness (Israel cut the electricity to Gaza at the beginning of the war), it was immensely difficult to rescue and pull people from under the rubble. It was also hard for those who came to the scene to distinguish survivors from corpses.

All of us knew people who were seeking refuge in St. Porphyrius Church, but some—including some of my congregants in the church I pastor in Beit Sahour—had immediate relatives who were sheltering in the church. Nuha Tarazi-Awwad is originally from Gaza but has been living in Beit Sahour for many years, having married a man from there. She and her family are dear, longtime friends. Nuha had two sisters and two brothers who were still in Gaza, as well as other extended family members. Nuha's desire has always been to return to Gaza to visit her siblings and her childhood city. Long before this recent war, the Israeli siege made this impossible. For years she lamented to me in tears how she was not able to visit her home city. In fact, days before the war broke out, one of her sisters passed away and Nuha tried to apply for a permit from the Israeli military to go to Gaza, even if for only one day, to attend the funeral. Her request was rejected. How is this peaceful, elderly woman, who merely wanted to attend the funeral of her sister, a threat to Israel? Stories like Nuha's accumulate, and their pain accumulates, too. We inhabit this accumulated pain. This is the injustice of apartheid and segregation made personal.

We knew Nuha's siblings, who were occasionally allowed by the Israeli military to leave Gaza and visit Bethlehem and Jerusalem for a few days during Christmas or Easter. On these occasions, Nuha, like many other Gazan Christians who live in the West Bank, awaits anxiously, hoping that the permit is indeed granted for her relatives to visit the West Bank so they could reunite. The permits are never guaranteed. They are issued for a very limited period, typically for a few days during Christian and, more rarely, Muslim holidays. Israel claims that it is doing Palestinian Christians a favor by giving these permits, but our problem is not simply whether the permit is granted or not. The problem is that the system exists to begin with. Palestinians should not need a permit to travel from one city to another in our homeland. I should not need a permit to travel to Jerusalem from Bethlehem, just as Gazans should not need a permit to travel to Bethlehem, Ramallah, or Hebron. This systematized restriction of movement is a textbook illustration of occupation. This is apartheid.

Upon hearing of the attack, we called our friends to check on them. I called Shireen, Nuha's daughter and my colleague at the Bible College. "Is your family ok? Did they survive?" She said that one of her aunts (Nuha's sister) was injured, but that she was all right. Tragically, as the dust settled in the morning, we learned this was not true. Aunt Ellen was among those killed in the attack. I had the painful task of breaking this news to Shireen. We also learned that Nuha's other sister was injured in the attack and was forced to undergo hip replacement surgery *with no anesthesia*. Imagine the pain! Later in the day, we went to Nuha's house with church members and our bishop to console them. It was an impossible task. We had no words.

The attack shocked the Christian community in Gaza. One of the survivors, Ibrahim, explained: "The building that they bombed is beside the church. We just pray to God to end this war. . . . We thought we would be protected by the church but unfortunately the brutal Israeli occupation does not differentiate. . . . They have targeted churches, mosques, and hospitals. There is no safe place."

Yet Ibrahim was defiant, in faith, regardless: "We were baptized here, and we will die here."[3]

Church officials in Jerusalem were angry and called for protection. The Orthodox patriarch rightly called this a war crime: "Targeting churches and their institutions, along with the shelters they provide to protect innocent citizens, especially children and women who have lost their homes due to Israeli air strikes on residential areas over the past thirteen days, constitutes a war crime that cannot be ignored."[4] The world, meanwhile, was watching—largely justifying Israel's right to defend itself.

---

3. Gostoli and Abu Riash, "'We Were Baptised Here and We Will Die Here.'"

4. "The Patriarchate of Jerusalem Condemns Israeli Airstrikes Targeting Humanitarian Institutions in Gaza," The Patriarchate of Jerusalem, October 20, 2023, https://tinyurl.com/yu274yt9.

Our Family Is Under the Rubble

The attack was devastating. I was angry, like so many Palestinians. I was angered by the cruelty of the killing. I was angered by the injustice. I was angered by the pain I witnessed in Nuha's heart, having wished just days before that she could be with her family. I was angry for the young man, whose story I learned, who lost his wife and two children in this attack after having their house destroyed earlier in the war. One can't help but think: "What if it was me?"

But I was also angry at God. *Why didn't God rescue or protect these innocent people? Why didn't God deliver as God often promises in Scripture? Where was God?*

Two days after the attack, I had to deliver my Sunday sermon in the churches I pastor. I wondered what I could possibly say in response. I grappled with how, if at all, I might comfort people. How do I answer these questions? I pondered. It was a service filled with sorrow and anger. Our congregations were truly lamenting, and many were in mourning. I included in our Sunday service portions of the funeral liturgy from our prayer book. I made sure to read the names of all the victims of the attack, for each victim in this war has a name, a story, and a dream killed. They are not merely numbers. They are people precious to God. This is why I read their names, and I want to share their names here: Yara, Viola, Abdilnour, Tareq, Lisa, Suheil, Majd, Ghada, Ellen, Marwan, Sulaiman, Sama, Alya', Issa, Julie, George.

I preached in anger. Pastorally, I searched for answers. I preached,

We prayed for their protection, and God did not answer us, not even in the "house of God" were church buildings able to protect them. Our children die before the silence of the world, and before the silence of God. How difficult is God's silence!

In our pain, I had to find words to express how we felt in the psalms of lament. And I cried out:

My God, my God, why did you forsake Gaza? How long will you forget her completely? Why do you hide your face from her? In the daytime I call upon you, but you do not answer; by night we find no rest.

Do not depart from the people of Gaza, for distress is near, for there is no one to help. O Lord God of our salvation, day and night we have cried before you. . . . Let our prayer come before you. . . . Incline your ear to our cries . . . for surely you have been satisfied with afflictions. Our souls and our lives approach the abyss. . . . Our eyes melt from humiliation. We call upon you, Lord, every day. We stretch out our hands to you. Why, Lord, do you reject our souls? Why do you hide your face from us? (adapted from Psalms 13, 22, and 88).

We search for God on this land. Theologically, philosophically, we ask: Where is God when we suffer? How do we explain his silence? But . . . in this land, even God is a victim of oppression, death, the war machine, and colonialism. We see the Son of God on this land crying out the same question on the cross: My God, my God, why have you forsaken me? Why do you let me be tortured? Crucified?

God suffers with the people of this land, sharing the same fate with us. As Palestinian theologian and pastor Mitri Raheb wrote in his article, "Theology in the Palestinian Context," which appeared in an Arabic book I edited:

"As for the God of this land, he is not like all the gods. His land is plowed with iron. . . . His temples are destroyed by fire. . . . His people are trampled underfoot, and He does not move a muscle. The God of this earth is hidden from view. You search for His traces but do not see them. You long for Him to split the heavens and come down to see. To listen, to be compassionate, to be saved. The God of this land does not repel brutal armies, but rather shares one fate with his people. His house is demolished. His son is crucified. But his mystery does not perish. Rather, he rises from the ashes, and with the refugees you see him. He walks, and in the dark of the night he raises springs of hope. Without this God, Palestine remains a scorched land . . . it remains a field of destruction. But if God tramples its foundations, he will only make it a holy land, a land in whose hills the good news of peace resounds."

In difficult times, we comfort ourselves with God's presence amid pain, and even amid death, for Jesus is no stranger to pain, arrest, torture, and death. He walks with us in our pain.

God is under the rubble in Gaza. He is with the frightened and the refugees. He is in the operating room. This is our consolation. He walks with us through the valley of the shadow of death. When we pray, our prayer should be that those who are suffering will feel this healing and comforting presence.

We have another comfort, which is the resurrection. In our brokenness, pain, and death, we repeat the gospel of the resurrection: "Christ is risen." He became the firstfruits of those who have fallen asleep. When I saw the pictures of the bodies of these saints in the white bags in front of the church, during their funeral, Christ's call came to my mind: "Come, you who are blessed of my Father, inherit the kingdom prepared for you from the foundations of the world" (Matthew 25:34).

In front of images of death and pictures of the deaths of children, I was reminded of the immortal call of Christ: "Let the little children come to me and do not forbid them, for the kingdom of God belongs to such as these" (Mark 10:14). If there is no place for the children of Palestine and the children of Gaza in this cruel and oppressive world, then they have a place in the arms of God. Theirs is the kingdom. In the face of bombing, displacement, and death, Jesus calls them: "Come to me, you who are blessed by my Father. Let the children come to me, for theirs is the kingdom." This is our faith. This is our consolation in our pain.[5]

This sermon was the beginning of the concept of "God in the Rubble in Gaza." It was a pastoral theme that I used, in sermons and conversations, to express the anguish we felt during those days. It was

5. The sermon was translated into English and published as Munther Isaac, "God Is Under the Rubble in Gaza," *Sojourners*, October 30, 2023, https://tinyurl.com/5fc33hvm. The interior quotation from Mitri Raheb is in Munther Isaac, *An Introduction to Palestinian Theology* (in Arabic) (Diyar, 2017), 83 (translation mine).

my attempt to comfort the listeners. It was my attempt to draw God nearer to our wounded humanity. This conception of God spoke to our people and also to the world. It showed that God is the victim of the violence of empire. It highlighted God's solidarity with humanity in its pain and suffering. The answer to the question, "Where is God when we suffer?" is that God suffers with humanity and shares its pain and anguish. This is the mystery of the cross. This might not be a satisfying message philosophically. But it can be true in an experiential way, and those who suffer can experience the presence of a God who draws near us in time of pain and suffering.

Christmas During a Genocide

In chapter 6, I described the international attention that our church in Bethlehem received in the seasons of Advent and Christmas. I used that sudden platform to cry out to the churches and world to end the genocide. But in the midst of all of that, we remained a church community, and I was their pastor. And with Christmas approaching, no one was in a mood to "celebrate." Instead, it was a period of mourning, brokenness, and fear, for all Palestinian Christians. The patriarchs and heads of the churches in Jerusalem decided together that Christmas celebrations would be confined to prayers only:

> These are not normal times. Since the beginning of the war, there has been an atmosphere of sadness and pain. Thousands of innocent civilians, including women and children, have died or suffered serious injuries. Many more grieve over the loss of their homes, their loved ones, or the uncertain fate of those dear to them. . . . Yet despite our repeated calls for a humanitarian ceasefire and a de-escalation of violence, the war continues. Therefore, We, the Patriarchs and Heads of the Churches in Jerusalem, call upon our congregations to stand strong with those facing such afflictions by this year foregoing any unnecessarily festive activities.[6]

6. "Statement on the Celebration of Advent and Christmas in the Midst

No decorations. No Christmas trees or Christmas tree lighting. No streetlights or music processions from scouts' groups. Just prayer. The heads of the churches in Jerusalem were able to sense and discern that people were in a state of mourning. No one was in a mood to celebrate. This was a pastoral cry, and it was also a message to the world.

"Why Christmas Is Canceled in Bethlehem," read the headline in the *Washington Post*, after the meeting with the Palestinian Christian delegation that I led in November of 2023.[7] But it was not Christmas that was canceled. The celebrations were canceled. Nevertheless, this became a headline that captured the attention and imagination of the world, including the Western press. How can Christmas be canceled in the place where it all started? I insisted, in response, that canceling Christmas in Bethlehem is not the headline. *The genocide in Gaza is.*

To church leaders in Bethlehem, this was an opportunity to rediscover the true meaning of Christmas. There were no distractions. My friend Fr. Rami Asakriah of the Catholic church in Bethlehem shared with me that to him prayer provided the only moment of hope during those dark days. It was a time to witness the solidarity of God with the oppressed as one of the most important elements of the meaning of Christmas.

Every year, we place the traditional Christmas manger scene in our Lutheran church in the first week of Advent. Having preached on the theme of "God Is in the Rubble," I suggested to our young families at the Christmas Lutheran Church in Bethlehem that we create a special manger from rubble, resembling a destroyed house in Gaza similar to the images we were seeing in Gaza on a daily basis. I explained that this is one of the meanings of Christmas: Jesus was born among the occupied and oppressed as a sign of solidarity. We discussed the idea, and the families supported it. The Saturday before the first Sunday of Advent, four families met in the church, and together with our children we created this special manger. We

---

of War on Gaza," The Patriarchate of Jerusalem, November 11, 2023, https://tinyurl.com/4zyjwkw4.

7. Ishaan Tharoor, "Why Christmas Is Canceled in Bethlehem," *Washington Post*, November 29, 2023, https://tinyurl.com/24rdtzhj.

called it "Christ in the Rubble." It was a special time of bonding and reflecting. It also allowed us to teach our children to think beyond ourselves during the Christmas season.

The result of our work was a memorable and iconic nativity scene, and the image of Christ in the rubble captured the imagination of the world. But first, it captured *our* imagination. We sat down and gazed at it. One of the young women with us promptly began singing a well-known chorus in Arabic, "Ya Rabbal Salam"—which translates: *Lord of Peace, rain peace upon us. Lord of Peace, fill our land with peace.* There were tears in our eyes. And we said a prayer for Gaza in our hearts.

The next day in church, the rest of the congregation was surprised and shocked by what we had created. It blew them away. Some were in tears. Some found it too harsh for the Christmas season, typically associated with joy and celebration. I said to the congregation in my sermon that I was sure they were surprised and that I realized this was a difficult image. It is possible that it takes away the joy of Christmas. However, I argued that this is *precisely the meaning of Christmas*. I reflected in my sermon that "this manger teaches us the meaning and importance of Christmas in more than one way. With death, destruction, and rubble defining and shaping our reality, this is how we welcome Jesus into our world. And if Jesus had been born in our land today, I wonder, would he have entered our world any other way?" I then continued:

> This is a time to rediscover the true meaning of Christmas. The circumstances of Palestine two thousand years ago were not very different from the circumstances in Palestine today. Then, Palestine was under the Roman occupation, and there were revolutions, and even children were massacred. When Jesus was born, he was not born in Rome, but in Bethlehem, with those under occupation. He was not born into conditions of comfort or luxury. His birth was very difficult. The story began with a census ordered by Augustus Caesar. It is a colonial method par excellence, meant to locate and control, just like Israel today uses magnetic cards and colored identities to control Palestinians.[8] Because the

8. To learn more on how Israel has over the years divided the Palestin-

Holy Family was from Bethlehem, they had to travel from Nazareth to Bethlehem, so that each could be counted in their city of origin, similar to our experience today as Palestinians when we apply for these magnetic cards in the military bases, each in the region where he or she is registered. While Mary was pregnant with Jesus, the Holy Family had to travel to Bethlehem, simply because an unjust ruler from a distant land decided to make such a decree. When Jesus was born, another ruler, Herod, went mad, and in his obsession with power ordered the killing of the children of Bethlehem. "A voice was heard in Ramah, weeping and loud lamentation, Rachel weeping for her children; she refused to be comforted, because they are no more" (Matthew 2:18). As for Jesus's family, they took refuge in Egypt (out of all places) and miraculously escaped this massacre. They were displaced. They became refugees in Egypt, similar to the fortunate Palestinians today who were able to escape Gaza to Egypt. The Christmas story is a very *Palestinian* story! Its vocabulary is census, control, empire, occupation, Caesar, Herod, military, refugees, pain, exhaustion, and massacred children (not trees, lighting, or Santa).

Christmas is the birth of Jesus with us, specifically in our distress and pain. It is the coming of Jesus to be born with the "afflicted, perplexed, persecuted, and struck down" (2 Corinthians 4:8-9). It is God being with the lowly to exalt them and the hungry to satisfy them (Luke 1:52-53). It is that Jesus came in order "to proclaim good news to the poor, liberty to the captives, recovery of sight to the blind, to set at liberty those who are oppressed" (Luke 4:18). This is the true meaning of Christmas. We should not strip it of its meaning. "Jesus in the rubble" communicated this in a special and vivid way.

In times of war, destruction, cruelty and injustice, we need to remember that God sides with the weak and the oppressed.

---

ians using magnetic cards and colored identities, see Linah Alsaafin, "The Colour-Coded Israeli ID System for Palestinians," *Al Jazeera*, November 18, 2017, https://tinyurl.com/yuusv37d; Helga Tawil-Souri, "Colored Identity: The Politics and Materiality of ID Cards in Palestine/Israel," *Social Text* 29, no. 2 (2011): 67-97.

Christmas is God's solidarity with the oppressed, the distressed, and those suffering from injustice. In Christmas we remember that God stands with the marginalized.

"Jesus in the rubble" is the presence of Jesus with those who suffer. It is God showing solidarity with the oppressed. "Jesus in the rubble" is a ray of light and hope from the heart of pain and suffering. It is the radiance of life from the heart of destruction and death.

In Gaza, God is in the rubble. If Christ were to be born today, he would be born under the rubble. "Jesus in the rubble" is an invitation to see the image of Jesus in every child killed and pulled from under the rubble, in every child who is fighting death in destroyed hospitals devoid of the components of normal health hospitals, and in every child in an incubator.

Christmas celebrations were canceled, but through this manger we communicated that Christmas itself was not and will not be canceled, as in it we have hope, and hope can never be canceled. Jesus is Emmanuel, God is with us. But it is precisely that God is with those who suffer today.

"Jesus in the rubble" is a message of hope. As we contemplated this image, we were reminded that in the midst of war, rubble, destruction, and death—Jesus is the light of the world. And this very same Jesus who escaped a massacre as a baby, went on to challenge the empire, face its leaders in defiance, and challenge and defeat the ultimate enemy—death itself.

The message of "Christ in the Rubble" was heard by millions around the world, but it also spoke to the hearts of our people. We needed to humanize the children of Gaza, especially when the world continued to rationalize and justify their killing. We needed to reclaim their God-given honor and dignity. This is at the heart of the teachings of Jesus, in Matthew 25:35-40, when he reminded us that "as you did it to one of the least of these my brothers, *you did it to me.*" Jesus here reminds us that he is the hungry, the thirsty, the stranger, the naked, the sick and the prisoner. He is the one who is oppressed and deprived of opportunities. He is the victim of unjust structures. He is the refugee and he is displaced. He is the one who is lonely and sad. In these words, Jesus cries out to the world, and we cry out with him, calling on the world to see Jesus in the children of Gaza, and all the victims of wars, and in those who are under the rubble, in the refugees and the sick. In a war that has established that world leaders do not view us as equal in value and dignity, Jesus tells us the opposite. The simple phrase "You did it to me" reminds us of the image of Christ in *us*, and of his presence with *us*. And this is an honor for us, in the face of the world's humiliating and shameful attitude toward us. No one can take this away from us.

A Voice for the Voiceless

After the first Sunday of Advent, and after I preached about Christ in the rubble, I posted pictures of our special Christmas manger on my social media. To say it went viral is an understatement! The image of baby Jesus under the rubble became an iconic image; it was an image seen around the world. Within a few days, the image was reported on by CNN, the *Times* (London), Sky News, *Al Jazeera*, CBS, MSNBC, ABC, TRT World, the *Los Angeles Times*, the *Washington Post*, the *New York Times*, and *Time*, to name only a few. I lost count of the number of interviews I did in those days. It was over a hundred. Journalists from Denmark, Brazil, Japan, Indonesia, the Netherlands, Norway, France, Germany, Saudi Arabia, Lebanon, Egypt, and other countries showed up in front of our church or called. In all these interviews, I made sure to emphasize two points: First, this manger is God's solidarity with the oppressed. I repeated over and over that if Jesus were to be born today, he would be born under the rubble in Gaza. Second, this manger is what Christmas looks like in Palestine today: homes destroyed, families displaced, and children pulled from under the rubble. I pleaded over and over that all we wanted for Christmas is a cease-fire. The theme "If Christ were born today, he would be born under rubble" was highlighted in many news headlines all over the world.[9]

9. See, for example, Mallory Moench, "Bethlehem Reverend Delivers 'Christ in the Rubble' Christmas Sermon amid Gaza Conflict," *Time*, De-

The media attention was overwhelming and tiring. There was also an element of amazement. What in this image captured the imagination of the world? Why does the world seem to be more interested in a Christian symbol of baby Jesus in a manger of rubble than in the actual children of Gaza who are pulled from under the rubble? I also felt some guilt. Was I drawing too much attention and as such drawing attention *from* Gaza? All I wanted was to point to Gaza. And one Sunday morning during Christmas, when more than five media outlets were filming and recording my sermon, I looked at the cameras and said: "Why are you here? The headlines are in Gaza. Go to Gaza. The cancelation of Christmas is not the headline; the genocide in Gaza is. Go to Gaza." Of course, I knew that international journalists were not allowed to enter Gaza throughout the war. I was simply trying to make the point that this manger is pointing to a real and harsh reality that demands our attention, empathy, and action. I was hoping that my message would get to those watching behind the cameras.

Others were not so moved by the image of Christ in the rubble and protested wrapping Christ with a keffiyeh. Some took issue with my provocative statement that if Jesus were to be born today, he would be born in Gaza under the rubble. Some questioned my biblical knowledge, instructing me that Jesus was born in Bethlehem, not Gaza (as if I, a Bible scholar and pastor *from Bethlehem*, needed such an education). Many journalists asked me directly when they

---

cember 24, 2023, https://tinyurl.com/ycy3sscd; Yara Bayoumy and Samar Hazboun, "'God Is Under the Rubble in Gaza': Bethlehem's Subdued Christmas," *New York Times*, updated December 27, 2023, https://tinyurl.com/umjruj8m; Bethan McKernan and Sufian Taha, "'If Jesus Was Born Today, He'd Be Born Under the Rubble': Bethlehem Set for Forlorn Christmas," *Guardian*, December 24, 2023, https://tinyurl.com/54r4m4f2; Monjed Jadou, "'If Christ Were Born Today, He Would Be Born Under Rubble, Israeli Bombing,'" *Al Jazeera*, December 7, 2023, https://tinyurl.com/cbbvf63b; "Lutheran Pastor: If Jesus Were Born Today He Would Be Born in Gaza Under Rubble," *CNN*, December 22, 2023, https://tinyurl.com/2sbps88f; Jay Gray, Kayla McCormick, and Yuliya Talmazan, "Deserted Streets and Shuttered Stores as Israel-Hamas War Looms over Bethlehem at Christmas," *NBC News*, December 25, 2023, https://tinyurl.com/57v4prwe.

visited our church about the "Palestinian Jesus" or the "keffiyeh Jesus." The irony not to be missed is that the very same church in which we created "Christ in the Rubble" was built 120 years ago by German missionaries, sponsored by the German Empire then, with stained glass windows featuring a blond, blue-eyed German Jesus! German Jesus is ok; Palestinian Jesus is not ok!

There were two common questions: Am I politicizing Jesus? And why didn't I wrap Jesus with an Israeli flag, symbolizing God's solidarity with the Jewish children killed as well?

I tried to make it clear that in Palestine faith leaders cannot avoid political discussion, but at the same time, I was not politicizing Jesus so much as I was humanizing Jesus and the Palestinians. I was sending a human message about God's solidarity with the oppressed. As for wrapping Jesus with an Israeli flag, a question I was also asked by a German diplomat who attended our Christmas service, I answered by first acknowledging that all lives are equal and precious, and that I sincerely lament the death of Israeli children on October 7. Moreover, if Israeli parents say they feel that God is in solidarity with them in their loss and pain, then I believe that this is not only within their right but a good and commendable thing. Jesus is not the exclusive property of one people group!

Having said that, the number of Israeli children murdered on October 7 was thirty-six. The whole world stopped, and a war was waged in revenge. Germany projected the Israeli flag onto the Berlin Wall in solidarity. Meanwhile, by Christmas, more than ten thousand Palestinian children had been murdered in Gaza. I told the diplomat then that I have not seen the Palestinian flag on the Berlin Wall or any other monument in Europe, and wondered whether our children are less valuable? Are they less human? At a time when the world continues to justify and rationalize the killing of our children, it is my obligation as a man of faith to speak for those children, and to highlight their worth. They are precious to God. We see Jesus in each child pulled from under the rubble. This is why we have Jesus in a keffiyeh in the rubble. Through the image of Christ in the rubble, we attempted to speak for the voiceless and marginalized, and in particular, the children of Gaza.

Christianity Today featured a cover story for its March 2024 issue written by Mike Cosper, the senior director of media at the magazine. In that cover story, Cosper called "Christ in the Rubble" a manifestation of antisemitism, arguing that the keffiyeh, the national symbol of Palestine and Palestinians, is a symbol of terrorism and ideological violence:

> But to wrap him in a keffiyeh goes beyond an effort in solidarity, embracing not just partisanship or nationalism but a symbol of violence that expressly sees the destruction of Jewish life as a key to history. It is the symbol of a movement that glorifies as martyrs those who strap bombs to their chest and blow up school buses. It is not a profound expression of identification or solidarity; it is an obscenity.[10]

Cosper completely disregards Palestinian pain. He claims to know our motives, even claiming that we are deceitful. Such a dehumanizing article, with its blatant yet casual anti-Palestinian racism, featured in the most prominent evangelical magazine, makes me both angry and sad. It makes me angry because it is an outrageous distortion of the meaning of the keffiyeh and of who Palestinians are. Cosper, who in the words of Ben Norquist wrote about the keffiyeh "with the doctrinaire certainty of an expertise he does not have," has no right telling us or the world what the keffiyeh symbolizes. Instead, it is for Palestinians to tell him and the world what the keffiyeh means to us. This is a combination of arrogance and racism. Further, this posture by Cosper makes me sad because of its lack of empathy, even apathy and numbness, to the extent that he and *Christianity Today* cannot seem to make themselves (and their readers) empathize with Palestinians, even Palestinian Christians, in one of the darkest moments in our lives, and instead vilify our whole community. To be sure, Cosper empathized with those killed on October 7. But as Norquist argues in his response to Cosper:

10. Mike Cosper, "The Evil Ideas Behind October 7," *Christianity Today*, March 2024, https://tinyurl.com/2znexw2a.

When it comes to Palestinian sorrow, Cosper appears disinterested in appealing to Jesus' identification in suffering. He doesn't make the same connection between the violence against Christ's body and the violence against the more than 30,000 Palestinians gone from the earth in Gaza. Nor does he invite his Christian readers to mourn with those left behind. He makes a gesture or two, but always in the service of some critical point. In fact, he criticizes Palestinian attempts to draw close to Jesus and to wrestle in their hearts and minds with the devastation.[11]

Sadly, while Cosper attempted to expose the "evil ideas behind October 7" in his cover story and has very vocally critiqued antisemitism, I wonder if he is aware of the anti-Palestinian hatred and bigotry in this article. How someone who is so invested in exposing church abuse and critiquing antisemitism can oppose one form of bigotry and hatred while peddling another is beyond me.

To be clear, wrapping Jesus with a keffiyeh or claiming that he is a Palestinian by no means denies his Jewishness. But let us remember that Jerusalem, Bethlehem, and Nazareth are Palestinian cities today. Further, as people who live under the Israeli occupation, we draw inspiration from the fact that Jesus was born under Roman occupation. This fact brings the experience of Christ nearer to the experience of the Palestinians living under occupation today: God stands in solidarity with all those who suffer injustice. When we say that Christ is in the rubble, it is a message that God stands in solidarity with all the oppressed!

In the end, Christ is God incarnate and is not the exclusive possession of any people group. No one people group can monopolize Christ for themselves. Christ is for all, "He is Lord of all" (Acts 10:36). And when it comes to suffering, Jesus is a refuge and comfort for all who suffer.

11. Ben Norquist, "Jesus' Comfort Is for All Who Suffer: A Response to Mike Cosper and *Christianity Today*," Religion News Service, March 18, 2024, https://tinyurl.com/33fzmvmz.

Bringing "Christ in the Rubble" from Bethlehem to the World

"Christ in the Rubble" became our message from Bethlehem to the world in the midst of this genocide. I have already alluded to the sermon I gave the day before Christmas, in which I called out the world and the church for their complicity in this war. In that sermon, I expanded on the meaning of the scene before us: "Christ in the Rubble." This was our message to the world:[12]

> In Gaza today, God is under the rubble.
>
> And in this Christmas season, as we search for Jesus, he is to be found not on the side of Rome, but our side of the wall. In a cave, with a simple family. Vulnerable. Barely, and miraculously surviving a massacre. Among a refugee family. This is where Jesus is found.
>
> If Jesus were to be born today, he would be born under the rubble in Gaza.
>
> When we glorify pride and richness, Jesus is under the rubble.
>
> When we rely on power, might, and weapons, Jesus is under the rubble.
>
> When we justify, rationalize, and theologize the bombing of children, Jesus is under the rubble.
>
> Jesus is under the rubble. The rubble is his manger. He is at home with the marginalized, the suffering, the oppressed, and displaced. This is his manger.
>
> I have been looking at, contemplating this iconic image. . . . God with us, precisely in this way. *This* is the incarnation. Messy. Bloody. Poverty. This is the incarnation.
>
> This child is our hope and inspiration. We look and see him in every child killed and pulled from under the rubble. While the world continues to reject the children of Gaza, Jesus says: "Just as you did it to one of the least of these brothers and sisters of mine,

---

12. For the full text of the sermon, visit "Christ in the Rubble: A Liturgy of Lament," Red Letter Christians, December 23, 2023, https://tinyurl.com/yxb74nch.

you did it to me." "You did to *me*." Jesus not only calls them his own, he is them!

We look at the holy family and see them in every family displaced and wandering, now homeless in despair. While the world discusses the fate of the people of Gaza as if they are unwanted boxes in a garage, God in the Christmas narrative shares in their fate; he walks with them and calls them his own.

This manger is about resilience—*Sumud*. The resilience of Jesus is in his meekness; weakness, and vulnerability. The majesty of the incarnation lies in its solidarity with the marginalized. Resilience because this very same child, rose up from the midst of pain, destruction, darkness and death to challenge empires, speak truth to power, and deliver an everlasting victory over death and darkness.

This is Christmas today in Palestine, and this is the Christmas message. It is not about Santa, trees, gifts, lights . . . etc. My goodness, how we have twisted the meaning of Christmas! How we have commercialized Christmas! I was in the United States last month, the first Monday after Thanksgiving, and I was amazed by the amount of Christmas decorations and lights, all the . . . commercial goods. I couldn't help but think: They send us bombs, while celebrating Christmas in their land. They sing about the Prince of Peace in their land, while playing the drum of war in our land.

Christmas in Bethlehem, the birthplace of Jesus, is this manger. This is our message to the world today. It is a gospel message, a true and authentic Christmas message, about the God who did not stay silent, but said his word, and his Word is Jesus. Born among the occupied and marginalized. He is in solidarity with us in our pain and brokenness.

Christmas allowed us to meditate on the meaning of the incarnation in a fresh and meaningful way—as the embodiment of God's presence, Immanuel, among the occupied, and those who suffer and mourn. Immanuel, God is with us: God visited our world, and God visited us precisely in our pain, weakness, and fear. The Christmas message is: Do not be afraid, I am with you!

The message of Christmas is also that Jesus is the Word of God. What we could not fathom throughout this genocide, especially in its early stages, is the silence of the world in the face of the mass killing of children. The incarnation allowed us to proclaim that God is not silent, even if it seems so to us in our distress and pain. We shouted in our oppression: Why are you silent, Lord? Have we forgotten that Jesus is the *Word* of God? Jesus is God's answer to our prayers and calls. God spoke his Word, and the Word is Jesus. It is a word of hope, compassion, and justice. It is the word of salvation. Jesus the Word challenges the silence of the world—and his Word is life. His Word is hope.

The Cross and the Solidarity of God

The message and image of Christ in the rubble accompanied us throughout the war and beyond Christmas. In fact, we kept the manger in its place in our church and decided not to remove it until the war was over. The longer the war has lasted, the more shocked we have been by the world's complicity and seeming acceptance of the continued killing of Palestinians. It was hard to fathom that all the efforts to end this war came to nothing. It was traumatizing to continue to witness image after image of children pulled from under the rubble. We ran out of words trying to console our friends in Gaza when we were fortunate enough to have a connection to call or text them.

By Easter, as I've shown in chapter 6, a genocide was normalized. The killing of a hundred in a strike in Gaza was no longer "breaking news." The fact that people were literally being killed by starvation seemed like just another headline. This was the context for our Easter "celebrations." If Advent and Christmas bring us the image of the manger, Holy Week and Easter direct us to other images from God's life of solidarity with the oppressed. We turned to the cross.

On Holy Saturday, the day before Easter, I preached these words from our church to a global audience:[13]

13. For the full text of the sermon, see "Easter Vigil for Gaza, Bethlehem,

These are dark, dark days. In times like this, we Palestinians look at the cross, identify with the cross, and see Jesus identifying with us. In Easter, we re-live his arrest, torture and execution at the hands of Empire—with the complicity of a religious ideology of course.

In the Easter story, we find comfort and empowerment in knowing that Jesus identifies with us.

We have kept this rubble in our church since the time of Christmas, because Gaza is still under the rubble, and because our people and our children in Gaza are still being pulled from under the rubble.

Yesterday I watched with anguish a cruel scene of a child pulled from under the rubble. He miraculously survived the bombing, and while he was being pulled out, he was saying: "Where is the water? I am thirsty."

This reminded me of the words of Jesus on the cross, when he cried out: "I am thirsty." He cried out "I am thirsty" in solidarity with those being massacred by famine, siege and bombardment. Jesus stands in solidarity with all the victims of wars and forced famines, caused by unjust and tyrannical regimes in our world. It is the cry of everyone oppressed by the injustice of humanity, its silence and its inability to put an end to tyranny and injustice.

Jesus shouted, "I am thirsty," so they gave him vinegar to drink. They added more pain to his pain, more anguish to his anguish. Today, while Gaza screams, "I am thirsty," they drop aid from the sky, stained with the blood of innocents. Some were killed by drowning while trying to pull the dropped aid from the sea. How cruel. Gaza is thirsty, and they give Gaza vinegar.

We searched for God in this war. We cried out to Him, and there is no answer, it seems, until we encounter the Son of God hanging on the cross, crying out: "My God, my God, why have you forsaken me?" Why did you let me be crucified? Alone? While I am innocent?

March 30th, 2024, Rev. Dr. Munther Isaac," Red Letter Christians, April 2, 2024, https://tinyurl.com/mn53jvmh.

This is the cry of feeling abandoned. I am sure this is how Gazans feel today. Abandonment by world leaders—not only Western, but also Arab and Muslim leaders abandoned us. Many in the church also watched from a distance, like Peter did when Jesus was arrested. Peter wanted to be safe; he lacked the courage . . . similar to many church leaders today, who say one thing behind closed doors and another in public.

Yet it is in this cry—"My God, my God, why have you forsaken me?"—that we experience God, that God draws near to us, and it is in this cry that we feel his embrace and warmth. This is one of the mysteries of Easter.

In this land, even God is a victim of oppression, death, the war machine, and colonialism. He suffers with the people of this land, sharing the same fate with them. "My God, my God, why have you forsaken me?" It is a cry that has resonated for years in this land. It is the cry of every oppressed person hanging in a state of slow death. It is a cry that Jesus shared with us in his pain, torment, and crucifixion. Today we place the cross on the rubble, remembering that Jesus shared the same fate with us, as he died on the cross as a victim of the colonizers.

And it became dark. The universe became dark in grief over the absence of truth. The universe became dark, lamenting the absence of justice. The cross is the ultimate injustice. Today, the universe is saddened by the silence of decision-makers and their racism, and by the silence of many who did not speak a word of truth, out of fear, armed with the theology of neutrality and silence, under the name of peace and reconciliation. There are still those who have not openly called for a cease-fire. We received a letter of "solidarity" from large churches in Europe that did not even call for a cease-fire! I told them this is an absolute insult. . . .

We are carrying a heavy cross. And our Friday has lasted way too long . . . but we know from the experience of Jesus that this suffering is not for the glorification of suffering. We know that suffering is always a path to glory and life. It is a stop in the road to resurrection. We walk with Jesus the road to Golgotha. We are empowered by his solidarity, but we look for Sunday.

The Empty Tomb and the Victory of God

I continued my sermon by shifting the focus from the cross to the empty tomb. This was a difficult message, because it felt so "unreal"; it felt like wishful thinking. The message of the cross was so real to us. We felt it. We lived it. But can we in the midst of pain and suffering think beyond our Good Friday? Can we even dare to imagine Sunday? When we are waiting for Easter Sunday, our faith is really tested. This is when the stories of the gospel really confront us, daring us with a dare to believe. I dared to believe that Sunday is coming, and I dared to challenge those listening in Bethlehem and around the world that Sunday will ultimately come, and that the final word belongs to God:

> What gave Jesus this strength? This resilience and power—to the extent that he forgave his oppressors? To the extent that he said, "Your will be done," and went voluntarily to the cross? I believe his resolve and determination—his resilience—came from trusting his Father's will, and from knowing that his Father is able to raise him from the dead—and that He will ultimately do that! He will raise him. His faith sustained and empowered him. He was defiant in the face of empire; he faced the cross, and even death, with confidence and steadfastness.
>
> I must admit—it is so difficult today to hold on to faith, and to hope. We cannot see Sunday. It seems an impossibility. We are swallowed by the darkness of the tomb. It is so hard to speak of the resurrection now. We are mourning. Our siblings in Gaza are literally dying from starvation. But we cannot lose our faith in God. This is our last resort. As such, we have to fight to keep this faith. We cannot lose our faith. We have to look at the empty tomb. We must remember the empty tomb.
>
> Today, I preach to myself with the psalmist: "Why are you cast down, O my soul, and why are you in turmoil within me? Hope in God; for I shall again praise him, my salvation and my God."
>
> The Resurrection gives us hope. Christianity is faith that hopes. Hope is not a denial of reality. We are not blind to our reality, and we as Palestinians realize the corruption and evil of

the world—probably more than anybody else. But we must refuse to let this be the last word.

Christ is the Risen One—this is the final word. Christ is risen, and this changes everything. The empty tomb is our hope. Behind the apartheid wall, and specifically in the Church of the Holy Sepulcher, there is an empty tomb that reminds us that the last word is not death but life. Not darkness but light.

The empty tomb reminds us that evil, injustice, and tyranny cannot have the last word. If Christ had remained in his grave, Caesar and Pilate would have triumphed. Rome would have won. The oppressors would have been victorious. But Christ is risen. The empire is defeated, and even better, death itself is defeated.

Despair and fear do not have the last word. Because we believe in the God of resurrection, and in the God of justice, the God of love, we believe that justice, truth, and righteousness will cover the earth as waters cover the seas.

Because we have faith—we do not live in despair. Because we have faith, we will not accept the prevalence of darkness but fight evil with good. Faith is the only thing they cannot take away from us.

When we declare on Easter Sunday, *Al-Maseeh qam* (Christ is risen), we declare that the final word belongs to God. We declare that justice is served. Truth is vindicated. The empire and its allies lost. Today, after two thousand years, by carrying the cross we defeat and even mock the empire and its theology. We took the symbol of Rome's power, and the means of its humiliation of others, and made it the symbol of our strength, victory, and steadfastness in the face of death, and this is because *Al-Maseeh qam*—Christ is risen.

The resurrection urges us to rise and act! Because we know that the final word belongs to God, we rise and act. We build. We preach life because we know life wins. We preach love because we know love wins. We preach peace, because peace wins. We preach life because death is defeated. Jesus stared death in the face and defeated it. And therefore, we rise and act. . . .

So today let the way of the cross be our way. Let the way of sacrificial love be our way. The crucified Jesus, who sacrificed his life for the sake of those he loved, calls us to costly solidarity, the costly solidarity of love. This is a call to action, for the church to be the church—to follow in the footsteps of the crucified savior.

The cross is God's solidarity with humanity in its pain and suffering, and God's solidarity must become our solidarity. The followers of Jesus risk all to speak truth to power. This is not about making a statement. Jesus did not say: I was hungry, and you prayed for me and made a statement! Jesus said: I was a prisoner, and you came to me! We must find ways to make a difference. We must act, pressure, lobby, hold powers and leaders accountable, mobilize. We must live as people of the resurrection. Today, the land of the resurrection calls you to act, in hope and love. Together, we are committed to end this genocide. Together we are committed to work for truth and justice. We know we will prevail. "*Al-Maseeh qam.*" Christ is risen. Amen.

God in the Midst of Suffering

This chapter is an attempt to respond pastorally to the questions that arise in times of severe pain and suffering. How do we make sense of our faith in a God who is almighty, and who is able to protect, yet does not?

We cannot, and should not, blame God as the sole reason for all the suffering in our world. Many times, if not most of the time, it is our collective fault as humanity. In a time of genocide, and when children are killed or kidnapped, we need to point the finger at ourselves. We have created and nurtured cultures of hate, revenge, and supremacy. We chose to be silent in the face of injustice. We chose neutrality. We idealized might and pride. We allowed the weapons industry to control governments and entire economies. We enabled modern coloniality. We allowed lobby groups to buy politicians. We sold ourselves to gain power and influence. "Those conflicts and disputes among you, where do they come from? Do they not come from your cravings that are at war within you? You want something and do not have it; so you commit murder. And you covet something and cannot obtain it; so you engage in disputes and conflicts" (James 4:1-2).

Yet God could have stopped all of this, and he did not. This was our crisis. It is the age-old question: "Where was God?"

For those experiencing the pain, and who choose to hold firm to their faith, the issue shifts from a philosophical one into the realm of experience. They experience God in the midst of their suffering. This is why the psalmist prayed:

> Even though I walk through the darkest valley,
>   I fear no evil;
> *for you are with me;*
>   your rod and your staff—
>   they comfort me. (Ps. 23:4)

The psalmist did not say, "Even though I walk through the darkest valley, you deliver me." Sometimes, God does deliver. Most of the time, he does not. But all the time, he is present. This is the promise. The promise is not deliverance but presence. This needs faith.

When asked about the question: "Where was God during the Holocaust?" Rabbi Jonathan Sacks gave one of the many answers that he heard from those who survived it:

> This one came to me from Holocaust survivors, many of whom told me they felt that God was personally with them, giving them the strength and courage to survive. There were people who lost their faith at Auschwitz. There were people who kept their faith, and there were people who found faith in Auschwitz.

This is not about comparing one genocide with another. The Holocaust represents one of the most grievous evils of human history. For people to testify that they experienced God even in the midst of the evil horrors of Auschwitz is truly amazing. Rabbi Sacks continues:

> So that is where God was: in the commands, in the sanctity of life that was so cruelly and devastatingly unheard, and in the hearts of some of the survivors who found God, giving them the strength.[14]

14. Jonathan Sacks, "Where Was God During the Holocaust?" Jonathan Sacks, April 2020, https://tinyurl.com/pavs3y8j.

The presence of God in the midst of suffering is a declaration of faith—a declaration that I tried to make through my sermons, advocacy, and writings. I do not claim to even come close to the experience of those in Gaza, or those who experienced October 7. I do not claim to know what it is like to live in the midst of a genocide. I cannot imagine being in the shoes of those in Auschwitz, Namibia, Armenia, Syria and Iraq, or Rwanda. I draw conclusions from my faith and understanding of the God who became man in Jesus of Nazareth, and who was crucified and who experienced pain and suffering. As Sri Lankan theologian Vinoth Ramachandra writes:

> To believe that the Creator God was uniquely present in the crucified Christ means to believe that God has chosen to identify himself as God in a human corpse. He has chosen to define his deity in weakness. God is revealed not as the one who inflicts suffering or avoids suffering, but who suffers.[15]

I also draw conclusions from the experiences of those who survived and lived through wars of genocide. For it is they who told us of experiencing God's presence. In this war, the people of Gaza have demonstrated remarkable faith. They would literally come from under the rubble thanking God and accepting his will. Many times they were heard crying out in Arabic, "Hasbiy-allah wa ni'mal Wakeel"—which literally translates as "God is sufficient for us! Most excellent is he in whom we trust!"

On Christmas, I draw inspiration from a Facebook post by one of those taking refuge in the Orthodox church. He wrote then:

> The days pass in an indescribable way, and we feel fear, anxiety, and insecurity, in supernatural circumstances that no human being can bear, and the whole world celebrates Christmas and lights the Christmas tree, and we celebrate Christmas, but in a difficult and terrifying atmosphere, *but we have the joy of Christmas in our hearts.*

15. Vinoth Ramachandra, *Sarah's Laughter: Doubt, Tears, and Christian Hope* (Langham Global Library, 2020), 60.

Oh Jesus, your birth is drawing near, a day of joy, love, and salvation, but we live in sadness and pain. We pray that your Christmas will be the Christmas of peace, the Christmas of joy for our country and our people, and we will celebrate this Christmas despite the harshness of the scene, despite the terror and fear that reminds me of the terror and fear of the shepherds when the angels appeared to them to announce to them the most beautiful good news, the good news of Christmas, the birth of the child Jesus. Shine your light upon us and light our country with love and peace, and comfort the afflicted.

Peace, O child of Christmas, to our people who have lost peace.

I commented on these words then as follows:

This is true faith. This is steadfastness. This is the resilience and insistence of celebrating *despite* the harshness of the scene. These words come from someone who does not know if he will survive this war. But the war, with all its ugliness, did not steal his faith. It did not steal his joy in Christ. This is faith that all the armies of the world cannot defeat, because this child was not and will not be defeated by all the armies of the world.

My faith is in a God who transcends nationality, race, and religion, and who sides with the oppressed, who is present with those who suffer in the worst of times. God is in solidarity with *all* the oppressed and *all* the victims of injustice, and draws near to them. This is not—in fact, this is the opposite of—the concept of a tribal and racist God who favors peoples and nations based on their ethnicity or nationality or religion. In the book of Exodus God says to Moses, "I have observed the misery of my people who are in Egypt; I have heard their cry on account of their taskmasters. Indeed, I know their sufferings" (Exod. 3:7). These words apply to all who suffer and cry out in pain and anguish to God. Jesus's gospel proclamation is to bring good news to the poor, *all* the poor, and to proclaim release to the captives, wherever there are captives of injustice and oppression, and to set free those who are oppressed, anywhere there is oppression (Luke 4:18).

And as God identifies with humanity in its pain and suffering, the very same humanity is reclaimed and celebrated, the same humanity that was crushed by the brutal force of empire and injustice. Ramachandra reminds us:

> However, for the post-Easter church, this is the turning point of history. This shameful death of an obscure outcast, unnoticed by any Roman historian, is the point at which God has broken the power of evil in his world and opened the way for freedom for all. Instead of being another of the countless forgotten victims, Jesus was remembered, and his story told and retold for centuries to come. His solidarity with all other forgotten victims, victims of terror and torture, all who are considered dispensable to protect the security and comforts of those who think they matter, *enables them to be remembered too.*[16]

"Christ in the Rubble" is not a claim of any inherent righteousness in Palestinians, or a claim that God sides with the Palestinians because they are Palestinians. "Christ in the Rubble" is a Palestinian cry from the midst of suffering, and a faithful declaration of the presence of God with those who are under the rubble in Gaza. It is a statement from the midst of suffering that we see the image of God in those pulled from under the rubble. It is an application of the concept of the God who sides with those who suffer injustice in times when those going through unbearable suffering in Gaza cried out to God for help and comfort.

---

16. Ramachandra, *Sarah's Laughter*, 58 (emphasis added).

8

The Moral Compass of the World

These were the concluding words, heard around the world, of Irish lawyer Blinne Ní Ghrálaigh, who represented the case of South Africa in the public sitting of the ICJ held on January 11, 2024, in the case entitled Application of the Convention on the Prevention and Punishment of the Crime of Genocide in the Gaza Strip:

> In a powerful sermon, delivered from a church in Bethlehem on Christmas Day—the same day Israel had killed 250 Palestinians, including at least 86 people, many from the same family, massacred in a single strike on Maghazi refugee camp—Palestinian Pastor Munther Isaac addressed his congregation and the world. And he said: "Gaza as we know it no longer exists. This is an annihilation. This is a genocide. We will rise. We will stand up again from the midst of destruction, as we have always done as Palestinians, although this is by far maybe the biggest blow we have received."
>
> But he said: "No apologies will be accepted after the genocide. . . . What has been done has been done. I want you to look at the mirror and ask, where was I when Gaza was going through a genocide."[1]

1. "Public Sitting Held on Thursday 11 January 2024, at 10 a.m., at the

The case was comprehensive and conclusive. It appealed to international law and included detailed evidence of Israel's acts and intentions in warfare that resembled genocide, and concluded with this appeal to the conscience of our humanity.

I was overwhelmed with mixed emotions upon discovering that my sermon was quoted by the ICJ. There was immediate fear—will the Israeli authorities retaliate against me? Fear then turned into gratefulness that my voice could potentially make a difference toward ending the genocide. I received numerous messages and calls from friends and family, thanking me for my witness throughout this period. The small Palestinian Christian community in particular felt a sense of empowerment, that our voices were being heard and had the potential to impact international decisions about our livelihood. The next Sunday in church, I made sure to declare that it was not just me quoted in the ICJ, but our church and broader community as well. My voice is their voice.

Later, as I reflected on that moment and how widely the sermon "Christ in the Rubble" reached, I was reminded of the power and impact of the pulpit, especially when preachers preach from a place of humility, conviction, and courage. The quotation is an acknowledgment of the importance of morality, ethics, and humanity in public discourse. "Where was I when Gaza was going through a genocide?" is a prophetic challenge to our world and to our humanity. This is a challenge that has been made historically whenever brutality and injustice prevail, whether in Palestine or anywhere else in the world. It is a cry against silence when a moral voice is needed. This was particularly true for Gaza, given that genocide was unfolding before the eyes of the whole world. Our humanity is in danger when our approach to contexts of war and mass killing is devoid of compassion and empathy, especially when it includes the killing of children in masses. The moral and human dimensions of catastrophes of such

---

Peace Palace, President Donoghue Presiding, in the Case Concerning Application of the Convention on the Prevention and Punishment of the Crime of Genocide in the Gaza Strip (South Africa)," International Court of Justice, January 11, 2024, https://tinyurl.com/mpwfy3jk.

massive scale must be at the center of our politics and public discourse. This is what I attempted to invite through my sermon. It was a call for humanity to reclaim its humanity, from the town in which the divine became man, to particularly show us how to be fully and truly human. Jesus of Bethlehem was the embodiment of love and compassion. The call of "Christ in the Rubble" was precisely that: for humanity to embrace love and compassion as elements of what it means to be truly human.

The "Christ in the Rubble" manger and sermon, and the activism of Palestinian Christian leaders throughout the war on Gaza and for the past decade, are also a summons to the *church* to act in compassion and defend the oppressed. The church must be at the forefront of the battle against desecrating the *imago Dei*, especially when this desecration is enacted with theologies and ideologies of supremacy that evoke the name of God. Silence in the face of atrocities of this scale cannot be our response as people of faith. We must speak out. We must humanize the oppressed and dehumanized. We must reclaim the *imago Dei* in victims of wars and violence, who have become flash news and mere numbers in a world dominated by consumerist culture and apathy. Our humanity is at stake. And for us Christians, the credibility of our Christian witness is also at stake. We cannot, as Christians, be silent when atrocities are committed, especially when these atrocities are committed in the name of our God.

The Moral Integrity of the World

In that very same sermon, I declared that Gaza has become the moral compass of the world, by which I mean a test of global moral integrity. In this way Gaza has divided our world. This, I believe, is a good thing, for we need to know where people stand when it comes to the killing of tens of thousands of children. Gaza has divided our world not on the basis of religion, ethnicity, or politics. Rather, it has created a moral wedge.

Gaza is not the only place tormented by wars and violence, and our world has certainly witnessed more violent wars in the last century, at least in terms of the numbers of people killed and displaced. This reality, however, should not make such atrocities permissible. We should not compare the suffering of people groups as if there is a competition. What drove me to emphasize this point that Gaza is a global moral test is the unique fact that this genocide was broadcast live for the world to see. It is not as if the horrors were discovered later, long after the fact. Rather, the world has become desensitized to the brutal images of children killed in Gaza, day after day after day. The devaluation and dehumanization of Gazan lives unfolded in a very public manner.

We must never get used to any form of violence, or to children dying in war zones, as if such things are an inevitable part of life. Our collective humanity is at stake here. We must never stop lamenting, protesting, and working toward ending violence. If we stop doing so, then something is seriously wrong with our humanity. Decision makers must act morally to stop violence. Sadly, the weapons industry still dominates our world. The culture of "might is right" still dominates our world. Racism and ideologies of supremacy still dominate our world. We have not learned. This is why the mobilization of people in the streets, places of worship, and campuses around the world remains essential. These grassroots movements have become a source of hope in a world that seems to be numb to violence and resigned to accepting the death of children.

In May 2024 I was honored to be invited by an old friend who is a campus minister at Harvard to address the "Peoples' Graduation." Her church hosted this special ceremony for students who were not allowed to walk in MIT, Emerson, and Harvard commencements in 2024 due to their participation in Gaza solidarity encampments. Some of the students had requested that I be invited. When I addressed the more than 270 students and professors who participated in that event, I reminded them of the power of their voices:

> If world leaders—and many faith leaders—are silent, the streets of the world are not silent. The streets have spoken, and today university students have spoken as well. And the word spoken is that of justice and humanity.

What is happening in universities in the United States and in many places around the world is truly powerful and unprecedented when it comes to Palestine. Remember: in history, universities always mobilized for change. And, in the past, university students have always been on the right side of history. And they have always been resisted. This is why politicians are trembling in fear because of your movement. The world that sings of freedom of self-expression—we see it trembling and shaking, and they even send security forces to suppress these demonstrations. It is hypocrisy itself, and it is fear and the realization that this is the beginning of the end.

What you are doing is extremely important! You are on the right side of history. Be assured of this! Today you are the conscience of your country. Keep speaking the truth. Be creative, nonviolent, and strong. Keep the righteousness of our cause—that of justice and liberation—in sight and mind. Keep the people of Gaza in your mind and hearts.

The world today, specifically the Western world, needs your guidance. It needs your values. It needs your courage. This is a world that lacks moral credibility and courage, and is controlled by warlords who profit from the death of children. Western politics suffers from moral bankruptcy. But you can be, as you have been in many previous experiences, the hope of your peoples and their politicians.

The Credibility of Our Witness

"Never again!" is an often-repeated phrase in reference to what our response as humanity *should* be in the face of wars of genocide and mass destruction. We can think of the Holocaust, the genocide against the Armenians, and the Herero and Nama genocide in Namibia as examples that evoke this kind of response. I have personally visited Auschwitz and was shaken to my core by being in the extermination ovens and witnessing the site where Nazis committed evil horrors against the Jews in Europe. The response that stirred at my core was "Never again!"

Yet, as a Palestinian, I've come to understand "Never again!" as merely a slogan that politicians repeat with no real intent of heeding. If the empires of our world, including the superpowers of today, designate certain people as dispensable and their extermination as serving the interests of the empire, then "Never again!" becomes "Yet again!"

If we say, "Never again!" about events in the past yet allow the displacement of millions in Sudan, China, and Gaza, our words remain hollow. "Never again!" should mean that *never again will we allow mass destruction, displacement, and genocide against any peoples.* While millions of people remain dispensable, it is clear that our world has not yet learned this lesson. When it comes to Palestine, and the creation of Israel in part as a righting of the horrors of the Holocaust, "Never again!" for the Jewish people cannot be achieved by committing horrors against the Palestinian people. You cannot redeem one evil by committing another!

Gaza has not only divided our world but it has also created what Palestinian Christian scholar Daniel Bannoura calls a "theological crisis" for the church.[2] In fact, a large part of why I am writing this book is because I am deeply troubled by the church. It is not a stretch to say that the credibility of our Christian witness is at stake when the church is silent and, even worse, complicit in the face of a genocide. This is particularly true when it comes to many churches in the West. The very same people who for years lectured Palestinians on human rights and international law, and who for years lectured us on antisemitism, nonviolence, and Judeo-Christian traditions and values, turned a blind eye to a genocide.

Needless to say, I am also troubled by the response of Arab countries to the war on Gaza. They could have done more. Wealthy Arab countries could have utilized their leverage to a much greater extent to stop this war. Muslim faith leaders could and should have spoken more, and in fact many, many Muslims have shared with me that they wish their clergy spoke out as I did. By calling out the global church, I am not singling out the church. Yet my focus and calling are to speak to my siblings in faith and challenge them, because I am convinced

---

2. Daniel Bannoura, "CATC2024 Day 2: A Call for Repentance—Daniel Bannoura," Christ at the Checkpoint YouTube Channel, June 3, 2024, https://tinyurl.com/2p8nhrce.

that Gaza is a moral issue for the church, and it is precisely the credibility of our Christian witness that is at stake.

"Never again!" should also include "Never again!" to the weaponization of the Bible as a tool for the empire, for teaching and enforcing domination of some people by others. The Bible was tragically and shamefully used to justify many forms of oppression in the past, including slavery and apartheid. It has also been used to justify colonialism, and in Palestine today it continues to play a role, as Mitri Raheb argues:

> Christian theology has played a role in almost all settler-colonial projects, including North America, South Africa, and Australia . . . yet Palestine continues to be the exception. While no one would dare today to cite the Bible to justify settler colonialism in Australia or North America, many Christians and Jews have been doing exactly this for nearly two hundred years, continuing to do so this very day in Palestine.[3]

"Never again!" has once more become "Yet again!"

Christianity and violence should not go hand in hand, at least theoretically. The teachings of Jesus are very clear. The teachings of Paul and the apostles are very clear. There is no place for violence for the followers of Jesus. Yet an honest assessment of even the last 150 years will clearly reveal that many who claimed to be Christians committed some of the worst atrocities in our world: the Belgians in Congo, the Germans in Namibia, the French in Algeria, the Bosnian Serbs in Bosnia-Herzegovina, the genocide against the Tutsi in Rwanda, the Guatemalan genocide against the Maya indigenous people, and of course the Holocaust against the Jewish people in Europe. As I have shown in detail in chapter 4, the Bible and theology have played a significant role in this war of genocide in Gaza. The shameful irony is that Western Christians dare to portray Muslims, or the religion of Islam broadly, as violent! We should listen to Jesus: "Or how can you

---

3. Mitri Raheb, *Decolonizing Palestine: The Land, the People, the Bible* (Orbis Books, 2023), 22–23.

say to your neighbor, 'Let me take the speck out of your eye,' while
the log is in your own eye? You hypocrite, first take the log out of your
own eye, and then you will see clearly to take the speck out of your
neighbor's eye" (Matt. 7:4–5).

To be clear, I fully believe that when Scripture is used to justify
genocide or promote ideologies of supremacy, this use has nothing to
do with the teachings of Jesus nor the essence of the Christian faith.
Yet, shamefully, the church has aligned itself with empire throughout
the centuries. It has chosen the path of power and influence. One
would expect Christians to have learned the lesson. We have not. The
war on Gaza is another piece of evidence that this "theological crisis"
still exists in many Christian churches and traditions.

You Did It to Me

A few days before my ordination as a pastor in the Evangelical Lutheran Church in Jordan and the Holy Land in January of 2016, an
old friend of mine sent me a prayer that he hoped would inspire me
and shape my ministry as a pastor. It was a prayer that is commonly
known as a "Franciscan Blessing"—a prayer that has been with me
since then, challenging and guiding my life and ministry. It reads:

> May God bless you with anger
> at injustice, oppression,
> and exploitation of people,
> so that you may work for
> justice, freedom and peace.
>
> May God bless you with tears,
> to shed for those who suffer pain,
> rejection, hunger, and war,
> so that you may reach out your hand
> to comfort them and
> to turn their pain to joy.
>
> And may God bless you
> with enough foolishness

> to believe that you can
> make a difference in the world,
> so that you can do
> what others claim cannot be done,
> to bring justice and kindness
> to all our children and the poor.[4]

Anger can be a blessing. Tears can be a blessing. So can foolishness. This is a prayer against the passivity and fatalism that characterize much of our world and church life today; the feeling that we can do nothing in the face of evil, resulting in surrender to injustice as the norm. It is a challenge to our lack of faith in the God who taught us that if we have faith like a small mustard seed, then we can move mountains. There is so much injustice in our world, oftentimes at our doorsteps. We can choose to ignore it, be silent and not take a position (which is in itself a position). Or we can choose—empowered by the spirit, guided by our kingdom ideals, and led by our faith in a just and good God—to weep, kindle holy anger, and be foolish enough to believe we can make a difference. Gaza has cried out to the world for the last seventeen years, and in particular for the last twelve months, for justice and compassion. Some responded. Some sacrificed. Some stood in solidarity. Many were silent, passive, and numb.

Over the years, and more so in the last year, Matthew 25:31–46 is a passage that has guided my understanding of the teachings of Christ and what it means to follow Jesus and be a Christian. In this passage, Jesus is teaching about judgment day, and he clearly says that on that day people will be judged based on how they treated those in need:

"Come, you who are blessed by my Father, inherit the kingdom prepared for you from the foundation of the world, for I was hungry and you gave me food, I was thirsty and you gave me some-

4. The prayer often referred to as a "Franciscan Blessing" was written by Sister Ruth Marlene Fox, OSB, in 1985. She composed it for a graduation breakfast at Dickinson State College (now Dickinson State University) in North Dakota. She called it "A Non-Traditional Blessing." See Dan Miller, "A Non-Traditional Blessing," The Almond Tree, July 22, 2016, https://tinyurl.com/3th7s6kp.

thing to drink, I was a stranger and you welcomed me, I was naked and you gave me clothing, I was sick and you took care of me,
I was in prison and you visited me." (Matt. 25:34–36)

I could make the argument that the people Jesus describes here are
the victims of unjust structures. In a perfectly just society, there
should be no persons who are hungry or thirsty, no strangers, no
naked persons, no uncared-for sick, and no prisoners, for a society
is judged by how it cares for the marginalized. Jesus's words here
are fully in line with the prophetic tradition of the Hebrew Scripture,
where the prophets taught that justice in a community is measured
by how that community treated the widow, the orphan, the poor, and
the stranger (e.g., Deut. 24:17–22; Zech. 7:10).[5]

Jesus then claims, in an affirmative manner, that those who do
not do these works of compassion and justice will be cast away:

Then he will say to those at his left hand, "You that are accursed,
depart from me into the eternal fire prepared for the devil and his
angels; for I was hungry and you gave me no food, I was thirsty
and you gave me nothing to drink, I was a stranger and you did
not welcome me, naked and you did not give me clothing, sick
and in prison and you did not visit me." (Matt. 25:41–43)

Jesus could not have been more explicit and direct, and when we spir-
itualize this passage in our readings, we miss the radical nature of his
message. Christians over the years have done their best to turn this passage around, often determining who is a good Christian and who is not
by a particular set of dogmas and beliefs. They have managed to shape-
shift the teaching of Jesus—that the true mark of Christian discipleship
is love, self-denial for the sake of others, and compassion—privileging
instead how orthodox our doctrines are, the size of our churches, or the
wealth we accumulate. The true mark of the way of Jesus, according to
this passage, is love, compassion, and service to others.

5. See Munther Isaac, *From Land to Lands, from Eden to the Renewed
Earth: A Christ-Centered Biblical Theology of the Promised Land* (Langham
Monographs, 2015), 93–96.

Jesus does not stop here. He, then, in the most shocking and provocative manner, unites himself with the "least of these," treating our responses toward the victims of unjust societies as though we ourselves are the perpetrators and Jesus himself the victim:

> "Truly I tell you, just as you did it to one of the least of these brothers and sisters of mine, *you did it to me*. . . . Truly I tell you, just as you did not do it to one of the least of these, *you did not do it to me*." (Matt. 25:40, 45, NRSVue)

You did it to me!

A similar strong warning is echoed in another parable of Jesus, that of the rich person and Lazarus in Luke 16. The parable is known for Jesus's vivid description of eternal damnation, which is the fate of the rich person in the story. Notice how Jesus introduces the characters of the story:

> "There was a rich man who was dressed in purple and fine linen and who feasted sumptuously every day. And *at his gate* lay a poor man named Lazarus, covered with sores, who longed to satisfy his hunger with what fell from the rich man's table; even the dogs would come and lick his sores. (Luke 16:19–21)

Jesus highlights that Lazarus was literally at the gate of the rich person. In other words, Lazarus was within the gaze of the rich person. He must have seen him every single day. The sin of the rich person that merited his eternal damnation, according to Jesus, was not his richness, but his apathy toward Lazarus, who represents the poor of the world. Again, Jesus could not have been more explicit. Apathy and lack of care for the poor bring judgment!

As Christians, who claim to follow Jesus, we must take these warnings seriously. The church must be the embodiment of active love and compassion. The church must not turn away from the problems of our world, but rather ought to strive to end injustice. Christ called those who follow him to act in solidarity with the marginalized, as if it was Christ himself who is hungry, thirsty, naked, and imprisoned. Tragically, the church not only oftentimes fails to do so but in some cases is part of the problem. When the horrors in Gaza were unfolding "at the gate" of our world, visible to all on our TV screens and mobile devices, many responded with apathy. Beyond apathy, scores of Christians went as far as justifying, at times endorsing, the genocide in Gaza. This is a theological crisis.

Where Was the Church?

I have lamented throughout this book that the prophetic voice of the church—the voice of courage that speaks truth to power—was audibly absent in this war. Not only was the church missing the mark prophetically, it was lacking pastorally as well. People are traumatized. They are seeking answers. They are looking for a voice of guidance. They want to experience the comforting presence of God. Instead, in many cases what people got from the church was apathy, silence, or a justification of the war couched in a problematic rhetoric of self-defense and Islamophobia.

During the first year of the genocide, numerous people shared with me that they stopped going to church because of Gaza. Both Palestinians in the diaspora and non-Palestinians recounted traumatic experiences, difficult conversations with their pastors and priests, and hurtful things said from the pulpit. It was heartbreaking for me as a pastor to listen to these painful experiences. I was angry that the church, rather than being a place of comfort where lament could take place, did more harm against its people during such a difficult time.

At the same time, I continue to be amazed by the positive responses to the "Christ in the Rubble" manger and sermon, in Palestine and around the world. "Christ in the Rubble" originated as a pastoral response to the unfolding genocide in Gaza. It was my attempt to console my people amid an unimaginable catastrophe. I was trying to emphasize that God is near, and that Jesus is so near to the children of Gaza that, in fact, he became one of them. I needed to humanize the children of Gaza for my congregation, especially when the world continued to rationalize and justify their killing. Our community needed to reclaim their God-given honor and dignity, to see Jesus in each child pulled from under the rubble.

I have received thousands of messages from all over the world expressing thanks and gratitude, not necessarily for advocating for Gaza, but for speaking directly to the humanity and experiences of Gazans. I believe that God used "Christ in the Rubble" to break open callous hearts and bring comfort and peace to broken souls all over the world. I heard this in person and on social media, from people of diverse backgrounds and faiths. Atheists talked to me. Muslims and Jews as well. Arabs, Brits, Americans, and South Africans. The pain transcended boundaries, and so did the comforting message of "Christ in the Rubble." There was so much pain and vulnerability. And there was much brokenness. In fact, I was shocked by the number of people who told me that I became their "virtual" pastor during the year that genocide unfolded in Gaza and that my sermons sustained their faith.

An experience that I will never forget is meeting a Palestinian Muslim couple in London who had waited long in the queue after my sermon at Bloomsbury Baptist Church to greet me. They introduced themselves; the husband was from Nazareth and his wife was from Gaza. As the husband introduced himself, his wife stood behind him, not able to contain herself. She was visibly shaking, and through her sobs said, "if it was not for your words during this crisis, I don't know how we would have survived. Thank you." I was in tears. I was broken by her brokenness. But I was grateful that God had used my words to bring this family some small sense of comfort.

Pastorally, people needed to hear that God is the God of justice, that God is in solidarity with the oppressed and the marginalized, and that God is actually against violence and oppression! The weaponization of religion by people in power during this war drove many around the world away from their faith. I have always argued that the answer to the question "Where is God when we suffer?" is found in another question, which is: "Where is the church?" I remember the first time I was haunted by this question was when I visited the Holocaust Museum in Jerusalem, accompanied by a Jewish friend. I was deeply troubled, and my Christian upbringing led me to ask over and over: "Where was the church?" Later, I discovered that the church in Germany and Europe was not simply missing but was complicit in the Holocaust. And for Dietrich Bonhoeffer, standing on behalf of the weak is not merely part of the mission of the church; it is the criterion by which Christianity stands or falls:

> Christianity stands or falls by its revolutionary protest against violence, arbitrariness and pride of power, and by its apologia for the weak. I feel that Christianity is doing too little in making these points rather than doing too much. Christianity has adjusted itself much too easily to the worship of power. It should give much more offense, more shock to the world, than it is doing. Christianity should take a much more definite stand for the weak than for the potential moral right of the strong.[6]

Where there is injustice, the church must speak. Where there is oppression, the church must side with the oppressed. Where there is marginalization, the church must humanize the marginalized. Where there is pain, the church must bring comfort. Where there is need, the church must show generosity and compassion. The church is the voice, hands, and feet of Jesus on earth. We are called to continue his ministry on earth. The church must be visibly present in its solidarity with those suffering from injustice. We must

> learn to do good;
> seek justice,
> > rescue the oppressed,
> defend the orphan,
> > plead for the widow. (Isa. 1:17)

We must

> speak out for those who cannot speak,
> > for the rights of all the destitute.
> Speak out, judge righteously,
> > defend the rights of the poor and needy.
> > > > (Prov. 31:8–9)

---

6. *The Collected Sermons of Dietrich Bonhoeffer*, edited and introduced by Isabel Best (Fortress, 2012), 183.

Gaza in 2023 and 2024, and indeed for the last seventeen years, was one test of many in our world. It has become the preeminent global test case. And although I have lamented the silence of many, I must also acknowledge the prophetic witness of the church in its response to Gaza. For in many instances, the church was where it was supposed to be—where it belongs—and that is in the streets!

Thousands all over the world gathered in prayer and protest calling for a cease-fire. Many organizations and movements mobilized, organizing vigils and protests. The Gaza Ceasefire Pilgrimage was exceptional and moving. Launched by a Christian from New Zealand, it inspired movements in forty different locations around the world, where thousands engaged in a peaceful and prayerful show of solidarity with the people of Gaza by walking the length of the Gaza Strip during Lent.[7] Churches for Middle East Peace organized several vigils in Washington, DC, including one before the visit of Netanyahu.[8] There were many vigils for Gaza all over the world. Some demonstrated in front of weapon factories and were arrested.[9] Some organized sit-ins in the US Congress and were also arrested.[10] Thousands demonstrated nonviolently, wrote to their policy makers, campaigned, and pressured politicians.

Some decided to visit us in Palestine in the most difficult of times. I, like many Palestinian Christians, will never forget the solidarity visit from a group of twenty global Christian leaders during Christmas. The majority of the group, thirteen out of twenty, were South Africans. It was led by Rev. Frank Chikane, a veteran of the anti-apartheid struggle in South Africa and a personal hero of mine whom

7. To learn more about this initiative, visit https://tinyurl.com/2wr22xvt.

8. "Prayer for Justice and Peace at Netanyahu Address," Churches for Middle East, July 24, 2024, https://tinyurl.com/4kkpkh6v. Before the vigil, more than two hundred global bishops and Christian leaders issued a call to world leaders to institute a permanent Gaza cease-fire, halt arms sales to Israel, and prevent a broader regional war; see https://tinyurl.com/we4r9pm3.

9. Shane Claiborne, "Good Trouble on Good Friday, Part 2," Red Letter Christians, April 7, 2024, https://tinyurl.com/mtazj2hr.

10. John Nichols, "Christian Peacemakers Are Ramping Up Their Faith-Based Call for a Cease-Fire," *Nation*, April 15, 2024, https://tinyurl.com/2m5m29jt.

I am honored to call a mentor.[11] The visit came in response to an invitation by the Kairos Palestine group, and the original goal was to try to visit the borders of Gaza (this did not materialize due to the severity of the war then), in addition to spending Christmas in Bethlehem with us, knowing that we had canceled our Christmas celebrations. The group made many visits in Jerusalem and Bethlehem and was present when I delivered my "Christ in the Rubble" sermon. During the sermon, I said to them:

> To our friends who are here with us: You have left your families and churches to be with us. You embody the term accompaniment—a costly solidarity. "We were in prison and you visited us." What a stark difference from the silence and complicity of others. Your presence here is the meaning of solidarity. Your visit has already left an impression that will never be taken from us. Through you, God has spoken to us that "we are not forsaken." As Father Rami of the Catholic Church said this morning, you have come to Bethlehem, and like the Magi, you brought gifts, but gifts that are more precious than gold, frankincense, and myrrh. You brought the gift of love and solidarity.[12]

My community was moved by the activism of one thousand African American pastors who, representing hundreds of thousands of congregants in the United States, penned a letter to the White House that made a moral case for a cease-fire. The letter reflects the growing solidarity between African Americans and Palestinians, as African Americans are increasingly recognizing the similarities between the oppressive ideologies they face and the oppression that Palestinians face. Commenting on the statement, Barbara Williams-Skinner, co-convener of the National African American Clergy Network, whose members lead roughly 15 million Black churchgoers, said: "Black

---

11. Frank Chikane's autobiography played an important role in my life: Frank Chikane, *No Life of My Own: An Autobiography*, rev. ed. (Picador Africa, 2012).

12. Munther Isaac, "Christ in the Rubble: A Liturgy of Lament," Red Letter Christians, December 23, 2023, https://tinyurl.com/yxb74nch.

clergy have seen war, militarism, poverty and racism all connected." Rev. Cynthia Hale, the founder and senior pastor of Ray of Hope Christian Church in Georgia, said: "We see [Palestinians] as a part of us. . . . They are oppressed people. We are oppressed people."[13]

These examples, among others, reminded me that many in the church were not silent! My experience resonated with that of the prophet Elijah, who complained that all abandoned him and that he was left alone, only for God to rebuke him and open his eyes to the fact that not all had bowed down to worship Baal. As I write this, not all have bowed to the logic of war and supremacy, and many have spoken up—often at a cost—about the tragedy facing Palestinians. They have kept alive the prophetic tradition of speaking truth to power.

It is telling to see so much international solidarity with Palestinians coming from communities in marginalized or colonial contexts. Oppressed people understand suffering when they see it, because they have been on the receiving end of ideologies and theologies of supremacy and control. It should come as no surprise that it was South Africa that led the case against Israel in the ICJ. They understand apartheid. They understand settler colonialism. They understand solidarity. South African support meant so much to us as Palestinians, something I made sure to communicate in person during my visit in 2024 to South Africa. In my sermon in Cape Town Cathedral, where Archbishop Desmond Tutu commonly organized and preached against apartheid, on a Sunday morning packed with worshipers, I, covered with the Palestinian flag and wearing the keffiyeh, said:

> I have come here to say thank you. Thank you to South Africa for your support and courage. Thank you for your political support in the ICJ. . . . I know it came with a costly price. Thank you to people who have been going out to the streets. We hear you. Thank you to the church. . . . People who experienced colonialism and apartheid have the gift of empathy. The SA in prayer words and action have

---

13. Maya King, "Black Pastors Pressure Biden to Call for a Cease-Fire in Gaza," *New York Times*, January 28, 2024, https://tinyurl.com/4nw69ve7.

been one of the very few signs of hope during this time of distress in the midst of this genocide. It is a powerful sign of integrity.[14]

During the same visit, I was privileged to meet Naledi Pandor, South Africa's foreign minister, who was instrumental in application of the ICJ case. Speaking in front of hundreds of activists in an anti-apartheid conference for Palestine, I thanked the minister by placing my own keffiyeh on her shoulders. This was a symbolic act that led to many tears and thunderous applause in the hall. I said:

> Please accept a very symbolic gift as a token of love, unity and solidarity—the keffiyeh. I know everyone in South Africa seems to be wearing one. But there is symbolism in what I am about to do. To take the keffiyeh from the shoulders of a Palestinian and place it at the shoulder of a South African leader and acknowledge that today you carry our cross with us upon your shoulders.

This is the power of solidarity.

I am not surprised to see a growing number of Jewish supporters of the Palestinian cause around the world, and especially in the United States. In one instance, hundreds of Jewish activists were arrested in Washington, DC, for staging a sit-in against the war in Gaza on Capitol Hill, a day before Israeli prime minister Benjamin Netanyahu was to address a joint meeting of Congress.[15] The demonstration was organized by the group Jewish Voice for Peace (JVP), and their actions stem from the Jewish ethos and prophetic tradition, as well as Jewish experiences of exclusion, persecution, and attempted extermination throughout history. In a statement about the sit-in and arrests, JVP quoted Rabbi Abby Stein, an Israeli American activist and member of the Jewish Voice for Peace Rabbinical Council, who said:

14. "Munther Isaac at St. George Cathedral in Cape Town—May 2024," YouTube, https://tinyurl.com/2x9m29tv.

15. Ayana Archie, "About 200 People Protesting Gaza War Arrested in Congressional Building, Police Say," *NPR News*, July 24, 2024, https://tinyurl.com/3jhrpusy.

The most important commandment in all of Judaism is *pikuach nefesh*, the commandment to save a life. Our Jewish tradition compels us to raise our voices and call on our leaders to do all they can to save the lives of Palestinians in Gaza now.

During the sit-in, over a dozen rabbis wearing hand-made prayer shawls emblazoned with "Never Again for Anyone" led the group through prayer and songs of peace and justice. Hundreds of Jewish and a small number of Christian protesters wore red shirts with the message "Jews Say Stop Arming Israel" and "Not in Our Name," and displayed banners calling for an end to genocide.[16] Their public witness was an incredibly profound prophetic act of recognition that "Never Again" cannot be true unless it is "Never Again for Anyone," and it is clearly rooted in a painful Jewish experience of persecution.

Blessed Are Those Who Speak Truth to Power

In June 2024 I visited the city of Philadelphia and was humbled to be recognized by the city council for my work for peace, upon the initiative of council member Nicolas O'Rourke.[17] I had the chance to address the council and thank them for this recognition. During the day, I became aware that the city council had granted $24 million from federal tax money to the State of Israel. I was perplexed, and even more so when I visited some streets in Philadelphia that are marred by poverty and homelessness. I could not be silent. My recognition meant nothing. And so, when I addressed the council to thank them, I also made sure to add the following:

16. "400 American Jews Mark Netanyahu's Arrival with Congress Sit-In, Calling on Biden and Congress to Stop Arming the Israeli Military as It Wages Genocide in Gaza," *Jewish Voice for Peace*, July 23, 2024, https://tinyurl.com/3h95hchf.
17. Jack Tomczuk, "Council Member Apologizes Following Outburst over Gaza Testimony," Metro Philadelphia, June 13, 2024, https://tinyurl.com/3bdfrnde.

Please accept my candid remark. I am aware that this city council granted $24 million from federal tax money to Israel. This is money that is used for war and revenge. Let us be clear: this war is not about self-defense. This is a vengeance campaign. We are all accountable before God for how we spend and invest in our talents.

Honorable city council members: invest in peace not apartheid. Invest in people, education, and transformation, not in war and segregation. This is how you can actually contribute to peace and justice.

You could have heard a pin drop in the council chamber.

Seeking justice entails unavoidably the concept of speaking truth to power. There may be no other place today where this is true more than in Palestine. One of the points I have emphasized throughout this book is that, for far too long, the Zionists and their Western allies have framed the reality in Palestine as a "conflict," and even worse, a "religious conflict." This framework has given the impression that we are dealing with a dispute between two entities of approximately equal power. And for too long, the Western world has lectured Palestinians on peace, tolerance, and reconciliation.

We have been told that we must accept the other, our occupier. Palestinians have been instructed, time and time again, to give room in our discourse for the Israeli side of the story. We have been labeled radicals for not teaching about Israel and acknowledging its presence in our national narrative, when in fact it was the establishment of the Zionist state of Israel that set a precedent in refusing to acknowledge the legitimacy of Palestinian presence in the land and forcibly removing us from it. Within this logic, colonialism is normalized and ethnic cleansing deemed a natural, unfortunate consequence of wars. Apartheid is considered a conflict. And genocide is declared to be self-defense. And throughout decades of violent military occupation, it has always been deemed the fault of Palestinians for not accepting the "compromises" of our colonizers.

We have been trying to solve a conflict, *when in fact there is no conflict in Palestine, and there is certainly no religious conflict in Palestine.*

We do not have a conflict. We have oppression. We have apartheid. We have an ideology and reality of Jewish supremacy from the river to the sea.[18] We do not have a conflict, but we are dealing with Zionist settler colonialism. What was committed in Gaza is a genocide. We need to call things by their name.

We cannot move forward if we fail to acknowledge this. In fact, by denying these facts, one is clearly choosing the ways of empire: supremacy, domination, and elimination.

Similarly, speaking truth to power means that we need to acknowledge and name all forms of Zionism for what they truly are. Palestinian theologian Tony Deik has made a compelling argument that Christians must take a clear moral and theological stand against Christian Zionism:

> At the core of what Christians are commissioned to proclaim to the world, in word and deed, are the goodness, righteousness, and love of God, as evidenced in the person of Jesus Christ. Now this simple-yet-powerful proclamation is completely incompatible with Christian Zionism. And here I don't mean only dispensational Christian Zionism. Rather, I mean the full scale of soft- and hard-core theologies used to legitimize the Zionist settler-colonial project: from the dispensational all the way to the liberal, and including the continuously evolving post-holocaust and post-supersessionist theologies and biblical interpretations. These theologies neither proclaim God's goodness nor God's love, let alone God's justice and righteousness. Rather, these theologies proclaim that God is a racist. This might be a strong accusation, but I'm not making a straw man argument here. The burden of the proof is on Zionist theologians to tell us otherwise: to tell us how, especially after Jesus Christ, God can still have a special relation with a particular nation or race—including the giving of land inhabited by other people—and be a just and fair

---

18. "A Regime of Jewish Supremacy from the Jordan River to the Mediterranean Sea: This Is Apartheid," B'Tselem, January 12, 2021, https://tinyurl.com/4msybce7.

God who is not a racist. On what basis does God favor a particular nation over another, especially after Jesus Christ?[19]

Zionism is an ideology and a movement that engaged in settler colonialism by establishing a state for the Jewish people on someone else's land, systematically and deliberately committing ethnic cleansing of the Palestinian people. Zionism has established a system of apartheid, enforced by an aggressive military occupation. In Gaza, the Zionist Israeli government carried out a genocide. Justifying such acts is at the core of Zionism as a political ideology. And to my Christian readers I ask: Can we really put the word "Christian" before all this? Are colonialism, ethnic cleansing, apartheid, and genocide compatible with Christian ethics and the teachings of Jesus? Many Jewish people protest that these tactics are incongruent with their *Jewish* ethos and values. I wish more Christians would confess this simple yet profound truth. This is precisely why we need to call out Zionism for what it truly is, and make it an interfaith priority to combat Zionist theology with a holistic vision of justice and equality.

A *Kairos* Moment

In August 2024, I visited the United States, and this time I spoke mainly to churches and activists. I was inspired by the warm reception I received and was humbled to see the impact of my words over the last year. I was particularly moved by the noticeable presence of Jews and Muslims in almost all the churches I visited. This is not the typical audience when I speak in churches in the United States; and it was clear that new alliances were being made. Gaza was uniting people across religious divides who found commonality in their hunger and thirst for justice.

During this visit I spoke at the famous Riverside Church in New York City, the place where Martin Luther King Jr. used to speak regu-

---

19. Tony Deik, "CATC2024 Day 4: Missiology After Gaza; Christian Zionism, God's Image, and the Gospel," Christ at the Checkpoint YouTube Channel, June 3, 2024, https://tinyurl.com/syj23t5s.

larly, and where he made his famous speech, "Beyond Vietnam." The church was packed, and I sensed palpable anger, pain, and a passion for justice in the audience. In my talk, I said that the moment we live is a *kairos* moment for the church:

It is very common in theological circles to speak of a Kairos moment. Kairos could mean an appointed time for the purposes of God, or an opportune time. It is time in which the faithful need to have discernment about unfolding drama of history, and act prophetically. One of the most profound prophetic and kairos moments in biblical tradition is in 2 Samuel 12. It happened when the prophet Nathan had to confront King David with his sin of greed, adultery, murder, exploiting the vulnerable, and taking what is not his own. To do so, Nathan gave a story, with a clear message, that was followed with a strong conclusion:

"And the Lord sent Nathan to David. He came to him and said to him, 'There were two men in a certain city, the one rich and the other poor. The rich man had very many flocks and herds, but the poor man had nothing but one little ewe lamb that he had bought. He brought it up, and it grew up with him and with his children; it used to eat of his meager fare and drink from his cup and lie in his bosom, and it was like a daughter to him. Now there came a traveler to the rich man, and he was loath to take one of his own flock or herd to prepare for the wayfarer who had come to him, but he took the poor man's lamb and prepared that for the guest who had come to him.'"

The Bible then says that David burned with anger against the man. He said to Nathan, "As the Lord lives, the man who has done this deserves to die; he shall restore the lamb fourfold because he did this thing and because he had no pity."

Nathan's response is so profound, so courageous, and so prophetic. It is also so much needed today. Nathan said to David: "You are the man!"

"You are the man!" This is Nathan's challenge to the empire of his time. It took courage. But he had to speak truth to power. He had to uncover the exploitation of the vulnerable, even if it meant challenging his own king. This was Nathan's "kairos moment." What is happening in Gaza and Palestine today is a "kairos moment" that demands a similar prophetic courage. This is a "You are the man!" moment.[20]

It is time to call things by their name. Israel has committed war crimes, indeed, a genocide. Its military occupation of Palestine *is* apartheid. Zionism is racism. Israel is a settler-colonial entity. We must call things by name. And we must stand with those who are suffering under these specific forms of violence. This is not the time for neutrality. South African pastor and anti-apartheid activist Frank Chikane's challenge to the church in the 1980s in response to apartheid in South Africa applies today to Palestine:

> The church, to be church in the world today, must reject the dominant ideology of the powerful and take the way of the Cross. This, of course, will mean that it will have to take the side of the weak, poor and powerless in the world.[21]

The church, to truly be the church, must take the side of the oppressed and the marginalized. There are times in which the church cannot be neutral. There are times in which neutrality serves to empower the oppressors. When Christians hide behind slogans of peace and reconciliation to avoid taking sides, they serve the purposes of the aggressor. Taking sides can often be costly. Solidarity is by definition costly. Jesus never sought comfort or conformity. His ways were always controversial and sacrificial, and I am surprised by how much Christians and church leaders try to avoid precisely these two things: controversy and sacrifice.

My talk at Riverside Church was certainly emotional and uplifting, and I cannot deny the sense of awe I felt to speak from the place where

20. To listen to the talk: "Silence Is Complicity: Rev. Dr. Munther Isaac Calls upon U.S. Churches—August 14, 2024," The Riverside Church YouTube Channel, August 16, 2024, https://tinyurl.com/5xaesst3.
21. Chikane, *No Life of My Own*, 74.

Martin Luther King challenged the logic of wars and the militarization of the United States in his famous "Beyond Vietnam" speech. I could not at the time but feel sad. Here I was, fifty-seven years after that powerful historic speech, still arguing against militarism in the United States. According to a report by the Watson Institute for International and Public Affairs at Brown University, the United States provided $17.9 billion in military aid to Israel from October 7, 2023, to September 30, 2024.[22] Let this number sink in for a moment. It is ironic that a country that has a day to commemorate the life and legacy of MLK continues at the same time to go against his prophetic appeal against wars and violence. The same applies, by the way, to how archbishop and Nobel Prize–winner Desmond Tutu is remembered in many church circles: he is honored and respected in every way, with the exception of when he talked about Palestine and called out Israeli apartheid.[23] If $17.9 billion is not enough to make faith leaders realize the kind of *kairos* moment we live in, I don't know what will. Imagine the good that could have been done with this amount of money, in the United States and the world! This is why I made sure to call out faith leaders in the United States in my talk at Riverside Church, for it is American tax money that funded this war of genocide:

> I am here in the US. This is a different context, because we all know too well that this war of genocide would not be possible without the financial and military support of the US and without the political cover of the US. Friends, it is your money, and it is the officials you have elected. In your silence over those decisions, you are telling us in essence that you approve how your Congress and president spend your money, and that if money is spent on apartheid and genocide, you don't mind.[24]

22. Muhammet Tarhan and İbrahim Hamdi Hacıcaferoğlu, "US Provided $17.9B in Military Aid to Israel Since October 2023," Anadolu Agency, October 30, 2024, https://tinyurl.com/4954zxr4

23. Chris McGreal, "When Desmond Tutu Stood Up for the Rights of Palestinians, He Could Not Be Ignored," *Guardian*, December 30, 2021, https://tinyurl.com/mxwj65jj.

24. "Silence Is Complicity: Rev. Dr. Munther Isaac Calls upon U.S.

CHAPTER 8

Repentance

In chapter 6, I spoke about the "Call for Repentance" that a group of Palestinian Christians made at the beginning of the war. A few months later, a group of influential progressive evangelicals responded to our call. It was an honest response and a declaration of repentance. In it, they stated:

> We confess that we have failed to recognize the ways we have operated according to the logics of white supremacy; accepting the false narrative that Palestinian and Arab people are our inherent enemies.
> We confess we have valued Palestinian and Arab lives less than others.
> We confess that we have equated the State of Israel with the Israel of the Old Testament.
> We confess that we have been afraid. Fearful of what others may say or think if we speak up, fearful of consequences to us—without thinking too deeply of the costs that you have paid.
> We confess that we have let the sense of being so dwarfed by the powers of Israel/Palestine, the pervasive influence in America of dispensational eschatology, and the elephant of American militarism, that we have chosen silence rather than courage.
> We confess that we have accepted the forced displacement of Palestinians from their homes and ancestral lands.
> We confess that we have failed to speak up for a just settlement that allows all to live in peace and security.
> We confess that we have done far too little to counter the dominant theology that supports the Israeli occupation and violence against those made in the image of God.
> We confess that all too often particular theological perspectives have fueled blind support for the State of Israel and its actions. We recognize and accept Israel's existence as a nation-

Churches," The Riverside Church YouTube Channel, August 14, 2024, https://tinyurl.com/y4m8uhwm.

state. Theologically, however, we do not believe that the modern state of Israel is the same as ancient Israel portrayed in Scripture, nor do we envision the modern state as a harbinger of Christ's return. We reject all theological perspectives that promote Christian Zionism and justify Israel's oppressive policies and practices towards Palestinians.

We repent. Repentance is a process. For some of us, this repentance journey began decades ago. For others, the journey began six months ago. Regardless of when our journey began, we commit ourselves today to sit together for mutual learning and dialogue, debate, and rigorous examination of biblical, theological, and political issues. We long for our assumptions and biases to be exposed, for teachability and deep love, in order to act out of deeper/more faithful convictions. We want to learn and to listen to you, so you might help us be freed from our silence, paralysis, and unrecognized prejudice. As we all do our work in varied lands and contexts, we hold in common the reality of the love, mercy, and justice of God in Jesus Christ that is with us now and always.

We repent of our feeble advocacy, ignorance, and/or silence about this war, and about the underlying oppression of Palestinians. This leads us to humble dependence on God's mercy. In the light of the suffering, resurrected Lord who laid down his life to defeat all the powers of death, vengeance, hostility, and oppression and rose again so that we can live reconciled to God and each other, we repent of all theologies and practical support that justifies oppression, hostility, vengeance, erasure, and death in the name of Christ.

We stand in solidarity with, and in compassion for, all who are suffering the death of loved ones, the daily violence and brutal injustices, and the oppressive forces that are erasing hope. Many of us have expressed our solidarity with such statements as that from INFEMIT, from the Archdiocese of South Africa, from Churches for Middle East Peace and from the global Gaza Ceasefire Pilgrimage, but we here now express our further solidarity.

We call for an immediate and sustained ceasefire, the unconditional end to the genocide in Gaza, ethnic cleansing in the West

Bank, and an end to Israeli Occupation. We support a solution that leads to the restoration of political and social rights, self-governance, and the right of all Palestinians to self-determination.

Finally, sisters and brothers, we recognize that you have stood—and continue to stand—as faithful and courageous followers of Jesus of Nazareth, the Christ, amidst the long and daily horror of Gaza and the West Bank since Nakba, and even more intensively since October 2023. Though we have been inadequate in our solidarity with you, we now join you in faith and hope in the God who is seeking to remake our narratives for the thriving of all peoples in Palestine and Israel and beyond, and for the well-being of the entire creation. With you, we plead: Lord, have mercy on us![25]

I pray and hope that there will be more changes of heart, mind, and soul like the one of this group, not merely for the sake of Palestinians but for the sake of the credibility of our Christian witness. I pray that such a repentance is accompanied with activism, active solidarity, and peacemaking. It is high time Christians unite for the sake of justice and righteousness in Palestine.

This War Has Lasted Far Too Long

After my Christmas message, friends of mine approached me and asked if I would join and endorse their planned Lenten campaign to advocate for a cease-fire. My initial thinking at the time was that surely this war would be over by Lent. I never imagined that it would last until Easter. Yet here we are, passing the one-year anniversary of the war while completing this manuscript, still pleading and calling for a cease-fire. In many ways, it feels as if we are simply calling for the world to humanize Palestinians.

This war has lasted for far too long. Many other means could have achieved very different outcomes. Negotiations and diplomacy did

---

25. "Response to: A Call for Repentance; An Open Letter from Palestinian Christians to Western Church Leaders and Theologians," INFEMIT, April 22, 2024, https://tinyurl.com/y2yn8u7r.

achieve something in the beginning, when there was an exchange of detained Palestinians and Israelis. Despite the many efforts for a cease-fire agreement, nothing substantial was achieved after that first deal. The longer the war stretched on, the more scores of people were killed, including Israeli hostages. While the West continued to blame Hamas for not accepting the terms of a cease-fire, there was little doubt among Israelis that it was Netanyahu and his revenge-thirsty warlords who were extending this war for their own political gains.[26] In fact, Biden himself said, seven months into the war, that there is "every reason" to draw the conclusion that Netanyahu is prolonging the war in Gaza for his own political self-preservation.[27] In my opinion, we should blame everyone for this continuous horror— Israelis, Palestinians, Americans, Qataris, Egyptians, Iranians, and all other stakeholders. They are all to be blamed for not prioritizing human lives over politics. Far too many people have suffered due to the interests of a few in positions of power.

"This war will end if Hamas releases the hostages," is a comment I received frequently on social media from Zionist agitators. Surely, I want to see the Israeli and Palestinian hostages released. But are we positive that if Hamas released the Israeli hostages the war would be over? There are no Israeli hostages in the West Bank, but that has not stopped the routine killing of Palestinians, confiscation of land, and continuous colonization of Palestine over the last seven decades. This war did not begin on October 7, and returning to where things stood prior to October 7 would not resolve it. There must be a comprehensive solution to the Palestinian question that is based on justice and equity, in accordance with international law. We must reach the conclusion that the future of Palestinians and Israelis is one. Our shared future will be "either the cycle of violence that destroys both of us or peace that will benefit both," as the Kairos Pales-

26. Orly Halpern, "Scenes from Israel, Where Protesters Blame Netanyahu for the Deaths of Hostages," *Time*, September 2, 2024, https://tinyurl.com/cyznm7fk.

27. Julian Borger and Andrew Roth, "Biden: 'Every Reason' to Believe Netanyahu Is Prolonging Gaza War for Political Gain," *Guardian*, June 4, 2024, https://tinyurl.com/4pd84ce7.

tine document puts it.[28] There can be no future, let alone prosperity and security, for one side without the other. We must arrive at a place in which there is no apartheid, no supremacy, and no "might is right." If you want to see the Israeli hostages released, you must also want all Palestinian hostages released.

Moreover, we cannot and should not advocate for a cease-fire without also calling for those who committed war crimes to be held accountable. Otherwise, what kind of a world are we leaving for our children, if we surrender to the idea that the powerful can kill and displace because "they can," and then get away with it?

And, yes, we must arrive at a place where Jews feel secure. Antisemitism is evil. There should be no place for racist hatred ideologies in our world. And I will be the first to admit that some forms of antisemitism exist among Palestinians and pro-Palestinian groups and individuals. But antisemitism is not a Palestinian problem as much as it is a Western problem. Further, the response to antisemitism cannot be exclusion and supremacy, or support of apartheid and colonialism. Safety is not achieved by committing a genocide. Wars only sow hatred and resentment. The fact that the world keeps allowing Israel into this position of bullying and massacring others is an indictment against those who claim to be supporters of Jews. They are jeopardizing the future of all peoples in the region. This cannot be the mark of genuine friendship toward the Jewish people. In fact, I am shocked by the antisemitic discourse even among those who support Israel. Trump infamously claimed that Jews who do not support him "hate Israel" and "their religion,"[29] and that Jews are to blame if he does not win the elections,[30] while Biden claimed that Jews can only be safe in Israel, saying on several occasions that "were

---

28. "Kairos Document: A Moment of Truth; A Word of Faith, Hope and Love from the Heart of Palestinian Suffering" [Bethlehem, 2009], https://tinyurl.com/2d8864jr, section 4.3, p. 8.

29. Jill Colvin, "Trump Says Jews Who Vote for Democrats 'Hate Israel' and Their Religion," *AP News*, updated March 19, 2024, https://tinyurl.com/c4wn4p8v.

30. Gregory Krieg and Kit Maher, "Trump Says at Antisemitism Event That Jewish Voters Would Bear Some Blame If He Loses in November," *CNN*, September 20, 2024, https://tinyurl.com/3v9pwdam.

there no Israel, there wouldn't be a Jew in the world who was safe."[31] I hope I do not need to convince you of the antisemitism in these claims. Trump is playing the "blame it on the Jew" tune again! And does Biden really believe that Jews will perish if they remain in the United States or Europe, and as such they must move to Israel so that they can be safe? This is the same racism inherent in the slogan that can be considered the root cause for this tragedy we find ourselves in: "A land without people for people without land." This is such a racist statement on multiple levels. Not only did this statement dehumanize the indigenous Palestinians by framing the land as empty, it also considered Jews as not belonging to the places they lived in for generations. German, British, and Russian Jews were considered as "people without land." Is this not antisemitism?

The Way Forward

This war has created brutal catastrophes on multiple levels, one of those being the horrifying numbers of Palestinians murdered. Behind each person killed is a dream killed, and wounds and scars of these deaths will take generations to heal. The level of destruction is so enormous it will take decades to rebuild Gaza.[32] Close to two million Palestinians are currently homeless, as their homes are partially or completely destroyed. Assuming they survive the genocide, the question that will haunt them is: What does the future hold? Where will they live? The enmity, hatred, and resentments between the two peoples in the land have increased to a level that makes one wonder if healing and restoration are still possible.

In July 2024, the Israeli Knesset voted to affirm its opposition to the establishment of a Palestinian state. The resolution stated that

31. Sophie Hurwitz, "Why Does Biden Keep Making the Same Dangerous Comment About Jews?" *Nation*, March 6, 2024, https://tinyurl.com/yh6vzaa3.

32. Joseph Krauss and Sarah El Deeb, "Gaza Is in Ruins After Israel's Yearlong Offensive. Rebuilding May Take Decades," *AP News*, October 9, 2024, https://tinyurl.com/3s8m4aad.

"the establishment of a Palestinian state in the heart of the Land of Israel would constitute an existential threat to the State of Israel and its citizens, perpetuate the Israeli-Palestinian conflict and destabilize the region."[33] In other words, Israel officially stated the obvious, publicly declaring that they have no intention of pursuing a two-state solution. One ethnocratic state is what Israel has been working altogether to achieve for years, especially through the covert annexation of the West Bank through settlement expansion. Israel officially declared that the only viable solution adopted by the international community and the United States is no longer on the table. Needless to say, neither the United States nor the international community responded firmly to this. Some countries made "statements" while others were "concerned." This decision by the Israeli Knesset shows the paralysis of the international community when it comes to Israel.

So, what is the way forward? Let us consider first the political options that stand before us. This is when understanding the reality as settler colonialism, rather than as "conflict," is crucial. We cannot begin talking about the future until we admit that we were wrong all along to think of the situation as a conflict. We cannot speak of a future solution without addressing the reality of apartheid. We cannot imagine a solution that does not involve recognizing that war crimes have taken place and those who committed these crimes must be held accountable. We cannot talk about a future state without acknowledging Zionism as a racist ideology that seeks to subjugate the Palestinians, not to live with them.

According to Rashid Khalidi, settler-colonial confrontations with indigenous peoples have only ever ended in one of three ways: "with the elimination or full subjugation of the native population, as in North America; with the defeat and expulsion of the colonizer, as in Algeria, which is extremely rare; or with the abandonment of

33. Noa Shpigel, "With Gantz's Backing, Israel's Parliament Passes Resolution Opposing Palestinian Statehood," *Haaretz*, July 18, 2024, https://tinyurl.com/mu5mv59j.

colonial supremacy, in the context of compromise and reconciliation, as in South Africa, Zimbabwe, and Ireland."[34]

Option one, the elimination or full subjugation of the native population, horrifies me. The genocide in Gaza made us fear that this could become a reality one day, and that the world would permit such an outcome. Yet, despite all odds, Palestinians, who are survivors by nature, have managed to remain in the land, and today the numbers of Palestinians and Israelis in the land are almost identical, albeit with huge disparities in power, rights, and wealth. This status quo is unsustainable. For years, Palestinians and international political experts have warned that things would eventually explode, and they did. Now we fear it could happen in the West Bank, or even in East Jerusalem, which could be even more catastrophic. We are hoping, praying, and working tirelessly against this possibility.

Option two, the defeat and expulsion of the colonizer, is very unlikely given the unconditional support of the world powers for Israel. In all cases, driving a people out of the land cannot be the way forward. Restorative justice for the Palestinians does not necessarily mean driving Israelis out of the land. Justice is restorative, not retributive. The goal is justice and equality, not revenge, and the ultimate ideal is to share the land as neighbors, with equal rights and without subjugation. Very few Palestinians advocate for Israelis to be removed from the land. This is why option three, namely, the abandonment of colonial supremacy in a context of compromise and reconciliation, makes the most sense from both a practical and a faith-based standpoint.

Colonial supremacy and apartheid must come to an end. The separation wall must be torn down. Before we build, we must dismantle. This should be the first and immediate step after the ceasefire and the beginning of the rebuilding of Gaza. International talks about peace and reconciliation cannot resume until we have fully dismantled apartheid in Palestine. I would even argue that we should not spend time discussing the details of specific solutions unless it is

34. Rashid Khalidi, *The Hundred Years' War on Palestine: A History of Settler Colonialism and Resistance, 1917-2017* (Holt, 2020), 239.

established that apartheid or any ideology of supremacy must come to an end first, and that we work toward that end.

A lot has been said about the one-state and two-state questions. I believe that ultimately it is up to Israel to decide. Israel has created a tragic dilemma wherein the current status quo is unsustainable. By refusing a Palestinian state, Israel has chosen to maintain a status quo that only leads to more violence and bloodshed. You cannot suffocate and oppress millions, in their own homeland, and expect no resistance. Israel is creating new Gazas now in the West Bank. Palestinians are suffocated in isolated and walled-off communities in which the Israeli military controls all entrances and exits of our major cities, as well as the land and the roads surrounding them. Israel is killing the possibility of any life with dignity and self-determination for the Palestinians in their own land. Yet by denying the Palestinians a state of their own, which is the consensus solution of the international community, Israel will ultimately realize that a single state with equal rights is the ultimate result of their policy. Palestinians have nowhere to go, aside from being granted emigration status to foreign countries. Those remaining are here, steadfast in our land. Thousands were murdered and millions displaced over the years, but we have remained in our land, while many of those displaced have not given up on their right to return to their land and homes.

The moment we now live in represents a true test for the international community: Should international law be upheld? Do human rights matter? If they do, we are obligated to comply with them. If not, then decision makers should be clear that there are those like Israel and its allies who are above the law. And in this case, the church must speak out. The appeal of Archbishop of Canterbury Justin Welby in the wake of the ICJ ruling about the illegality of the occupation is commendable:

At a time when the world is marked by increasing violations of international law—and commitment to a rules-based system is in question—it is imperative that governments around the world reaffirm their unwavering commitment to all decisions by the International Court of Justice, irrespective of the situation. International law protects our shared humanity, and safeguards human dignity and flourishing. To resist a world where actions such as torture, hostage-taking and indiscriminate violence become the norm, we must apply the law without fear or favour in all circumstances. But for too long it has been applied and upheld in a selective manner that threatens our common peace and security. Now is the time to reverse that deeply damaging trend. . . . It is clear that ending the occupation is a legal and moral necessity. I pray that all UN member states respond positively to this Advisory Opinion by ensuring their individual and common actions are consistent with it—and pave the way for the realisation of the Palestinian people's fundamental right to self-determination.[35]

I, like other Palestinian Christian leaders, have been critical at times of Archbishop Welby. Yet his passionate appeals for a ceasefire throughout the war are clearly an indication of a leader who is guided by Christian principles and compassion. And I strongly support this statement and the logic behind it, namely, that we need to live in a world where the rule of law is agreed on and implemented. Currently, the ICJ represents this common framework. The alternative is not just chaos but the rule of the logic of empire—that might is always right. As Christians who are guided by the ethics of Jesus, we must be the first to challenge the logic of empire. And we must also challenge those who, from positions of privilege and superiority, conveniently use religious texts to endorse self-entitlement as if they are above the law. And in a time when decision makers seem content to render Israel exempt from international law, we must speak up, organize, and demand justice.

Rather than discussing a one-state or two-state solution, we must work on global boycott, divestment, and sanctions (BDS) actions against Israel. Such actions are not discriminatory but rather function to pressure Israel, an occupying state, to comply with in-

---

35. "Archbishop of Canterbury Statement on the ICJ's Advisory Opinion on Israel and the Occupied Palestinian Territories," Archbishop of Canterbury, August 2, 2024, https://tinyurl.com/kda9a3wy.

ternational law. The BDS movement needs grassroots mobilization. The people must take the lead, as it is clear that most politicians will not, and university students around the world can be an instrumental force in this movement. We cannot achieve justice in Palestine without this true and costly solidarity from the people of the world. Our collective humanity compels us to join in shared work toward ending colonialism and apartheid.

And my vision is that people of faith will lead interfaith campaigns toward this end. Such efforts would be a true manifestation of interfaith prophetic solidarity and activism. It is the kind of interfaith solidarity that we witnessed in the struggle against racism and segregation in the civil rights movement, and in the struggle against apartheid in South Africa. And we are beginning to witness this kind of struggle forming around the world for a free Palestine. When I saw Christians, Jews, and Muslims gather together at Bloomsbury Baptist Church in London and Riverside Church in New York City—in solidarity with the people of Gaza, hungry for justice and righteousness—it felt like a taste of the kingdom of God.

For Christians, costly solidarity goes beyond words and acts of charity. Solidarity, by definition, entails sacrifice. It is stepping out of places of comfort. It is accepting the radical call of Jesus to deny oneself for the sake of love, and showing the world a better way of being the true humanity God intended us to be. It is the kind of solidarity that gets one criticized, falsely accused, slandered, and possibly even arrested—all for the sake of righteousness. Did not Jesus say:

> "Blessed are those who are persecuted *for righteousness' sake*, for theirs is the kingdom of heaven" (Matt. 5:10)?

Just as I declared that Gaza has become the preeminent moral test case of our world, similarly, we can say that justice for Palestinians, the end of apartheid, and true peace in the land are a righteous cause. Actualizing justice and healing for Palestinians who have survived years of brutality and dehumanization is a call of righteousness.

EPILOGUE

Hope, Survival, and Sumud

C an we dare to hope? Should we even preach "hope" in the midst of a genocide?

How can we talk about hope when we have lost more than seventeen thousand children in Gaza?

How can we talk about hope when millions have lost their homes?

How can we talk about hope when settler attacks are on the rise?

How can we talk about hope when the person who led the Gaza genocide, and one of the architects of an apartheid reality, is received and welcomed in Congress as a hero?

How can we hope when Arab leaders watch and do nothing to stop the bloodshed?

How can we hope when ideologies of supremacy and exclusion dominate our world?

How can we hope when many churches side with the empire, repeat its rhetoric, and play its tune, all while claiming they are on the side of peace?

How can we hope when the Bible continues to be weaponized against the Palestinian people?

How can we hope after seventy-six years of an ongoing Nakba?

I must admit that over the course of last year, I began to doubt myself and the validity of preaching hope, even if I have done so perhaps more than anybody else during this war. I have written and spoken much about hope. But I have begun to wonder: Is it fair to ask people to have hope when their existence is at stake? Instead, I have often opted to talk about "survival." The goal is to survive, one day at a time. Survival makes more sense. Survival is more real and authentic. And in a war of genocide, in a context of seventy-six years of settler colonialism and an ongoing Nakba, survival, though a long shot, seems like the thing to strive for. We hope to survive the Nakba. Gazans hope to survive the genocide. It is very difficult for many Palestinians to even talk beyond this.

But—hope?

In a passionate talk at the Christ at the Checkpoint conference in Bethlehem in May 2024, during the height of the genocide, young Palestinian theologian Lamma Mansour challenged the audience to "still hope." It was a moving talk that challenged us to continue to hope despite all odds, and help the world imagine a different reality:

> We cannot allow our vision of what is possible to be dictated by the powers and principalities of this world. We cannot leave the task of imagination to oppressors. This living hope that we have in God empowers us to envision a different reality; to challenge the imaginations of exclusion and supremacy.[1]

When we stop hoping, we declare that we give in to tyranny and oppression, allowing the oppressors of the empire to shape our reality. When we stop hoping, we accept that injustice is the norm. Hope in this sense is a struggle. It is painful. It is illogical. It even feels wrong, at times. But we cannot surrender to the alternative.

Sumud is the Arabic word for steadfastness. It is commonly used to refer to Palestinian steadfastness in the face of the assaults of Zionism. *Sumud*, in its essence, encompasses Palestinian resilience. It is about refusing to forget the past. It is about rootedness in the land that can be shaken but never uprooted. *Sumud* is Palestinian refugees holding

---

1. Lamma Mansour, "CATC2024 Day 4: A Christ-Centered Response in Times of War—Dr. Lamma Mansour," Christ at the Checkpoint YouTube Channel, June 5, 2024, https://tinyurl.com/54ksywf3.

to their right of return, but it is also beyond that. It is about preserving memory, such as when a descendant of the 1948 Nakba wears the *thub* (Palestinian traditional dress) of the village and continues to name the village of her parents or grandparents as their place of origin.

Yet the path forward seems to be marked with more suffering and pain. Until then, we will continue to fight for our existence and survival, and to hope against hope that our children will be able to, and choose to, live in this land. And we will continue to pray.

Years after the Nakba, and even after the Gaza genocide, we will not give up our hope and desire to live in dignity in our land. Hope and *sumud* go hand in hand. The Kairos Palestine document says:

> One of the most important signs of hope is the steadfastness of the generations, the belief in the justice of their cause and the continuity of memory, which does not forget the "Nakba" (catastrophe) and its significance.[2]

The prophet Habakkuk resembles and embodies this *sumud*. In his pain and anguish, he refused to surrender to despair. In the conclusion of the small book of Habakkuk, which was characterized by his lament and even questioning of God, he declared in defiance:

> Though the fig tree does not blossom,
> and no fruit is on the vines;
> though the produce of the olive fails
> and the fields yield no food;
> though the flock is cut off from the fold
> and there is no herd in the stalls,
> yet I will rejoice in the LORD;
> I will exult in the God of my salvation.
> GOD, the Lord, is my strength;
> he makes my feet like the feet of a deer,
> and makes me tread upon the heights. (Hab. 3:17–19)

2. "Kairos Document: A Moment of Truth; A Word of Faith, Hope and Love from the Heart of Palestinian Suffering" [Bethlehem, 2009], https://tinyurl.com/2d8864jr, section 3.3.3, p. 6.

This is a statement of *sumud*. I can imagine the pain in uttering such a statement in a time of despair. He chose to speak this affirmation contrary to his feelings and his perceptions of reality. This is, in fact, a declaration of commitment to pursue God as one's only source of hope. Jesus said something similar when he encouraged us not to give up when it is justice that we are asking for. In a parable about prayer, Jesus told a story of a widow who relentlessly petitioned an unjust judge to grant her justice. This judge who, according to Jesus, had "no fear of God and no respect for anyone," refused the widow's request for a while, but finally gave up and granted her justice because the widow "kept bothering him." Jesus here invites us to bother God the same way this widow kept bothering this judge. It is amazing that Jesus is willing to compare God to an unjust ruler, in order to motivate his followers to pray and not give up in their demands for justice. So the parable concludes with these words:

> "And will not God grant justice to his chosen ones who cry to him day and night? Will he delay long in helping them? I tell you, he will quickly grant justice to them. And yet, when the Son of Man comes, will he find faith on earth?" (Luke 18:7–8)

Prayer, in a situation like this, is an act of *sumud*. Insisting on justice is *sumud*. Prayer, as such, is resistance. It is about resisting the surrender to the normalization of pain and injustice. We as Palestinians carry with us our generational wounds and pain from years of injustice. But in our *sumud*, which is grounded in our rootedness in the land of our mothers and fathers, in our faith in the justice of our cause, and in our faith in a just God, we, like this widow in the parable of Jesus, must hold firm to our faith that justice must be granted—that justice will be granted. Jesus's words compel us to pray, and pray without ceasing, until justice is granted. Jesus challenges us here to keep bothering God—the one who acts "with steadfast love, justice, and righteousness in the earth" (Jer. 9:24). Because we know who God is, we will continue praying and pleading.

In our call to Christians around the world to repent, we the twelve Palestinian Christian organizations made the following conclusion:

We also remind ourselves and our Palestinian people that our *sumud* ("steadfastness") is anchored in our just cause and our historical rootedness in this land. As Palestinian Christians, we also continue to find our courage and consolation in the God who dwells with those of a contrite and humble spirit (Isa 57:15). We find courage in the solidarity we receive from the crucified Christ, and we find hope in the empty tomb. We are also encouraged and empowered by the costly solidarity and support of many churches and grassroots faith movements around the world, challenging the dominance of ideologies of power and supremacy. We refuse to give in, even when our siblings abandon us. We are steadfast in our hope, resilient in our witness, and continue to be committed to the Gospel of faith, hope, and love, in the face of tyranny and darkness. "In the absence of all hope, we cry out our cry of hope. We believe in God, good and just. We believe that God's goodness will finally triumph over the evil of hate and of death that still persist in our land. We will see here 'a new land' and 'a new human being,' capable of rising up in the spirit to love each one of his or her brothers and sisters."

We Will Recover

Refaat Alareer was my age when he was murdered. He was a Palestinian poet, and professor of world literature and creative writing at the Islamic University of Gaza. He was a cofounder of We Are Not Numbers—a nonprofit organization that aims to amplify the voices of Palestinian youth living in Gaza and the refugee camps. He edited several books that had short stories, essays, photos, and poetry by young writers documenting their lives under Israeli blockade.[3] He was loved by his students.[4]

---

3. Sana Noor Haq and Abeer Salman, "Prominent Gaza Professor and Writer Killed in Airstrike, Weeks After Telling CNN He and His Family Had 'Nowhere Else to Go,'" *CNN*, December 12, 2023, https://tinyurl.com/yd9t57j3.

4. Alia Kassab, "Remembering Refaat Alareer, in the Words of His Student," *Al Jazeera*, January 16, 2014, https://tinyurl.com/ycyw4v7h.

On December 6, 2023, Refaat was killed by an Israeli Defense Forces (IDF) airstrike, along with his brother, his nephew, his sister, and three of her children. Refaat was survived by his wife and six children. His eldest daughter, Shaimaa, her husband, Mohammed Siyam, and their newborn baby were killed by an Israeli airstrike on their home in Gaza City.

Upon Refaat's killing, one of his poems, written in English, caught the attention of Palestinians and people around the world. He writes:

> If I must die,
> you must live
> to tell my story
> to sell my things
> to buy a piece of cloth
> and some strings,
> (make it white with a long tail)
> so that a child, somewhere in Gaza
> while looking heaven in the eye
> awaiting his dad who left in a blaze—
> and bid no one farewell
> not even to his flesh
> not even to himself—
> sees the kite, my kite you made, flying up above,
> and thinks for a moment an angel is there
> bringing back love.
> If I must die
> let it bring hope,
> let it be a story.[5]

I will tell his story, and that of honorable Gazans like Refaat, who empowered people with the gift of art, storytelling, and poetry, and who dreamed that the children of Gaza might even for a moment, in

5. "A Bilingual Poem from Gaza," World Literature Today, December 14, 2023, https://tinyurl.com/2fj2r2uk. (Alareer wrote his poem in English; D. P. Snyder translated it into Spanish.)

the midst of their brutal blockade, imagine an angel in the sky who will bring them love and hope. Refaat's wish was that his death would bring hope. I wish desperately that he and the tens of thousands killed in this brutal war had survived. I wish I did not have to tell his story. I wish he lived to write more poetry and empower more people to write and be creative. Refaat, however, alongside thousands of Gazans, was killed, and we must not stop telling their stories.

One of the things I have repeated over and over again in the last year is that we must not stop talking about Gaza. We cannot stop because we owe it to the people of Gaza. We owe it to their sacrifices. We owe it to the medical workers who worked nonstop in the most difficult circumstances, often giving their lives to save lives. We owe it to the first responders. We owe it to the mothers sheltering their children, and to the children who search tirelessly for food to give their mothers. We owe it to the ones who played music to cheer little children in the refugee camps. We owe it to the ones displaced over and over and over again. We owe it to their pain and suffering. We owe it to their *sumud*. We cannot stop talking about Gaza.

When I stood up in front of thousands of protesters in the streets of London, it was an emotional moment. And I declared:

> Never in my life have I been more proud and honored to be a Palestinian than this last year. I am proud of our *sumud*. I am proud of our solidarity with one another. I am proud of our unity. When I said in my Christmas sermon that we will be ok, and that we will recover, I said it because I know my people; I know who we are. Palestine is our homeland. We are deeply rooted there. For those Palestinians exiled around the world, Palestine lives in them.
>
> I also said it because I know who God is. We cannot, and will not lose our faith in a just and good God. We cannot, and will not lose our faith in the God of the resurrection. We will be satisfied. Righteousness will be achieved.

Sumud is our commitment, defiance, and resolve. Commitment to continue to work for justice, to advocate for life with dignity, and to choose to hope that we will recover from this atrocity. The loss is enormous. The destruction is massive. The pain is profound and the wounds are deep, to the extent that recovery seems an illusion. It feels like being in the bottom of a deep and dark pit. It feels like the tomb of Jesus on Saturday: death, darkness, and silence. But we choose to hope. To survive. To exist. To insist that God is good. We will recover, rooted in resilience, and demand justice for our people. We will recover.

Acknowledgments

I am deeply grateful for the unwavering support of my two congregations in Bethlehem and Beit Sahour, and the family of Bethlehem Bible College. Your encouragement, counsel, and prayers have been a constant source of strength throughout this journey.

A special thanks to Celia and Jennifer, whose meticulous editing of the manuscript has been invaluable. Your dedication and attention to detail have greatly enhanced the quality of this work.

I would also like to express my heartfelt appreciation to James, my editor from Eerdmans, for his insightful guidance and support. Your expertise has been instrumental in bringing this book to fruition.

To the clergy in Gaza who serve under the most difficult circumstances. Although we have never met in person, your resilience and dedication have truly inspired me. Your unwavering faith and commitment to serve in the face of adversity have been a beacon of hope and strength.

Lastly, to my beloved wife, Rudaina, who stood by me through every step of this journey. Your love, patience, and unwavering belief in me have been my greatest source of inspiration. Thank you for being my rock.

To God be all glory.